PENGUIN BOOKS

THE CREATIVE ECONOMY

John Howkins worked as a journalist before moving into TV and entertainment with HBO and Time Warner. He was chairman of CREATEC, Tornado Productions and BOP Consulting as well as the London Film School and has advised government and business in over 30 countries. He is the founder of the Adelphi Charter on Creativity, Innovation and Intellectual Property. In 2006 the Shanghai government established the John Howkins Research Centre on the Creative Economy. Previous publications include *Understanding Television*, *Four Scenarios for Information* and *Creative Ecologies*. For updates see www.creativeeconomy.com.

JOHN HOWKINS

The Creative Economy

Second Edition

PENGUIN BOOKS

PENGUIN BOOKS

Published by the Penguin Group
Penguin Books Ltd, 80 Strand, London WC2R ORL, England
Penguin Group (USA) Inc., 375 Hudson Street, New York, New York 10014, USA
Penguin Group (Canada), 90 Eglinton Avenue East, Suite 700, Toronto, Ontario, Canada M4P 2Y3
(a division of Pearson Penguin Canada Inc.)
Penguin Ireland, 25 St Stephen's Green, Dublin 2, Ireland (a division of Penguin Books Ltd)
Penguin Group (Australia), 707 Collins Street, Melbourne, Victoria 3008, Australia
(a division of Pearson Australia Group Pty Ltd)
Penguin Books India Pvt Ltd, 11 Community Centre, Panchsheel Park, New Delhi – 110 017, India
Penguin Group (NZ), 67 Apollo Drive, Rosedale, Auckland 0632, New Zealand
(a division of Pearson New Zealand Ltd)
Penguin Books (South Africa) (Pty) Ltd, Block D, Rosebank Office Park,
181 Jan Smuts Avenue, Parktown North, Gauteng 2193, South Africa

Penguin Books Ltd, Registered Offices: 80 Strand, London WC2R ORL, England

www.penguin.com

First published by Allen Lane 2001
Published by Penguin Books 2002
Reprinted with updated material 2007
This revised edition published in Penguin Books 2013
002

Set in 9.25/12.5pt Sabon LT Std
Typeset by Jouve (UK), Milton Keynes
Printed in England by Clays Ltd, St Ives plc

Contents

Preface: Who is Creative, and Why?

Who is creative? Who wants to be? Who can be? Everyone is born with a personal imagination and the raw instinct to test it by playing, asking questions and coming up with new ideas. Being creative is part of growing up and a sign of being normal. But then for years, when children went to school to be taught facts and how to behave, their creativity was relegated to the art class. Teenagers emerged more-or-less educated but their creativity was muted.

This downgrading of one of our most precious assets is no longer inevitable. School teachers are more willing to encourage self-expression and to answer questions, and more people go to university where they are expected to challenge conventional thinking. Companies want to hire people who have ideas. We are surrounded by crises of resources, energy, poverty and finance that desperately need clever, imaginative solutions. Creativity and its business-like cousin innovation are the most interesting and most profitable areas of the economy and the presiding genius of the internet. Creative thinking has become something that ordinary people want to do and are discovering they can.

When IBM asked 1,600 CEOs in 60 countries about leadership the CEOs said creativity trumps all other leadership characteristics and said it includes being 'comfortable with ambiguity', which is not something one associates with IBM. Samuel J. Palmisano, IBM's CEO, who commissioned the survey, said it was 'a wake-up call'.

You can sense the new mood in the people writing code and algorithms for dotcom businesses in California and in the digital start-ups and pop-up shops in London. It's visible in the immersive theatre and video installations throughout Europe, the fashion, online blogging and design networks in Shanghai and the geeks and artists discussing open source healthcare, biomimicry and ubiquitous computing at the SXSW (South by SouthWest) Festival in Texas. It is happening in low-energy power schemes in India and in design rooms in the favelas in Brazil and among the under-privileged children playing in the Notes of Peace orchestra in Bogotá.

It's in the mind of Cory Doctorow, online activist and novelist, who has a story and a research project about sending 3D printers to the moon to build structures for future landings. Instead of squirting ink on to a flat surface, 3D printers use plastic and other materials to build up a 3D object. His plan may seem far-fetched but the American army already uses backpack-sized 3D printers costing $550 in Afghanistan so soldiers can reproduce spare parts on the go. Audiences of *Skyfall* who watched James Bond's beloved Aston Martin DB5 car explode in flames might have guessed it wasn't a real car but few would have known the life-like model had been *printed* by a 3D printer in Germany instead of made out of traditional board and glue.

This book is about these people using their imagination and exploring the relationship between creativity and business and money. Creativity is not new and neither is economics but what is new is the nature of the relationship between them, and how the expression of one's own ideas, whether in traditional media, online or with a 3D printer, can be a source of both pleasure and profit. In the ten years since the first edition of this book, the opportunities to share ideas have increased, the cost of doing so has dropped and markets have expanded.

This book is about what we want and what we are good at. We face a daily choice which is measured at one end by creativity and at the other by repetition. Which do we want? It is a choice between thinking and not-thinking, between learning and not-learning.

People with ideas – people who *own* ideas – have become more powerful than the people who work machines and, in many cases, than the people who *own* machines. Yet the relationship between creativity and economics remains almost invisible. I decided to see if I could bring together all these elements – creativity, management, capital, wealth and welfare – into a single framework.

Bigger Scale, Wider Scope

We are living in extraordinarily creative and inventive times. I don't mean today's ideas are 'better' than yesterday's but that there are more people being more creative, seeing it as part of their identity, than ever before. We can measure the change by the numbers of people involved (scale) and the reach of what they do (scope). The core creative sectors contribute over 12 per cent of Europe's, America's and Japan's gross domestic product (GDP) and a higher proportion of their growth. America exports more value in terms of copyright than food, soft drinks, cars, computers and planes and Britain's fashion industry employs more people and makes more money than do its car or steel industries. In China, creative sectors contribute a fast-increasing 4–5 per cent, rising to 10–11 per cent in Beijing and Shanghai. Over a hundred countries have national plans for their own creative economy and almost every major city in the world claims to be creative, with some interesting exceptions.

The scope is bigger, too. When artist Elaine Shemilt asked Scottish crop geneticists for some of their genetic data, they expected she would produce beautifully artistic patterns, but she did much more than that. She stripped the data to pure pattern and visualized relationships that gave meaning to what the scientists had dismissed as background noise. She enabled them to see gene sequences they had not previously noticed, provoking them to think new theories about how genes develop in pathogens. Shemilt's use of her personal aesthetic to create new knowledge typifies the creative economy.

Creativity pops up anywhere one person, alone, taking a moment to think, comes up with a new way of doing something interesting. Sarah Collje in South Africa had the idea of adapting her grandmother's use of hay boxes for retaining heat to invent a Wonderbag that cooks food and she aims to save tonnes of carbon within five years. Will Allen, who started Milwaukee's urban farm movement, Growing Power, was being creative not only in his idea of building farms in the middle of derelict cities but also in his approach to hydroponics, his choice of crops and his invention of a new market.

The Scottish government has asked the 'creative talent here in Scotland, including a couple of people from computer gaming, to study terrorism'. In this new world of start-ups and pop-ups, it did not surprise me to discover that America's Central Intelligence Agency (CIA) has a venture capital arm whose first CEO started his career developing video games. In China, Li Wuwei, deputy chairman of the National People's Consultative Conference and a leading champion of the country's creative economy, asked the national committee for agriculture to implement creative thinking in farms nationwide.

When a sceptical official in China's Ministry of Education asked me to sum this up in a few words I offered three propositions for what I call a creative ecology. They form a trilogy: everyone is born creative; creativity needs freedom; freedom needs markets. He liked the name and the principles. A week later I got a similarly enthusiastic response from the president of Time Warner Sports Merchandising in Los Angeles. Since then, these propositions have formed the core of my work on creativity and innovation.

By setting yardsticks of freedom and markets we can evaluate how people manage ideas and how they learn to do something better and we can also evaluate the impact on social welfare. One cannot have too much art (one can have too much bad art, but that's a different matter) but when creativity grows in scale and scope and permeates society then it affects social welfare and equity. Freedoms can conflict. Markets can misallocate resources. Underlying these issues are the tensions between individuals who choose creativity as a way of life and those who desire familiarity and stability.

Ten Chapters: From Ideas to Assets

I start with an overview of the creative economy and show how creativity happens when an individual is trying to solve a problem (which word, which colour?) or to deal in something more personal and try to make their world more pleasing. I talk about people's search for knowledge and beauty (the *Twin Peaks*) (chapter 1). I make *Three Propositions* (*The Tripod*): 'Everyone is born creative'; 'Creativity needs freedom'; and 'Freedom needs markets' (chapter 2). I show how creativity leads to ideas that are personal, meaningful and new and list some characteristics of creative people (chapter 3).

Nobody has ideas in a vacuum, so I describe a *Creative Ecology* and its four factors of change, diversity, learning and adaptation (the *Quad*). A creative mind is an *Adaptive Mind*, continually learning and adapting, trying to understand and improve. We manage this process through relationships that range from mimicry to collaboration, competition and conflict (chapter 4).

The second proposition includes the freedom to manage one's relationship to an idea, so I explore management and how people work together and share ideas. The closer we get to markets and transactions, the more we need to negotiate contracts (chapter 5). I describe copyright, patents and other laws on intellectual property and show how they are changing in the light of new ideas about ownership and access (chapter 6).

Online markets are the fastest growing economy in the world, unaffected by the old economy's crises in debt and finance and by the old world's crisis of political governance. Many new developments in art, culture, media and innovation start online and only if they make sense online do they begin to have a physical presence. I describe what is happening with 'big data' and algorithms and the four basic demands of the online market (chapter 7).

These elements come together in the core markets of art, culture, design, media and innovation which I call the *heartlands* of the creative economy. I describe how these markets operate, their business models and value chains, and give market revenues (chapter 8).

Creative people have a voracious appetite to know what is new and interesting, and the best way to do this is to work together. I show how cities provide hot-house clusters for creativity and how the move from factory-sized production lines to brain-size thinking is changing the city's mood (chapter 9).

Creativity and innovation do not fit into conventional business

I

When Orcs Walked
Across Oxford Circus

IDEAS THAT JUMP

In 2009 the Mayor of London changed the way people crossed the city's busiest shopping interchange at the junction of Oxford Street and Regent Street. On that day, instead of huddling on narrow pavements squeezed around the edges, they were invited to walk diagonally across the middle. When Boris Johnson first proposed the idea, everyone laughed. Oxford Circus has over half a million visitors a day and is notorious for non-stop traffic. The idea of heading into its centre was absurd or, as Boris Johnson himself admitted, bonkers. Why would it work?

City Hall was confident because of the ingenuity of two people on opposite sides of the world, a film-maker in Wellington, New Zealand, and a fire-fighter in Los Angeles.

If you've read J. R. R. Tolkien's novel *The Lord of the Rings* or seen Peter Jackson's film trilogy, you'll remember the Orcs. Tolkien described them as 'squat, broad, flat-nosed, sallow-skinned, with wide mouths and slant eyes . . . degraded and repulsive'. To bring this mob to life for the opening film, *The Fellowship*, Jackson hired Stephen Regelous, the founder of a local New Zealand animation company called Massive Software.

Jackson and Regelous knew there were too many Orcs to draw by hand, as could be done for the main characters, and the then available crowd-replication software was primitive. Regelous realized he had to develop a new software algorithm that would give each one its own artificial intelligence and fuzzy logic so it could make its own decisions, enabling each Orc to appear to react to its neighbours and navigate its own path. Each Orc moved as if it was alive in its own way and with its own thoughts.

Tolkien's fans had been apprehensive but global audiences paid $871 million at the box office to see *The Fellowship*. The trilogy made $2.9 billion at the box office and about $2.2 billion from home video, totalling well over $5 billion. Film-makers voted *The Fellowship* 13 Oscar nominations and four wins, including one for Best Visual Effects.

The Fellowship heralded a new kind of film-making. Its script had four credited writers and about seven non-credited ones. Peter Jackson ran seven film units, nine music units and a production crew of 2,400. Some of the music was recorded in Watford, a small town outside London not noted for its musical talent but with the advantage of a disused town hall close enough to the London Symphony Orchestra. There's a story that Jackson never saw the third film from beginning to end until he was sitting in the Embassy Cinema, Wellington, for the world premiere on 17 December 2003. But what happened next had implications beyond film-making.

After the trilogy was completed, Stephen Regelous and his CEO Diane Holland could have put their software on the shelf and waited for the next producer to come calling. But they knew Warner's New Line production company had no interest in developing it. Hollywood likes to stay focused on its core business and seldom invests in technology. It prefers to sub-contract and out-source technology to others.

In every creative process there's a moment when an idea jumps out of its skin and takes root somewhere else. Peter Jackson said that his jump moment with *The Lord of the Rings* happened when instead of trying to make films that looked like *The Lord of the Rings* he realized it would be much better to go ahead and simply make *The Lord of the Rings* itself. The moment when Massive's new algorithm took off was when CEO Diane Holland had the idea of moving it from the world of film-making to real life.

She was living partly in a commune in Los Angeles and wanted to 'skim this idea into as many hands as possible'. So she contacted Ove Arup, one of the world's largest construction companies, which had a special unit to develop sustainable ecologies in Europe and China, and Ove Arup introduced her to Nate Wittasek.

Nate Wittasek is not a film-maker and does not see himself as creative. His mother used to buy him earlier film versions of the Hobbit and he remembers going to the local cinema with his family to see *The Fellowship of the Ring* but that was years ago. He had joined the Los Angeles Fire Department, where he specialized in fire safety, before moving to Ove Arup. He used computer models to show how people behave when they had to evacuate a building quickly but, like Regelous, he knew his existing software wasn't really good enough. It could show how wind or smoke flowed around an object but it could not map what happened if large numbers of people start to behave in irrational ways, as they do under stress. He was delighted to meet Diane Holland and for the opportunity to re-model Massive's algorithms to save people's lives. In a remarkably short time, the software became the global standard for designing buildings and enclosed spaces like air terminals and railway stations to take account of how people move when they find themselves in a strange place and have to get out quickly and start to panic. Then city planners came calling from Tokyo and London to ask if the model could be used to make street crossings safer.

The route from film-making in Auckland to fire prevention in Los Angeles to pedestrian crossings in London could have failed at any point if the people involved (and I have mentioned only a few of them) had been too busy or not interested, or given any of the familiar excuses people use for not doing something. But each person in the chain thought the idea was interesting and meaningful for what they were doing. Diane Holland took an idea from one context and applied it somewhere else. Nate Wittasek made the all-important connection between her idea and his job. This is how creativity happens. Someone takes a decisive step to grab an idea that seems interesting and can solve a problem or make something better. What matters is the picture, the meaning, you have in your head, first privately and then publicly. The link between what is desirable and what, suddenly, becomes possible.

KEYWORDS

I use *creativity* to describe a process of using ideas to produce a new idea. It happens whenever a person says, does or makes something that is new and interesting, either in the sense of 'something from nothing' (which is relatively rare) or in the sense of giving a new meaning to something. Creativity occurs whether or not this process leads anywhere; it is in the thought and the action. It is present when we dream of paradise; when we design our garden; and when we start planting. We are creative when we write something whether it is published or not; or invent something whether it is used or not.

Creativity has been part of the language of art for so long that the two words have become almost synonymous but they refer to different things or rather to different parts of the process. Artists do not have more ideas or better ideas but work with specific aesthetics and technologies which lead to specific kinds of work.

Creativity leads to innovation as often as to art. Both artists and scientists use the same thinking process to imagine (to visualize) and describe (to represent) their view of reality. Colin Ronan introduces his *Cambridge Illustrated History of the World's Science* with these words: 'To engage in science requires a vivid creative imagination, tempered by firm discipline based on a hard core of observational experience', which is a good description of creativity. Biologist Edward O. Wilson, one of the most distinguished scientists of the 20th century, defines creativity as 'the ability of the brain to generate novel scenarios and settle on the most effective'. He goes on to quote Nobel Laureate economist Herbert Simon: 'What chiefly characterizes creative thinking from more mundane forms are (i) willingness to accept vaguely defined problem statements and gradually structure them, (ii) continuing preoccupation with problems over a considerable period of time, and (iii) extensive background knowledge in relevant and potentially relevant areas.' Simon summarized these as daring, obsession and knowledge. The difference between artists and scientists comes in why they choose to think like this, how they present the result to the world and how they protect its economic value.

Innovation is a new product or process that can be exactly repeatable by anyone. Whereas creativity is personal and subjective and cannot be exactly repeated even by the original creator, innovation is public and objective and repeatable by anyone. Creativity often leads to innovation but innovation seldom leads to creativity. Innovation requires agreement whereas creativity is independent and often ambiguous (in economics, it is an exogenous variable). My own quick test for innovation is that it is creativity that has been cleared by a committee.

An *ecology* is a place with an identifiable population and a set of resources and nutrients (assets). Ecologies can be measured by the relationships and flows between members of the population; it is the relationships that matter and give an ecology its special nature. A *creative ecology* is a place where a population has sufficient resources and flows to be able to interact purposively to use ideas to produce new ideas. Creative ecologies can be measured by four criteria: change, diversity, learning and adaptation. They are the seedbeds for creative economies and like all seedbeds need tender care.

An *ecosystem* is a unit in ecology. Two of the most common ecosystems are habitats and niches. A habitat is an environment where many different populations live. A niche is a place within a habitat that is suitable for a specific population.

Creativity by itself has no economic value until it takes shape, means something and is embodied in a product that can be traded. This, in turn, needs a market-place with active sellers and buyers, some ground-rules on laws and contracts, and some conventions about what constitutes a reasonable deal.

A *creative product* is an economic good, service or experience resulting from creativity whose main economic value is based on creativity. It may have other characteristics of beauty, knowledge or other symbolic, intangible virtues but these are optional. The defining characteristics are twofold: it results from creative activity and its economic value is based on creativity.

A *creative economy* is a system for the production, exchange and use of creative products. Economics deals with the problem of how individuals and societies manage to satisfy their wants, which are infinite, with resources which are finite, and is primarily about the allocation of scarce resources. I calculate a creative economy's market value by looking at the number and value of transactions. In some markets, like music, fashion and computer code, copying is central to the process but in the arts the physical object or experience is usually more precious.

Many creative outputs, although not all, qualify as *intellectual property* (IP) with *intellectual property rights* (IPR). Governments and the courts define the nature of the property and an owner's rights. Intellectual property is not the same as any idea or bit of knowledge that we may happen to have but what a law says we know or have. The three most common kinds are copyright, patents and trademarks. *Copyright* law covers the expression of an idea in a qualifying work rather than the idea itself. Copyright accrues automatically to any qualifying work and does not need to be registered; it normally lasts for the author's lifetime plus 70 years.

A *patent* protects an invention and gives a monopoly which typically lasts 20 years. Whereas copyright accrues automatically, a patent has to pass tests of being novel, non-obvious and practical, none of which apply to copyright. Once registered, a patent gives stronger protection than copyright. A *trademark* does not require any artistic expression (as does copyright) or any expert skill (as does a patent) but covers any tradable symbol. Like patents, trademarks have to be applied for. Unlike patents, they can last for ever. Internet domain names are a form of trademark.

There are several ways of categorizing a creative economy. I use *markets* because I want to focus on how people sell and buy ideas and markets are the closest to what is actually going on. I am interested in whether people have access to markets, how markets work and if they are fair (or if regulation is required). Looking at markets allows us to look at supply and demand and to compare markets in different countries. It enables us to draw parallels with ecosystems as both depend on deciding where the boundaries lie and how permeable they are. Like ecosystems, markets are a map of how things relate to each other. They are both neither good nor bad, they just are. There is a tendency to say all ecologies are good and all markets are bad but this is sloppy thinking.

The term *creative industries* owes its popularity to the British government's decision in 1998 to award the title to 14 sectors: advertising, architecture, art, crafts, design, fashion, film, music, performing arts, publishing, leisure software, toys, TV and radio, and video games (regrettably excluding innovation). The list was a wake-up call to Britain and became a global standard, although almost every country tweaks it to promote its own success stories. China includes trade shows, Thailand includes food and spas, and America's lists usually include home furnishings.

It is now in danger of becoming a barrier to our understanding of how creativity and innovation actually operate. It ascribes industrial qualities to processes that are personal and subjective and not industrial at all. Only a few of the sectors are industries in the sense of making copies on an industrial scale, such as publishing, music, TV, film, fashion and games, and the growth of online media weakens even these industrial qualities. Art, crafts and design are not industries. It also assumes all creative people work in creative industries which is manifestly untrue. The Tripod principles say everyone has a creative capacity. As a result, Britain is now focussing less on creative industries and more on every job's level of *creative intensity*.

The World Intellectual Property Organization (WIPO) has a model of *copyright industries*, as does the US-based International Intellectual Property Association (IIPA), and there are lists of patent industries. I seldom use these terms because copyright and patents are only one factor in assessing value. The term *intangible industries* similarly singles out one factor but does not provide a complete picture. The people who print books and assemble smartphones and sell materials for 3D printers are also part of a creative economy.

UP THE LADDER OF DESIRES

There are many reasons why creative economies are expanding so fast in so many countries but the most compelling is the way we evolve as humans. The American psychologist Abraham Maslow suggested our needs ascend up a hierarchy starting at the base with our physiological needs for air and food and then, when they are satisfied, our physical needs for shelter and safety. Next come our psychological needs for love and belonging and emotional needs for self-esteem, respect and achievement. At the top, Maslow put our need for self-fulfilment. As each need is satisfied, so people become more conscious and desirous of the next one up. Linus Torvalds, who pioneered Open Source software, has a crisp modern variant: 'Every human motivation can be classified under survival, social life or fun'.

Towards the end of his life Maslow split the high-minded but possibly self-obsessed idea of fulfilment into knowledge (he used the word 'cognition') and beauty (aesthetics). I refer to these two fulfilment needs as Maslow's Twin Peaks. The need for knowledge is the need to understand and perhaps to be in control. The desire for beauty is more subjective and ranges from colours and shapes to that quiet satisfaction that something is well done and well made and cannot be bettered.

The two principles of knowledge and beauty can complement each other. Astronomer Fred Hoyle said that when Albert Einstein announced his theory of relativity, 'He put an issue of style ahead of all the confusion of detail . . . Of course, physicists never admit to style because the word brings a picture of Beau Brummell. But style it is.' They fight each other when musicians and artists portray beauty in ways that others find ugly. Cézanne, Van Gogh and Renoir were refused admission to the Paris art shows and Duchamp's original *Fountain* was thought to be a joke by him as well as others and thrown away (copies now sell for over $1 million). Damien Hirst provoked us to think about death by putting a dead cow's head and a swarm of buzzing flies in a cage together. Ugly stuff. We have no idea what future generations will find useful or beautiful.

Our basic physical needs are universal and clear-cut and we either do or don't have a roof over our heads but at each higher level a need takes on more of the quality of a want, which is desirable but not necessary. Some people want art, some people do not. People vary in their need, or want, for understanding and beauty. Air is a need; art is a challenge.

We should not be surprised if people whose material needs are largely satisfied and who have a high level of disposable income remix their ambitions and put a premium on these matters of the mind. It is also not surprising that markets emerge to meet these needs. Market economies are skilful at meeting people's various needs, especially in the field of entertainment where needs are so passionate and evanescent.

On the *supply* side, automation in the manufacturing industries and, to a smaller extent, the service industries has cut the demand for manual labour, so young people are looking elsewhere for work. Many turn to the creative sectors, which offer an attractive lifestyle and above-average economic rewards. New markets have arisen around digital technologies, each with its urgent needs for skills and ideas. Suppliers have become adept at charging for pleasure.

On the *demand* side, most rich countries spend more on culture and recreation than on food or clothing; only housing and energy cost more. Americans spend proportionately less, because they spend more on private education and healthcare. The Japanese spend more on entertaining themselves than on clothing or healthcare, and most clothes are chosen more for pleasure than for utility. From 2000 to 2010 the annual growth rate of the creative economy in rich countries exceeded that of the rest of the economy.

The greatest growth is not in the creation of new products but in their distribution and sale. The creative economy has been midwifed by digital technologies as well as by the upsurge in selling and retailing skills. Digital technologies have created new opportunities for content, a new universe of online networks, user-generated content and interactive media, hungry for information, images and stories. The low costs of digital technology allow people to make, distribute and exchange their own material alongside and increasingly inside corporate markets.

These desirable skills of individual creativity are being copied and borrowed throughout society. The use of the imagination, the management of intellectual capital, the best way to incentivize and reward creative people, the short time-scales and the response to success and failure, which only recently have got on the agenda of mainstream business, have always been the stock-in-trade of the creative person. Two trends are interwoven. Creative people are becoming more business-like; and business is becoming more dependent upon creativity.

play, swinging from delight to puzzlement to despair as they try to make things more comfortable for themselves. Childhood expert Tina Bruce says children's creativity develops in several stages, starting with a playful attitude to all activities, not just in formal play, and then moving to developing specific ideas and to making creative things. She suggests that when people feel nostalgic for childhood they are remembering this joy of learning what is new and interesting and recapturing the wonder of creativity.

Children develop by testing what is possible in a blurry mix of physical, emotional and mental sensations, searching for meanings. They become acutely sensitive to how things are, and then how things might be different and better. Gradually they become aware of the difference between what they feel and think and then in what they can say. Their creativity levels peak on average around ages three and four (Picasso said: 'The problem is how to remain an artist once we grow up'). Their consciousness of choices to be made continues to develop as does their confidence to choose between different possibilities. Gradually they learn how to manage outcomes and how to reconcile differences. The moment when a child begins to be conscious of this process and begins to think about specific meanings is the starting point of their own creativity.

Saying 'everyone is creative' does not imply that everyone is talented, which would be as silly as saying everyone who can walk can be an athlete or anyone who can write can write a best-selling novel. It simply implies that everyone is born with the instinct, the desire, to search for new possibilities that they personally find interesting and useful. Noam Chomsky and Steven Pinker interpreted children's aptitude for speech to argue persuasively that everyone is born with a 'language instinct' (Pinker) and a 'deep, universal grammar' (Chomsky). The same functional Magnetic Resonance Imaging (fMRI) techniques that supported their ideas have been used to suggest that children have a 'creative instinct' or 'deep universal creativity' that pushes them to make sense of what they see and, if they don't like it, to try to improve it. Turning this private, self-contained creativity into talent or achievement requires determination and hard work just as children need to work hard to learn how to write.

A good indicator of this creative instinct is that people answer 'Yes' to my Dreaming Questions:

Do you dream, do you have fantasies?
Do you think about how things might be *different*?
Do you often think of a *better* way of doing something?
Do you *want* to think of a *better* way?
Do you take pride in doing things *your* way?

CREATIVITY NEEDS FREEDOM

If our inborn creativity is to flourish, we need to be free to explore the ideas we want to explore and to do so without having to justify what we are doing. So the second proposition is that *creativity needs freedom*. We need internal freedoms of self-expression and external freedoms of circumstance. We need freedom to ask questions, believe or disbelieve, learn, explore possibilities, discover what is new and then adapt our thinking and our behaviour accordingly. It includes freedom from physical constraints such as hunger and poverty (Maslow's most basic needs) as well as from prejudice, censorship and interfering governments and other threats to the human rights of free speech and freedom of expression. One might add unhelpful schools to the list.

It can be summed up in the *freedom to manage one's relationship to an idea* so that we are able, first, to select which ideas we want to have a relationship with and, second, to manage the relationship in the way we want. We need freedom to be in charge of the journey because if we make our own discoveries we feel more involved (children who are forced to read a book at school often dislike the author for the rest of their lives).

Steve Lee and Sebastian Thrun at the secretive Google-X lab, which is researching artificial intelligence and the driver-less car, among other projects, talk about data that is *unstructured* and *unlabelled*. This proposition is about the freedom to choose data that is unstructured and unlabelled and to choose what to call it.

If we truly want to manage our relationships to ideas we have to be strong enough to get rid of bad ideas as easily as we embrace new ones. Personal enthusiasms can be blinding and dispiriting. There is nothing worse than being seduced by a bad idea.

I sometimes refer to the creative economy as an 'economy of failure', which can be a shock to people who are focused on success. The truth is that anyone who is free to play around with what is possible and what might be interesting, taking the next imagined step, will get it wrong more often than they get it right. Anyone who gets it right every time isn't really trying (or very lucky).

One person's favourite idea may seem ridiculous to another. Henry Ford and Walt Disney failed several times before they founded the companies that bear their names. Disney invented Mickey Mouse because he was angry he had lost the copyright to his earlier Oswald the Rabbit and had to start again. Bill Gates's first company was not a success although it wasn't entirely his fault. Rudyard Kipling was told by the Editor of the *San Francisco Examiner* that 'You don't know how to use the English language' only eight years before he won the Nobel Prize. Elvis Presley failed auditions and was advised to go back to driving a truck but changed his style and two years later got his first number one hit.

This freedom includes not only the familiar but the unknown. The principle of free speech encompasses the right to say things that others may disagree with or find stupid or even shocking. Voltaire reportedly said, 'I disapprove of what you say but will defend to the death your right to say it.' It is possible Voltaire himself never wrote these words, although they certainly reflect his views, and a more likely author is S. G. Tallentyre, who was actually an English woman, Evelyn Beatrice Hall, writing under a male pseudonym. Her pretence gives it added piquancy. We need freedom to be ourselves.

FREEDOM NEEDS MARKETS

A market tests value by enabling people to allocate resources of information, attention and money. In even the most basic street-market we make several decisions before any money changes hands. We discover it is taking place; we decide to spend time; we turn up; we wander around. We pay attention to what is on offer and look around for what is interesting. All markets are markets of time, attention and information before they are markets for buying. Herbert Simon and later Kevin Kelly came up with the idea of an attention economy in which people pay as much attention if not more than they pay money. It is revealing that we use the same word to pay attention and to pay money, and we always pay attention before we pay money (well, not always, but it is wiser to do so).

The histories of markets and economies are intertwined and support each other. The creative economy is as much about buying as about making. It is true that individuals can be wonderfully creative on their own, and state rulers and wealthy patrons have commissioned outstanding art, but a functioning economy needs many open market-places in multiple shapes and sizes. The exchange of ideas has low resource costs and low transactional costs as well as very fast transactional speeds. Many innovations in design, media and entertainment succeed as much because they create a new market as because they create a new product.

The totalitarian command economies in the USSR and in China from 1949 to 1979 stifled creative economies because they prevented people from developing and sharing their ideas unless those ideas were in line with the ruling interests. Thinking, asking questions and taking intellectual risks were seen as disloyal and stupid. Governments tried to control all data and all ideas in order to support their own policies instead of allowing individuals to check the truth.

The presence of an interventionist government by itself is not a problem if a country has a resilient public sector, independent institutions and a free press, and the government works in partnership with these and respects their freedoms, as the governments of Japan and Germany demonstrated when they built up their post-war economies. There is a strong case for saying that Japan and Germany recovered so quickly and became such major exporters because of their determined government. There is also a strong case for saying that they excel in innovation rather than in creativity for the same reason.

We can judge a market by three criteria: openness, fairness and

efficiency. An *open* market allows access to all-comers of all national-
ities whereas a closed market has barriers to entry against foreigners.
These barriers may be explicit, such as an import tax or visa conditions, or more subtle ones, such as bureaucratic and regulatory hurdles
that foreign companies find difficult to overcome.

A *fair* market is one in which all companies can compete on equal
terms and on the merits of their ideas. Companies that are monopolies or have a dominant position (absolute monopolies are rare) have
considerable power to tilt the market in their favour, such as cutting
prices below costs to stop a newcomer getting a foothold, known as
predatory pricing. Many incumbent companies try to distort markets
in their favour. A few countries, notably America, Britain and
Germany, have strong pro-competition, anti-trust laws but these are
difficult to apply when technology is developing fast and market
boundaries are blurred.

The third criterion is efficiency: can creators find buyers and can
buyers find what they want? An *efficient* market allows a full exchange
of information about a product's qualities, functions and price and
brings together sellers and buyers (or users and users). If buyers are
well informed about what's on offer then their purchases will have the
effect of resolving the demand and supply curves and lead to optimal
pricing. In practice, this level of transparency is rare because suppliers
are adept at managing market information in their favour and are
more interested in maximizing revenue by strengthening their market
position or maintaining a brand's exclusivity than in giving people full
information.

The economic crises in America and Europe have muted our enthusiasms for markets. The ideal of a free market has been found wanting
and it is felt that many markets are neither open, fair nor efficient. The
market freedoms which enabled economies to grow from the 1980s
onwards, led by the growth of advertising, the liberalization of media
and telecoms and the growth of financial data, expanded the range of
what was on offer. Many companies exploited these market freedoms
to encourage people to spend beyond their incomes and to buy things
they did not fully understand and, it might be argued, did not need
(although buying things one doesn't need is hardly new). As markets

are part of the problem so a better understanding of how they work and how they can be regulated is part of the answer. Currently, especially in Europe, governments have hardly begun to reform their market regulations on competition policy, tax, consumer protection and intellectual property to fit a creative economy.

By looking at markets, we can evaluate the size and nature of transactions. What is the market for art in China? What is the market for a singer-songwriter in America? In Brazil? Is the design business in Europe growing faster than in America? What is the market for an architect in China? We can see where markets allow competition and where new companies are squeezed out. Market analysis enables us to see the effects of copyright and patent laws on creativity and innovation, and to judge whether regulation is a help or a hindrance.

We can look at new developments. What is the market for self-published novels? How do the markets compare for physical books and e-books? What is the market for crafts in Indonesia? What is the market for 'frugal' housing? According to Bill Gross of Idealab, who has developed a cheap $2500 WorldHaus, it is $424 billion. What is the market for solar-powered lighting? According to the World Bank, 1.5 billion people have no electricity in their homes and unit prices are $8–20, so that's a $20–30 billion market.

3
The First Talent

OLD IDEAS AND NEW MEANINGS

We have seen how cleverer Orcs led to safer crossings. It is a story of how two or three people who were already on top of what they were doing were constantly thinking about how to do it better. Creativity is a complicated bundle but it can be summarized as using an idea to have another idea that is better in some way. The starting idea can be old or new, mine or yours, private or public, and the new idea can be just an interesting possibility but those two words – possible, interesting – are enough to start. Creativity happens whenever we give an old idea a new meaning and test how it might be used.

A TUMBLING MIX

The starting point is our personal, unique imagination. The next and most critical stage is the choice of a meaning, which involves naming and describing, although these names and descriptions are likely to change over time. Having a meaning is a necessary prologue to being interesting and being interesting is necessary for everything else. The third quality, novelty, might seem the most important of all three but something that is merely new is often not very interesting. I am going to describe each element in turn although the process is really a tumbling mix of all three. We look for what might be possible and what might be interesting and wonder if it is new.

Being Personal

Creativity starts as a quizzical impulse when we face a problem that needs to be solved for ourselves or others or when something is more or less satisfactory but we can't resist wondering if it still might be bettered in some way. This private niggle may not really be a problem but more of a question, a challenge that we decide to take up for the personal pleasure of expressing our opinion. Sam Mendes, director of the five-times Oscar-winning film *American Beauty* and James Bond's *Skyfall*, refers to the moment in directing a play or a film 'when you discover something that only you can do, only you can say'.

The German advertising writer and film-maker Hermann Vaske has asked an eclectic number of people why they were creative. Their answers showed they could not personally imagine any other way of living; and they meant living, not working. Poet and musician Laurie Anderson said: 'The alternative is *way* too boring'; conductor Daniel Barenboim: 'Because I'm very curious'; David Bowie: 'It has something to do with wanting to find a place where I can set sail and know that I won't fall off the edge'; musician Brian Eno: 'In this business not only do you get to fly your own plane, you can crash it and walk away from it'; David Carson, an American graphic designer, was more blunt: 'Why the hell not?'

Artist Christo said: 'I can't help it'; architect Frank Gehry: 'There is nothing else to do'; artist Damien Hirst, typically: 'I don't know'; artist David Hockney: 'I need to be'; and actor Dennis Hopper: 'I was desperate and lonely, there seemed no way out'. Vaske's fellow German, Nobel prize-winning novelist Günter Grass, spoke for many when he said: 'Because I have to.'

A few years later, the American author Kurt Vonnegut gave a similar view in a collection of essays called *A Man Without a Country*:

> The arts are not a way to make a living. They are a very human way of making life more bearable. Practicing an art, no matter how well or badly, is a way to make your soul grow, for heaven's sake. Sing in the shower. Dance to the radio. Tell stories. Write a poem to a friend, even a lousy poem. Do it as well as you possibly can. You will get an enormous reward. You will have created something.

For these people, and Vonnegut implies the opportunity is there for everyone, betting one's creative imagination against the world is a more secure proposition, and more fun, than becoming a little cog in a big organization or another bit in the information society. Creative people start within themselves and try to be true to themselves and they can be single-mindedly persistent even when the public do not recognize what they are doing. They tend to be passionately involved in what they are doing, whether they are full-time or part-time, paid or unpaid, and acquire a personal feeling for what works best in their medium; for what they personally want to work best.

When Igor Stravinsky was composing *The Rite of Spring* in 1911 he was living in a small room in a house in Clarens, Switzerland. Robert Craft has recounted how Stravinsky's landlady received complaints from the other tenants that he was playing the 'wrong' notes. Stravinsky retorted, 'They were the wrong notes for them but they were the right notes for me.' He walked out of the first performance when the audience jeered, just as his neighbours had done, but the 30-minute work is now recognized as one of the most profound musical pieces of the century.

There is a debate about whether creativity always depends on a personal insight or whether a group can be creative in any meaningful sense. It seems most knowledge and most expressions of knowledge reside in the head of an individual, and ideas are generally expressed by individuals, and that a group's knowledge is simply the knowledge of the individuals who comprise it. If so, a group can have an idea only metaphorically. But it is also true that people in a group can produce an idea that they could not have produced individually. Both processes seem equally valid. Individuals need groups just as groups need individuals.

The same question is asked of computers. Can a computer be creative? Super-computers are now capable of quintillions of operations a second but we should not confuse speed with intelligence. The real question is whether a computer can be creative in the sense of using an idea to produce another idea in a purposive sense. They score well on questions that can be reduced to data and logic, which is why IBM's Watson computer trounced two humans on the quiz show *Jeopardy* in

2011, but they fail miserably when confronted with a combination of words and pictures (or sounds) or with culturally ambiguous meanings. Computers can only operate according to the rules we give them and we have so far been unable to programme them to deal with non-linear, subjective information ('Computers are useless,' said Picasso, 'they only give answers'). In psychologist Daniel Kahneman's terms, they are much better at fast thinking than slow thinking. It remains to be seen whether these limitations will be overcome. Meanwhile, a computer, like any tool, can help us express a new idea (if reducible to data), and it is sometimes hard to draw the line between a human and a tool and an algorithm.

Playing with Names and Meanings

The person who has the makings of an idea has the first opportunity to say what it is (to name it) and to say what it means. Afterwards, others can make their own suggestions, which can be as creative as having the idea in the first place and can contribute more to its value.

We can see this in jamming. Josh Linker, CEO of Detroit Venture Partners, is a professional jazz guitarist who plays regularly with Paul Czarnik, CTO of Compuware, on keyboard. He says jazz musicians are adept at creating in tandem with others, alternately leading and being led. It's a good metaphor for how meanings emerge. If Linker pays attention only to his own playing and ignores what Czarnik is doing, he says the result is a discordant mess (I've heard him; it is). If he and Czarnik listen and play in response to each other, adding meaning, the result is music.

Collaboration gives people the opportunity to interpret an idea in their own way, bringing their own personal creativity, sometimes trying to help along the original meaning and sometimes trying to block it or twist it or use it as a springboard for another meaning.

How New is That?

Novelty is often regarded as the hallmark of creativity but its presence is not worth much. Being new is necessary but very far from sufficient, and being wonderful or beautiful or cheap or convenient attracts more attention and engenders more value. It may be pointless anyway to worry about degrees of novelty because it is difficult to trace origins accurately. The world is too vast and too fertile, literally too full of ideas, for us to be able to say definitely if any particular idea is original and another one is not as we continually use our stored memories, often unconsciously, to produce new and better meanings.

In his famous *Dictionary* of 1755, Samuel Johnson gave five meanings of the verb 'to create'. The first is 'to form out of nothing', which happens rarely and may be an echo of his contemporaries' belief in God-like originality, and the remainder describe ways in which people re-mix existing ideas. The levels of novelty vary from an idea that is new to the mind of the individual, as when a child thinks of doing things that to adults are familiar and obvious, to ideas that, as far as is known, are novel to everyone, though 'everyone' can be a market, a culture or the whole of human history. This latter sounds impressive but even these extremes are no guarantee that a new idea is interesting or useful to anyone.

In today's climate, what matters is not where you get an idea from, but what you do with it. The thinking in contemporary culture is wildly promiscuous, especially in art, entertainment and design. Hollywood is open to any idea from which to make a film. People write original scripts (*Inception*), adapt a novel (*The Girl with the Dragon Tattoo*) or re-make an existing film (*True Grit*). They love prequels and sequels (and not always in that order). They tell stories about real-life people (*The King's Speech*) and about aliens (*Avatar*). They even mix the two (*Mars Attacks*). Faced with a star who became a quadriplegic, Christopher Reeve, they re-make a classic film about a man in a wheelchair (*Rear Window*). They made a film about being inside the head of an actor (*Being John Malkovich*). They will take any idea, however simple or crass it may seem, as the start of a dream. They are unfazed by normal artistic or literary notions of what is right and wrong, original or borrowed or, indeed, new or old.

FLICK THE SWITCH

Re-mixing creativity requires us sometimes to *focus* and calculate and sometimes to let our minds wander and *drift* unconsciously. The two states are matched by two kinds of emotions. In the first people feel a sense of heightened alertness and in the second they feel the opposite and become less aware of everything else to the extent of being in a dream. Managing the creative process involves managing these two states and the switch between them.

There are interesting parallels with our understanding of sleep. We all sleep and we all know what it means to be 'asleep' but there is no medical or psychological consensus about what sleep actually is. It is generally believed to be a special case of unconsciousness. Is there a gradation from being unconscious to being asleep to being awake and to being conscious? And can we extend the range from being conscious to being creative? In other words, is creativity a special, heightened variety of consciousness?

The psychologist C. J. Jung followed Freud in describing the state of focus and heightened consciousness as a 'moment of high emotional tension' and drifting as a 'state of contemplation in which ideas pass before the mind like dream-images'. He believed the process could be managed. Neurologist Antonio Damasio, Van Allen Professor of Neurology at the University of Iowa, similarly suggests a circle of existence, consciousness and creativity. He sees benefits in letting the conscious mind generate its own patterns without becoming subservient to old knowledge or to too much logical analysis. Tests comparing people's ability to be creative when focused and when wandering show that wandering can be more productive in linking disparate concepts in surprising ways. Jennifer Wiley of the University of Illinois in Chicago says that 'too much focus can harm performance on creative or insightful problem-solving tasks'. Professor Wiley endeared herself to generations of Americans when she showed that (moderately) drunk students score above average in lateral thinking.

The two states match different kinds of brain waves. The more dream-like state is associated with waves in the lower, slower alpha range between 4–8 and 8–12 cycles per second (Hertz). Heightened consciousness and increased focus are associated with brain waves in the higher beta range between 12–15 and 15–18 Hz and with higher, faster gamma waves above 25 Hz. A steady profile of gamma waves indicates a singular focus, while a mix of the slower alpha waves and a few gamma spikes is associated with lateral thinking.

Psychologist Mihaly Csikszentmihalyi says: 'The creative excitement of the artist at her easel or the scientist in the lab comes as close to the ideal fulfilment as we all hope to, and so rarely do, achieve.' In *Flow* he describes states of 'optimal experience' as where 'skill matches challenge'. According to neurobiologist Charles Sherrington, the brain is an 'enchanted loom' which weaves an image of the external world. Our imaginations try to compare each new image with what we know already, reveal the differences and adapt accordingly. Creativity is not a single act but a combination of processes. We need both articulate reason and subjective dreams, contrasting what we know to be true and what could be true.

THE CREATIVE CIRCLE

The best-known catchphrase of creativity is 'Eureka', the Greek word for 'I have it', which people still exclaim when they discover something, whether a new theory or a lost key. The cry is attributed to Archimedes who had been asked by King Hieron to test whether a crown was pure gold or included silver alloys. He had puzzled about the problem for several months until, one day, stepping into a bath and seeing the water run over, he perceived a relationship between an object put into water and the mass, or weight, of the overflow. A solid gold crown would displace more mass than a composite one. According to legend, Archimedes was so excited that he leapt naked from his bath and ran into the street.

How can we generate a Eureka moment without the naked sprint? My own model is a five-fold mix of dreams and analysis, intuitive jumps and cold-blooded calculation spelled out in a list which I call 'RIDER'.

Review
Incubation
Dreams
Excitement
Reality checks

Review is taking stock of things, noticing what is curious, making connections, asking 'What is that?' and 'Why?' It is the conscious evaluation of raw materials, which economists call factors of production, including the attributes of our unconscious mind, which economists tend to ignore. It encompasses both ideas and things.

Incubation is letting our ideas sort themselves out. It is a time of rest and can last a few minutes or several months. The creative person recognizes when incubation is necessary and has sufficient resources of time, money or whatever is needed to provide it. One of the delights of the Christian and Jewish creation myths is that their authors believed that even God became tired and had to rest on the seventh day.

Dreams are unconscious wanderings and explorations of myth, symbols and stories, in night dreams and day-dreams, when we are free of constraints. Artist Francis Bacon called it 'drifting', in which he allowed his mind to be open to outside influences and unknown energies. Somerset Maugham said: 'Reverie is the groundwork of the creative imagination.' The philosopher and mathematician A. N. Whitehead said: 'Modern science has imposed upon humanity the necessity for wandering.' And in *The Lord of the Rings* J. R. R. Tolkien said: 'Not all those who wander are lost.'

Excitement is the adrenaline that powers intuitive jumps and half-calculated sideways movements, letting the mind loose to ask 'What if . . .?' without wondering whether the answer is sensible or crazy. It is close to Jung's moments of 'high emotional tension'. The trick is *not* to look before you leap.

We need *reality checks* to ensure our dreams and intuitions have not taken us too far away. We need to analyse and measure where we are, checking back to the problem and investigating the answers on offer. The rigour and timing of these checks, and how harsh we should be, need careful management. We may need to experiment, again and again.

There are several points about this list. The most obvious is that some steps are the direct opposite of others. Dreaming and checking are diametrically opposed and require different mind-sets. Creativity is a give-and-take, push-and-pull process of opening and closing, tightening and letting go. Trevor Nunn, the former Director of London's National Theatre and the director of the musicals *Cats* and *Les Misérables*, describes it as accelerating and slowing down. It involves taking risks and being opportunistic, using all one's qualities, both confidence and fear, both hard facts (data, the 'real world') and soft senses (dreams, intuition, gut feeling).

There is no magical order. Actually, there is no order at all. I have listed these elements in what might appear to be a rational order solely to make them memorable, but there is no rank, no hierarchy, no better beginning or worse end and we can start anywhere. Sometimes we need to start by dreaming and other times by analysing. Every time is different. The important thing is to start. Someone who wants a ready-made process, who waits for the whistle, who waits to be *told*, will create nothing.

SERIOUS PLAY

Children assume creativity is a kind of game and sensible adults feel the same. The Dutch historian Johan Huizinga invented the term 'homo ludens' as a play on the term 'homo sapiens' to suggest humans play before they think. The essence of play is that it is light-hearted and enjoyable; if it stops being fun, people stop playing. It is voluntary yet operates within given rules which everyone obeys absolutely even though the rules and the penalties may be arbitrary and silly. Play is both trivial and important. This often puzzles others who observe creative people at work: 'You don't look as if you're working!' In spite of being light-hearted and inconsequential, it is completely absorbing. It is uncertain and chancy; the opposite of routine and repetitive.

Film-maker David Puttnam says: 'The most exciting and creative period of my life was when I did a lot of tap dancing' – in the office, with his colleagues Alan Parker who later directed *Midnight Express* and Ridley Scott who made *Alien* and *Prometheus*. 'We spent hours practising tap dancing and in between we'd work out an ad. It was a fantastic thing. We'd be screaming with laughter, absolutely falling out and meanwhile creating some very remarkable work.' People who enjoy themselves are not only happier but they achieve more, faster. I tell this story nervously in case a company training manager decides to organize a tap-dancing session which misses the point. Puttnam's fun was spontaneous and mischievous.

Samuel Johnson's remark that 'It very seldom happens to a man that his business is his pleasure' is less true today than it was then. For creative people, business *is* pleasure and they would agree with Noël Coward that 'Work is much more fun than fun.' For many, their work is their life and they do it naturally and as if inevitably. Ideally, they have a high quality of work and a high quality of life and these two qualities intertwine and support each other.

Richard Feynman, Nobel Laureate and probably the greatest physicist of the late 20th century, decided early on while at Cornell University:

> I was only going to do things for the fun of it. Only that afternoon, as I was taking lunch, some kid threw up a plate in the cafeteria. There was a blue medallion on the plate: the Cornell sign. As the plate came down, it wobbled. It seemed to me that the blue thing went round faster than the wobble and I wondered what the relationship was between the two. I was just playing; it had no importance at all. So I played around with the equation of motion of rotating things and I found out that if the wobble is small the blue thing goes round twice as fast as the wobble. I tried to figure out why that was, just for the fun of it, and this led me to the similar problems in the spin of an electron and that led me back into quantum electro-dynamics which is the problem I had been working on. I continued to play with it in this relaxed fashion and it was like letting a cork out of a bottle. Everything just poured out and in very short order I worked out the things for which I won the Nobel Prize.

From this story, with its echoes of Archimedes' cry of Eureka, we learn three things. One, have fun. Two, always have a problem at the back of your mind. Three, don't skip lunch.

WHAT THINKING LOOKS LIKE

As people become more skilful at managing their talents, they develop distinct personality traits. One of the most articulate analysts of the creative spirit, Anthony Storr, believes they are characterized by a greater division of opposites than are other people and, equally important, that they are more aware of those opposites. They do not close off possibilities. Physicist Niels Bohr said that one of his father's favourite maxims was that 'Profound truths are recognized by the fact that the opposite is also a profound truth', and in his marvellous story 'The Crack-Up', writer F. Scott Fitzgerald said: 'The test of a first-rate intelligence is the ability to hold two opposed ideas in the mind at the same time, and still retain the ability to function.'

People who manage their creativity successfully, says Storr, are more determined and more skilful at exploring these tensions. They have a strong ego, tend to be more creative in their domestic arrangements and, if so minded, surround themselves with beautiful homes and gardens. Compared to the average person, they tend to be more independent; have a greater concern with shape and form; have a greater preference for complexity and asymmetry; have, in Goethe's words, a 'love of Truth'; and to be more overtly bisexual. Salvador Dali advised, 'You have to systematically create confusion, it sets creativity free.'

One of Britain's most successful TV producers, Peter Bazalgette, who became the Chairman of Arts Council England, says creative people have six characteristics. The first is open-mindedness: 'It means allowing your mind to wander in an almost dream-like way.' The second quality is independence of mind: 'Creative people are rule-breakers, not rule-makers.' Third is not being afraid of change. Next is 'The blank sheet of paper test. Creative people are challenged by a space and want to put something in it.' Fifth is a well-developed sense of humour. He agrees with Storr that creative people are competitive and ambitious. Swedish psychologist K. Anders Ericsson made a calculation, later popularized by Malcolm Gladwell, that the minimum effort to master a skill is 10,000 hours of practice, but perhaps 10,000 hours of curiosity and competition would be a better use of time.

As Bowie and Eno said in their replies to Vaske, it is about going to the edge, beyond the point where one keeps one's balance, and then peering over. The psychologist Erving Goffman spent a lifetime thinking about 'those existential moments of truth when character is gambled and people take risks sometimes wildly unjustified both to prove themselves right and, more profoundly, to prove themselves'.

Steve Jobs's extraordinary success demonstrated both qualities vividly. The Silicon Valley house magazine *WIRED* compared Jobs's Apple with Silicon Valley's core beliefs and said Jobs broke five sacred rules. One, the Valley says, 'Embrace open systems', but Jobs designed Apple's software so it only works on Apple devices. Two, the Valley says, 'Communicate, blog what you are doing', but Jobs never talked to the press and, according to *WIRED*, sued children who sent him ideas. Three, the Valley says, 'Play nice', but Jobs was utterly determined to build Apple and destroy competitors. Four, the Valley says, 'Love your customers', but Jobs did exactly what he wanted to do. Five, the Valley says, 'Coddle your employees', but Jobs famously screamed at almost everyone. *WIRED* might have added that Valley lore says, 'Focus on software', but Apple focuses on design and buys in a lot of software.

It is not easy to sum up creative people. The poet T. S. Eliot was a good example of personal oddities. He wrote harsh, elegiac poetry; worked competently in Lloyds Bank; wore rouge; enjoyed birdwatching and loved boxing. According to his biographer, Peter Ackroyd, Eliot was aware of the incongruities but had no interest in making them consistent or related to his literary work.

People disagree about most fundamental matters such as religion, morals, manners and sex but most cultures acknowledge creativity's primal importance as a generative power. It enlivens and makes distinctive what would otherwise be routine and repetitive. Socrates said the unexplored life is not worth living. When Shakespeare's Lear wants to express complete futility, he says, 'Nothing will come of nothing'. We admire creative people because they turn something into something new and we may fear them for the same reason.

When people stop being creative, they stop changing, stop learning, and in an important sense they stop living. As Bob Dylan sings, 'He who's not busy being born, / Is busy dying'. The Egyptian lawyer and economist Kamil Idris, who became Director General of the World Intellectual Property Organization, says: 'It is a simple formula: to live, we must create.' Without creativity, we could not imagine, discover or invent anything. We would not have fire, language or science. We would not be curious today about what we could do to make life better tomorrow.

One of Britain's greatest actors of the 20th century, Laurence Olivier, gave a majestic performance in *Henry V* one evening which reduced his fellow performers to wide-eyed admiration. After the final curtain, Charles Laughton and others went to Olivier's dressing-room to congratulate the great man, only to see him weeping. 'But, Larry,' said Laughton, 'you were marvellous.' 'I know,' Olivier said, 'but I don't know why.' Creativity isn't easy and, as Olivier knew, it is never exactly repeatable.

4
Where Ideas Take Root

CHOOSING THE RIGHT PLACE

The starting point of creative ecologies is the everyday observation that levels of creativity vary from place to place, with some being hospitable and others indifferent or uncomprehending or even hostile. Each place has a different degree of freedom, affecting who is allowed to speak and what they are allowed to say, and different market conditions which affect who is allowed to trade.

Each person, in turn, has their own attitudes towards these two conditions. Some put a higher value on the freedom to express their own personal view while others are more interested in what a market wants. This choice between expressing one's individual voice and adjusting it to take account of others is an age-old quandary. Whether someone feels a place is hospitable or hostile is therefore not an absolute but depends on the fit between the place and their own inclinations and the opportunities to be cleverer at spotting gaps and creating novelty.

The scientists who worked out the early ideas of what it means to have the right fit between a population and its environment were themselves in the right place at the right time. Nineteenth-century Britain, Germany and France had an abundant variety of naturalists, geologists, anatomists, ornithologists, biologists, zoologists, sociologists and medical doctors, as well as disputatious theologians to argue for tradition, always a useful corrective. One of the champions of the new science was Charles Darwin, who started corresponding with naturalists and scientists while still at school and set off for two years on the *Beagle* when he was only 22 years old. Darwin's life, from childhood rambles to his difficult decision when to publish, was as much affected by the environment as his personal instincts.

The man who discovered genes was not so fortunate. Gregor Mendel was born 13 years later than Darwin but lived in remote Silesia in what is now the Czech Republic and his isolation and the constraints on travel, apart from two years' study in Vienna, prevented his theories from being known. He had neither the freedom nor the means to meet others, and probably not much desire, and published only a few scientific articles. He died in a monastery and his papers were burned after his death. Mendel was extraordinarily creative but he never found the right niche and Darwin never knew of his discovery and others were unaware of it until many years later. A meeting between Darwin and Mendel is a fascinating might-have-been.

Ernst Haeckel, who developed and named the science of ecology, was born after Mendel and in the more interesting city of Potsdam, which was the court capital of Prussia and famous for its learning and science. He visited Charles Darwin in his home in Kent in 1866, a few years after the publication of *On the Origin of Species*. He travelled, though not as far as Darwin, and mingled with many artists, writers and scientists. The Swedish writer and painter August Strindberg, author of *Miss Julie*, one of the period's most scandalous plays, was an enthusiastic visitor.

Darwin had collected impressive evidence that offspring born to the same parents have different characteristics and that some survive and some do not (the struggle for existence). He judged that the ones who survived did so because they were more fit for their environment (the survival of the fittest). Because they lived longer, they had more offspring. He was a cautious writer and *On the Origin of Species* carefully avoided making firm conclusions about human evolution, leaving that to his later book, *The Descent of Man*.

Haeckel was more speculative and assertive. He liked to construct systems and find new relationships (he was the first to attach the word 'stem' to cells that are capable of renewing themselves and producing other cells). In 1866, the year he met Darwin, he coined the word 'ecology' to describe the study of how organisms relate to each other and to their environment. It shares with 'economy' the same Greek root of 'oikos', which means home but, instead of focusing on money, ecology refers to all kinds of resources and how they affect inhabitants' welfare. It looks at how *place* affects *behaviour*, both restricting and stimulating change.

THE QUAD

I have selected four attributes of ecologies which are relevant to why some places are more hospitable to creative relationships than others and more open to new ideas. They are: change, diversity, learning and adaptation. Together I call them the *Quad*.

They work in pairs. The first pair, change and diversity, happens whether we are aware of it or not, and we may have little control over it. The second pair, learn and adapt, is what we can choose to do, if we wish and have the freedom to do. Outsiders are probably more aware of a place's rate of change and diversity because they are physically evident but people on the inside are more concerned with the second pair of learning and adaptation.

Ecologies *change* and *diversify* as the cumulative result of people mixing and interpreting, accepting and throwing away. The rate of change increases if they are free to pick and choose, to copy this idea or experiment with that idea, and to say either 'Eureka! Let's do it!' or 'Well, I don't know, let's try something else.' They may well use an idea in ways that they know flouts the original intention. A graphic designer may see a colour on a dress and use it on a book cover (the dress designer probably copied the colour in the same way).

Every time people act like this they change the context and the meaning and thus the idea itself. Even ideas that are discarded leave their trace in their own minds as well as in the minds of others. The result is more ideas than anyone can handle or even imagine. Once begun, the process is hard to stop ('Ideas are like rabbits,' said novelist John Steinbeck. 'You get a couple and learn how to handle them, and pretty soon you have a dozen.')

We sort these ideas through a process of *learning* and *adaptation*. I want to differentiate between education and learning even though they are often used as synonyms. Education can be summed up as what someone does to somebody else. It is a system for teaching young people at school and university, always led by government and usually administered by government, to ensure everyone in the population shares the same basic knowledge and upholds the same culture, ethics and standards of social behaviour. It socializes people. It helps the majority of children to change from being self-obsessed infants to becoming aware of the interests and needs of others and it ensures most teenagers have the same basic cognitive and social skills. Then, at some point, education stops. People leave school or college and never go back.

Learning is different. It is personal in the sense of being self-interested, self-motivated and self-organized. We learn only if and when we want to. Learning is faster and more chaotic than being taught and it fails more often but, if managed, can be more productive. Learning is how a creative mind monitors itself. It is revealing that the English language has a word for a teacher but not for the person being taught, except as a target for the teaching, such as pupil or student; and it has a word for a learner but not for where they learn from. Education is about doing something to unnamed people while learning is about what we do to ourselves. Education is going to a university because all one's friends are going too (nothing wrong with that) and learning is joining an online educational service like the Khan Academy or Sebastian Thrun's Udacity or trying in any way at all to improve one's creative capital by the end of the day.

In the 1970s both America and Europe were beginning to explore the new worlds of fast, time-share computing. The technologies were common to both countries but people's attitudes to learning were very different and, in the end, the attitudes to learning were more important. In America, a fortunate generation of young American students got access to the first time-share computers in schools and on university campuses. Access appears to have been relatively easy, although sometimes the students had to show ingenuity to explain why they were practically living inside the labs. University staff seemed as enthusiastic as they were. There was a sense of hobbyists having fun but also of real potential to work in one of California's existing companies or start a new one. The learning was fast, open and cumulative.

A few years later the BBC launched a computer literacy project with a TV series, books and a supply of cheap but state-of-the-art personal computers. The first Acorn Micro was produced in 1981, the same year that Apple produced its first Macintosh (the 'A' of Acorn still survives in ARM, Britain's largest software company). For a time, Britain's bedroom geeks were as creative and innovative as America's campus-based geeks. But most schools and universities did not realize what was happening or were unwilling to help, home-grown electronics companies were few on the ground and home-grown investors even scarcer. The hard-studying students were isolated and unable to move to the next stage because they were caught in an ecology that lacked a capacity to learn.

'The capacity to learn' was a favourite phrase of an Indonesian writer and activist called Soedjatmoko, who referred to the BBC project as an example of teaching well but not learning well. His test bed was his own country. When Indonesia became independent in 1940 it had a population of 70 million. By 2010, this had risen to 230 million. The increase was both a blessing and a major challenge; it meant more workers but many more mouths to feed and more money needed for education and health. Soedjatmoko urged international banks to invest directly in people's learning abilities but they preferred infrastructure like roads, harbours and railways. Soedjatmoko believed passionately that society's capacity to learn was more important than externally donated political, financial or technological resources.

Having learned, the next step is to adapt, to change how we behave and what we do. Teachers can put information in front of someone and ask them to remember it and repeat it back but they cannot guarantee the information has any effect. It can go in one ear and out the other, as my teacher used to say. But learning implies change.

Walt Disney liked to say learning without adaptation was literally pointless: 'The future is not out there waiting to be discovered. It is created, created first in the mind and then in the action.' Disney was the Steve Jobs of his time. His response to a problem was a ferocious, no-holds-barred examination of possibilities, ignoring colleagues who pointed out that others had already produced an answer, until he came up with his own solution. He treated what others said as merely one input among many. Nothing was agreed until he had worked it out himself. Having worked it out, he made sure it was acted on.

Learning does not depend on its own structures but draws on everyone else's and does not have its own resources equivalent to education's schools and curriculum but scavenges for whatever it wants. It is an open process rather than a building or a list. When the design specialist Ideo launched its online platform for open innovation, Ideolab, it said it would always be inclusive, community-centred, collaborative and optimistic. It also said it would 'always be in beta', which is computer jargon for being in draft, unfinished, open to change and improvement. Software systems in beta are normally restricted to hackers and developers and not available for public use. Ideo was saying Ideolab will always be developing and always learning. This is how we learn and how we adapt ourselves and the environment, hopefully in our favour.

Moving In, Moving On

People's rate of learning and adaptation depends on their environment, which is partly a given and happenstance and partly a matter of choice. We make choices when deciding where to live and work and then by having relationships with others and taking actions which affect the environment in our favour.

The environment is a bundle (a rather large bundle) of habitats and niches, and niches within niches. The value of a niche is that it enables the inhabitants to know what has been done before, what is being done now, and what might be worth doing next. Only then can they tease out the best that they can do and know whether their ideas are going to attract interest and attention. Choosing a niche involves finding somewhere they can work at their preferred level of independence (freedom) and with their preferred exposure to what other people want (markets).

A move to a city is a move to a habitat and a move to work in a specific sector is like a move into a niche. The decision to move into a niche is more difficult to get right because it involves so many factors, ranging from people's lifestyles and morals to technology and money. Some people seem so well-fitted to their niche, so perfectly of their time and place, that they almost seem to create their personal sensory eco-system around them and to symbolize a new mood or style.

Choosing a niche is more a matter of lifestyle than money and life-style is a more powerful attractor than money. By lifestyle I mean people's habits, manners and morals and their attitude to freedoms and independence. It might seem that putting such personal matters above business calculations is rather self-indulgent but it is the most rational choice when personal feelings are so integral to the process. People often settle into a niche because they like someone who works there or they want to work in the same way as others. Alex Graham, the co-founder of British TV producer Wall to Wall, says his reason for starting his own company was not money but control: 'I wanted to be in control of the programmes I made.' Of course, the money is important because the rent must be paid but it's not the main reason, and people like him have other objectives.

Each niche has its own ethics on the ownership of ideas and the morality of copying. Each strikes its own balance between individual expression and the market. Each has its own level of tolerance to self-publicity and hype (in film it is expected but in code it is deplored). These ethics vary from country to country. America's entertainment contract for a 'work for hire', and China's buy-outs, which require a creator to give up all rights, would be anathema in France and Germany where creators expect to retain control over their work.

Niches vary in their scope for creative and financial independence. The creative economy depends upon very many people working on their own (sole traders) or in very small companies. In Britain, over 90 per cent of companies in arts, culture, design and media employ four or fewer people. The remainder work in a small number of gateway companies which wield exceptional market power because they own brands, have access to investment funds and control the gateways to distributors and buyers. Most gateway companies are large and some are very large, such as the major dotcoms, music, TV, film, book and media companies, but it is possible for a small company to be a gateway, as writers looking for an agent and artists looking for a gallery know well. The gaps between a sole trader and a gateway company can be chasm-wide in sectors which depend on selling in consumer markets but much more bridgeable in sectors which sell to clients. Even the largest multinationals often hire small funky design and advertising agencies.

A person's preference for being a sole trader or a corporate executive is a lifestyle choice, especially if it involves a choice between selling to consumers or clients, and usually precedes the choice of sector. Wanting to be a novelist and wanting to work in a group is not a job, as far as I am aware, and being a fashion designer by oneself, which used to be common, is now a dwindling possibility. Musicians who can stand up and perform in front of hundreds may be hopeless when faced with their manager (a source of many misunderstandings and financial battles). Architects and designers who can pitch persuasively to a client may go blank at the thought of selling direct to a high street consumer. A preference for a way of working determines a choice of sector more often than a choice of sector determines a way of working.

Questions of aesthetics are manifestly the touchstone of arts, culture and design. They will be present in the creator's imagination and in the mind of everyone else who works in the sector, if less passionately. Gallerists need to be as articulate (possibly more so) as their artists, fashion companies employ a hundred managers and media people to every designer, and digital managers need to understand what their programmers have done, if not how. If they do not feel the same excitement, they will not be able to sustain relationships and will not prosper.

Writers and even more so poets may be surprised to discover that software programmers regard code as having poetic qualities (a point well made in Kenneth Goldsmith's book, *Uncreative Writing*). The sensual elements of creativity are always present, even if the creative act itself has no obvious aesthetic and no obvious relationship with its final form. Many poets and writers believe their choice of technology for the act of writing affects their style even if it has no relationship to how their words are published.

The spread of digital coding has introduced new aesthetics which are not always welcome. Many film-makers who grew up on front-lit celluloid are uncomfortable with back-lit computer-generated images and many who work with a flat 2D picture plane are uneasy with 3D, which plays with depth. One reason why film and games companies seldom work together, in spite of seemingly compelling reasons to do so, is that their approaches to narrative are so different and neither of them wants to compromise. These tensions are often described in terms of a switch from analogue to digital technology but they are really about digital technology's effect on aesthetics. These choices are so basic and so personal that to get them wrong can cripple the sensibilities.

IDEAS FROM ELSEWHERE

The purpose of finding the right niche is to be able to develop the right relationships. It may be that creativity starts with private inspirations but even people famous for being solitary have usually acquired a stock-room of ideas from elsewhere. The true naïf artist or innocent inventor is freakishly rare. Most relationships fall into three groups: imitation, collaboration and competition.

The Most Intimate Kind of Copying

Children imitate what they see their parents do and later what they see other adults do in a kind of ambient awareness. They often imitate someone instinctively without knowing why but simply enjoy the experience and if the person being imitated also imitates the child then their mutual enjoyment is pure pleasure. Teachers build on this instinct to teach children how to read and write and how to behave. As their social circle widens, so people imitate friends and colleagues and indeed anyone who has high status in their peer group.

Richard Dawkins, author of *The Selfish Gene*, was once told he was imitating a colleague's mannerism and realized he had been unaware he was doing so. He believes such unconscious imitation influences how 'catchphrases, fashions, children's games, beliefs and even ways of making pots' spread around a community. He invented the word 'meme' to describe how a behaviour is transmitted in a population before anyone has coded or explained it.

Mimicking people is a good way to acquire their skills. A London business school once asked me to design a graduate course in computer animation. I soon discovered the potential employers were unenthusiastic because they believed the best way for anyone to learn animation was to work alongside someone who was more experienced and watch what they were doing. A CEO said he could tell if a novice was worth hiring within a few weeks of their watching-and-copying and that a trainee who had been working this way for six weeks would be as proficient as a graduate who had been at university for three years. It was a dramatic lesson: get close to people who are better than you.

When people join a new group they become alert to how the other members behave and pay attention to *how* people say things as much as *what* they are saying. They know that if they conform in these ways, they are more likely to be welcomed and included in those intimate moments when other people reveal their doubts and are open to disagreement.

Chinese blogger Isaac Mao, one of the founders with Chen Xu and Liu Yan of Shanghai's co-working pioneer XinDanWei, says one of the powers of online social networks is that they enable people to pump their mimicries into the creative ecosystem where they can be acquired, performed, passed on, re-tweeted and imitated again in a flash. Whether or not memes are the correct mechanism, it is true that imitation never stops. Mimicry is learning on speed.

Collaboration: Adding More Assets

It seems that the cultural formats which were dominant 100 years ago depended on one person's singular expression; that forms which evolved during the 20th century, such as mass media and popular entertainment, were a mix of single and collaborative work; and that newer formats depend on collaboration and co-authorship. This opening out has been both a cause and an effect of the increasing number of women working in the arts, culture, media and design.

Coding and programming are collaborative and interactive. The majority of software companies, including the most successful, are based on partnerships between two or three people (all men, as it happens, suggesting that in this respect male dominance continues). They dislike hierarchy and prefer small groups and flat management styles, a feeling summed up in a remark by Francis Galton, cousin of Charles Darwin, about the 'wisdom of crowds' and in Eric Raymond's declaration that 'Given enough eyeballs, all bugs are shallow', which is normally shortened to 'more eyes, fewer bugs'.

One of the most admired teachers of collaboration is Keith Johnstone, who taught improvisation at London's Royal Court Theatre for many years. In his classic *Impro*, which is revered within the theatre world but almost unknown outside it, he writes: 'People in a group are amazed when I explain that they're supposed to work for the other members, that each individual is to be interested in the progress of other members; yet obviously if a group supports its own members strongly it'll be a better group to work in.'

For Charles Leadbeater, who invented the term 'we-think':

The basic argument is very simple. Most creativity is collaborative. It combines different views, disciplines and insights in new ways. The opportunities for creative collaboration are expanding the whole time. The number of people who could be participants in these creative conversations is going up largely thanks to the communications technologies that now give voice to many more people and make it easier for them to connect. As a result we are developing new ways to be innovative and creative at mass scale. We can be organized without having an organization.

Valve is a small but critically and commercially well-regarded American games company which published its staff handbook in 2012 in this spirit of disorganized openness. The book is beautifully designed, which is as it should be if you are treating people with respect. It describes Valve as 'A fearless adventure in knowing what to do when no one's there telling you what to do', and prefers collaboration to hierarchy:

> Hierarchy is great for maintaining predictability and repeatability. It simplifies planning and makes it easier to control a large group of people from the top down, which is why military organizations rely on it so heavily. But when you're an entertainment company that's spent the last decade going out of its way to recruit the most intelligent, innovative, talented people on Earth, telling them to sit at a desk and do what they're told obliterates 99 per cent of their value. We want innovators, and that means maintaining an environment where they'll flourish. That's why Valve is flat. It's our shorthand way of saying that we don't have any management, and nobody reports to anybody else . . . Valve works in ways that might seem counterintuitive at first. This handbook is about the choices you're going to be making and how to think about them. Mainly, it's about how not to freak out now that you're here.

As well as maximizing their employees' potential, companies are exploring how to collaborate with customers. In 2010, Citroën asked its Facebook friends what they wanted for its new C1 car due to start production in 2012. BMW asked young Chinese would-be buyers of its cars to suggest new features and invited the six winners to its factory in Munich. Nike invites loyal customers to become involved in Nike-ID and customize their shoes (which gives Nike instant feedback on new trends). Many companies use online feedback forums. Since 2001 innocentive.com has dealt with thousands of challenges from motor neurone disease to solar power in isolated African villages. The Quirky site is more commercially oriented and promises two new consumer products a week.

As a result, all companies, large and small, want to hire people who like to work in groups. Nicky Binning, head of 'global mobility' at advisory firm KPMG (in other words, recruitment) says: 'It is the ability to understand what is in front of you, and work collaboratively, that counts. You have to work together as a team because it is likely that you are facing something you have never faced before.

There was a time when KPMG would hire accountants or IT technicians. Now, it wants people with emotional intelligence and analytic abilities allied to specific skills.'

There is a downside to collaboration as there is to mimicry. It can blunt the effectiveness of a group's more insightful and radical members at the same time as it increases the average levels of success overall, and the search for consensus can push radical ideas to the margins or ignore them completely. Edward de Bono's system of using multiple coloured hats cleverly gets around this problem by having a green hat for wacky ideas, which gives the hat-wearers confidence without undercutting their later contributions. It has also been shown that members of a group are more likely to remember what was discussed if they do have a personal stake in what was said. A group's effectiveness depends on a good mix of members and it should be large enough to offer diversity but not too large to stifle individual views. There is some evidence that it also depends on the male–female ratio: the more women, the better.

The age-old benefit of collaboration is summed up by Isaac Newton's remark, 'If I have seen further, it is by standing on the shoulders of giants'. It is refreshing to discover that this comment seems to date from at least the 12th century, so Newton was already practising what he preached. The Indian writer Rabindranath Tagore was more outspoken: 'Oh Fool, to try to carry thyself upon thy own shoulders!'

Competition

The American kinetic artist Liliane Lijn once told me how she had constructed one of her intricate mobiles. She is as imaginative as any artist and proficient as any engineer and she was concerned that the quality of the final construction met both criteria in ensuring the mobile's set of planes and spheres produced the desired effect. There was integrity and craftsmanship in her imagination and in her actions. She kept in mind her own standards and those of one or two other people who had faced the same problem and she wanted to do better than them.

We face two judges, ourselves and others. We want to meet our own high standards. Is this the best I can do? We also want the result to succeed in the market-place. Is this what people really want? In front of both judges, our own ambition and the judgement of others, we are putting forward our private ideas, so success and failure have a personal edge. The benefits of freedom come at a cost. Freedom gives us room to manoeuvre but the lack of signposts can be unnerving. The fear of failure is always present.

Facing up to the first judge is a lonely task even when one is surrounded by friends and allies, because the arbiter of one's own work is oneself. The person who conceives a new idea has to judge whether it is worth pursuing. Is it really new? Is it really better?

Having satisfied the first judge to the best of our ability, we can put our ideas into the market. The goal here is to convince others that the idea that we find most interesting, out of all possible ideas, is something they might also find interesting. Our idea has to meet everyone else's standards of novelty, meaning and interest. It has to fight in the market-place, which means we have to choose the right market and then succeed in that market.

Each sector has its own way of evaluating ideas and deciding what to do next. It is hard to succeed unless you are not only familiar with how the people around you make their decisions but also accept their criteria as being fair and reasonable (which does not rule out passionate, loud arguments on occasion). It is a two-way process, us judging others and others judging what we do. How we handle the give-and-take of these opinions will determine not only the success of our ideas but our ability to operate within the group.

Mad inventors are not mad because they have mad ideas but because they ignore other people's ideas. They ignore these two judges. They do not judge what they are doing and they do not care what everyone else is doing. They choose freedom above everything else but it is not enough. We need to manage that freedom purposefully.

5
Managing Ideas

THE ECONOMICS OF AN IDEA

There are people on both sides of the creative/business coin who believe creativity and business are incompatible and may even be mutually destructive. The managers' task is to manage this tension and to develop and enhance ideas rather than stifle them, whether as individuals trying to organize their relationship to an idea or as executives who want to optimize a company's negotiating power over an asset.

It is important to know what these assets are or could be. They're a mixed bunch, a floating population, of ideas and meanings. Some are public and up-for-grabs while others are private and controlled by people who come and go with their own personal views and expectations and resist being tied down, although occasionally their ideas can be caught in the net of a contract and sold on with confidence (there's more on assets in chapter 10).

Managing creativity starts with understanding the make-up of the various assets you already have or need from others. Together, they constitute an interlocking set of four value systems based on physical objects, intangible qualities, the ways they are experienced and the intellectual property rights attached to them. These four systems interact at all stages from the initial expression through to the market transaction.

The *physical* objects are the easiest to identify but their appeal and their value often lie in their *intangible* qualities. Both the object and its qualities contribute to the *experience*, which is also influenced by a range of factors on which the maker and the user, or buyer and seller, may have different views. The experience of reading, hearing music or using a website is the combined result of what is on offer and a user's personal feelings at that moment. Alongside these three systems, *copyright*, patents and trademarks operate a parallel world of values with their own idiosyncratic rules and sell-by dates.

The universality principle which says everyone is born creative results in very large numbers of producers, makers and buyers exercising their own decisions on these matters (spending time, paying attention, paying money). It also implies that they make decisions according to personal, subjective criteria whereas conventional economic theory assumes everyone wants to maximize their welfare in the same way. Ideas people are as rational as anyone else but they calculate their welfare differently. It is rational for sellers to forego revenues if they put a higher value on their market reputation; or for a buyer to pay more for novelty. Reducing what we want to a reality measurable only by money is an absurd over-simplification of human behaviour.

The ease with which ideas can be borrowed and copied multiplies the number of transactions and creates a positive relationship between people with the same idea. Whether a hundred other people have the same idea or share the same experience may have no effect on any one individual's ability to have it and experience it fully and, in many cases, may increase their enjoyment. The growth of the scale of the creative economy goes hand-in-hand with an increase in people's desire for shared artistic and cultural experiences, both in how they are produced and how they are experienced.

My enjoyment of something shared in this way does not 'rival' yours, and so public ideas that are shared by many people at the same time are called 'non-rival'. This shared experience can be a good thing or a bad thing, depending on your point of view, as it can increase people's pleasure but it can also lead to disparities in who is paying and in how much. It is in the nature of art, culture, design and media that there is often a skew between who pays and who enjoys. Benefiting from public ideas without paying is called 'free-riding'. Some markets depend upon a degree of free-riding but if the skew is too great the market becomes unsustainable. The skew is most evident in the market for physical products and services, such as 'free' entry to a museum, where the real costs are very high, but virtually trivial online where the costs of supply are so low.

The point of trademarks, copyright and patents is to restrict this kind of copying or free-riding either absolutely or for a price. In order for some people to benefit, others must go without. There is a fierce debate about the social utility of this exchange. Some say these monopolies are necessary to reward innovation and that intellectual property rights are a good way to allocate resources. Others say any constraint hampers creativity, drags down economic development, and is a misallocation of resources. The management of ideas involves making fine judgements: first, when to exploit the non-rival nature of ideas and, second, when to assert ownership rights and make an idea rival.

These products do not compete in conventional terms of objects and cash but more on the basis of what's recommended and what's available, itself a mix of equipment, access and previous capital expenditures. It follows that the law of diminishing returns, which states that each additional unit of production becomes more expensive to make, does not apply. The law assumes that production is dependent on limited resources and that therefore at some point the cost of producing one more unit would exceed the revenue obtained from selling it. The point at which marginal cost meets marginal revenue is called the equilibrium point. Such a trade-off makes sense in a world of limited resources and price competition but in an economy based on ideas and free-riding the costs of production are less important.

If we combine these factors, we can sketch a picture of the economics of ideas. Companies in the ordinary economy operate with scarce material resources over which they assert permanent property rights, and compete primarily on price. In the creative economy, individuals use resources which are infinite and over which they assert intellectual rights, which may be short-run, and which do not compete primarily on price.

We have moved from a world of diminishing returns, based on the scarcity of physical objects (the repetitive economy), to a world of increasing returns based on the infinity of possible ideas and people's genius for using ideas to generate new products and transactions (the creative economy). A company's control of products and prices becomes less relevant if production resources are freely available, if products are intangible, if price competition is negligible and if the market is driven by demand not by supply.

New Patterns of Work

It is a shift as dramatic as the rise of industrial manufacturing in Europe 200 years ago, when the French journalist and economist Jean-Baptiste Say invented the term 'entrepreneur' to describe someone who unlocked capital in land to invest in a factory or, as Say said, 'invest in the future'. He was interested in how people take advantage of moments of instability. The Austrian economist Joseph Schumpeter similarly believed that new ideas can flourish only if old ideas are pushed aside in a process he called 'creative destruction', which is a good description of how people develop new ideas to fit changing circumstances.

As manufacturing declines in Europe and America, these countries are shifting investments into creativity and innovation in a transition as fundamental as the switch from land to manufacturing. The period of large capital-intensive manufacturers and full permanent employment is coming to an end. The reasons are the increase in university education and the rise of personally held knowledge as well as globalization and the competitiveness of low-wage economies in other countries. As a result, freelance work, portfolio part-time work, sole trading, partnerships and micro-companies are becoming more common. Some people prefer these alternatives, while others do not but have little choice. In America, 6.7 million people work this way, 14 per cent of the working population, and in Europe, the percentage is 15 per cent. In the heartlands, the percentages are much higher, about 50 per cent. Accurate figures are hard to determine because many governments offer tax incentives to self-employed people to set up their own company, which has the effect of hiding the true figure.

This shift does not fit easily into countries' arrangements for tax and social security because government tax systems are based on jobs-as-employment rather than jobs-as-things-to-be-done. Self-employed and freelance people typically earn income from a range of different sources, some of which relate to the current year and some to jobs done years ago. As they move between their portfolio of projects, from working to not working and back to working again, and being both employed and self-employed, the tax and social security rules begin to creak. Government officials who have chosen to work in bureaucracies find it hard to understand this.

Dotcoms are especially troublesome if they operate internationally, as most do. American entertainment companies have always located their overseas operations in low-cost and low-tax countries. The internet has opened more opportunities as companies can set their sales and fulfilment operations in separate countries and use transfer pricing to minimize tax liabilities. American law supports this. Back in 1994 the Supreme Court ruled that companies only had to collect sales taxes in states where they had a physical presence (which encouraged Amazon to base itself in the small state of Washington instead of New York or California).

This presents a major problem for European governments as they face mounting public expenditures and falling tax revenues. The main offenders are global dotcoms, all American and all brought up on the Supreme Court's 1994 ruling, as few European dotcoms are big enough to make transfer pricing worthwhile. The OECD commented in 2012 that 'Many are questioning the fact that multinational enterprises, and in particular those that are IP-intensive, have effective tax rates dramatically lower than the statutory rates of the countries in which they operate.' The British tax authorities wisely decided to fight the dotcoms with their own weapons and asked British Aerospace to design a search-and-connect algorithm called Connect to identify international tax evasion which brought in $2.3 billion in its first year. But it did not solve the underlying problem that national tax authorities cannot keep up with global online corporations.

Europe's problem is not only the high levels of tax avoidance but the long-term decline in its capacity for work. In the global economic boom of the 1980s, the national profiles of the working population in Europe, America and Japan looked roughly the same. In 1980, 64 per cent of Europe's working population between the ages of 15 and 64 had jobs compared to 63 per cent in America and 68 per cent in Japan. Thirty years later, the figures have become startlingly different. Europe now has the smallest working population in percentage terms and the trend is downwards. There has been a significant decline in business employment, undercutting the main source of creativity and innovation, although the effects have been mitigated by a significant increase in government and public sector employment. Government jobs are proper jobs but they don't usually increase creativity, innovation or competitiveness. Overall, Europe's working population has drifted down to 60 per cent while America's had climbed to 76 per cent and Japan's to 75 per cent.

It is hardly surprising, since the growth of mass industrial manufacturing was the cause of permanent full-time employment, that its decline is causing it to diminish. Applying the rule of comparative advantage, which suggests countries should specialize in what they do best, the industrialized countries are concentrating on sectors where they add the greatest value, which is in upstream creative inputs, and contract the less skilled manufacturing tasks to low-cost countries in Asia and elsewhere. It remains to be seen whether this separation is sustainable and creativity can be managed separately from making and manufacturing.

MANAGEMENT LEVERS

Americans were the first to put management at the heart of a business and treat it as separate from the provision of capital or technology or the skills of finance and sales. Daniel Bell and others said that management's most powerful asset was information and the management of information was bringing about a 'post-industrial' society. Peter Drucker coined the term 'knowledge worker' and others talked of creative workers. Each term was a stepping stone to the creative economy.

They come together in a new triangle of work: the job of thinker, the just-in-time thinker and the creative entrepreneur. These, in turn, involve new kinds of offices and networks and a new set of financial assets:

The job of thinker
The just-in-time thinker
The creative entrepreneur

The network company
The temporary company
Clusters

Financing ideas
Hits and misses
Deals and contracts

The Thinker ('Thinking is a Proper Job')

Peter Jackson's Orcs helped Londoners to cross Oxford Circus safely because Nate Wittasek was thinking how to do his job better. Ben Cohen and Jerry Greenfield started Ben & Jerry's Ice Cream because they didn't like what was available and because Cohen, who has little sense of smell, wanted ice-cream with tasty chunks he could feel with his tongue. Tim Berners-Lee invented the World Wide Web because he wanted to contact new arrivals in the office without knowing their email addresses. Marc Zuckerberg had the idea for Facebook when he wanted to post comments about other people and Bo Yang started Douban because, sitting in a coffee shop one day, he wanted to know what the other customers were reading and listening to.

These 'commencement' incidents are trivial but each became the springboard of a new idea. Wanting ice-cream with chunks is personal. Wanting to comment on college friends is personal. If someone had told Mark Zuckerberg, even in jest, that he was on the verge of starting a corporation he might have frozen and would have found it hard to get advice. Bo Yang wanted to know what others were enjoying; as a result, 50 million people are now able do what he wanted to do. Many people become irritated when a computer does not do what they want but Tim Berners-Lee decided to fiddle around and work it out.

The job title is 'thinker' not 'thinking'. We all think in the sense that we use our brains but the job of thinker is a full-time occupation and as serious and dedicated as any. Computer expert Jeff Bezos gave himself the job in the early 1990s when he was working for a bank in New York and wondered how to exploit the internet's capacity to sell things. He had no experience of publishing but calculated that the number of book titles, so much bigger and more diverse than any other creative product, made books the ideal candidate, and in 1994 he started Amazon. When, three years later, he set up Amazon in Britain he bought a young online company called Bookspages that had been started by American and Irish entrepreneurs (one of whom later went on to start what became Britain's LoveFilm) as a launch-pad rather than an existing bricks-and-mortar retailer. He faced little competition because Britain's publishers and high street booksellers had put thinking low down their list of priorities. It is possible that some of them had thought like Jeff Bezos but done nothing about it, which is useless. Thinking is a proper job.

It often doesn't look like work. The American writer Ralph Waldo Emerson wrote in his diary: 'If a man sits down to think he is immediately asked if he has a headache.' A group of managers were once asked what they would do if they had their feet on the desk and the boss walked by. Everyone said they would take their feet off the desk. The questioner then asked: 'Does your boss like you to think?' to which the answer was, 'Sure.' 'Does he put a high value on you being original and thoughtful?'; 'Sure.' 'Do you sometimes think best by being relaxed – maybe staring into space, maybe staring out the window – maybe putting your feet on the desk?'; 'Sure.' Finally: 'So having your feet on the table may be a sign you are working at thinking?' 'No.'

It does not matter where you are. A BT/*Management Today* survey asked managers, 'Where do you have your best ideas?' What it called 'office work' generated a meagre 15 per cent of good ideas. The more productive occasions were 'At home' (17.8%), 'While commuting'

(17.1%) and 'During leisure activities' (16.9%). 'In the bath/shower' even scored 11.7 per cent.

The Just-in-Time Person

The term 'just-in-time' describes a logistics system that maintains low levels of stock in order to allow for last-minute customization and to cut down on warehousing costs, and obtains an item only if and when a customer wants it; in other words, 'just in time'. The system was introduced by Toyota and other Japanese car manufacturers when they began to export to America and is now standard practice worldwide.

I use the term to describe people with a specific creative skill who work only when and where they are wanted. They bring together three assets: their own expertise, their knowledge of a specific sector and their ability to slot into a group at short notice. Many arts and cultural organizations have always worked this way but almost all organizations now see the benefits.

The demand for just-in-time people increases as work becomes more oriented towards personal knowledge, more specialized and more collaborative. The advantage to clients is having the exact person one wants for as long as one wants, rather than financial gain (these people are not emergency stand-ins, nor are they cheap labour, although they are sometimes wrongly used as such). The advantage to just-in-time people is that they can concentrate on their own skills and be more flexible and opportunistic about who they work with. It also allows them to sell their services anywhere.

The trade unions oppose what they see as a casualization of labour. They fear their members will be hired and fired arbitrarily, lack employee rights, not be given any training and be paid less, and it is likely their fears are justified except possibly for the last point about money. Just-in-time workers have to assert their own rights by way of deals and contracts and have to select and pay for their own training. In spite of these concerns, the trend is unmistakable. The economic conditions and, in the public sector, the political conditions for large bureaucracies are fading fast.

People in a just-in-time operation face both centripetal and centrifugal forces. The centripetal forces draw them into a new project quickly and engender a strong team spirit, and as deadlines approach the energy is palpable. But because people's loyalties are divided between this and other projects, especially if the project is temporary, managers have to work harder to maintain cohesiveness and momentum. There is probably no better place to be than a project run on these lines if things are going well and no worse place when it goes badly.

The demand for just-in-time people is high and the rewards are good but many people don't like the hard work, the pressure or the risk. In Europe and America there is a shortage of skilled and university-educated workers capable of working in this way and an over-supply of low-skilled workers who are not capable or don't want to. The situation is worse in China, Brazil and developing countries where, in addition to the shortage, working on one's own can be seen as a sign of weakness. By 2020, it is estimated that industrialized economies will face a shortage of 10 per cent of skilled, flexible workers and China a shortage of around 15 per cent. China may close the gap but Europe and America may have a problem.

The Creative Entrepreneur

The workers in a factory may have excellent ideas about how to run their factory, possibly better than do the managers, but they cannot put their ideas into practice because they have no access to financial capital and their own intellectual capital is likely to be limited. Workers in a steel mill have never started or owned their own steel mill because the steel economy does not permit it. But creative workers can start their own business tomorrow because the creative economy encourages it.

Entrepreneurs in the creative economy operate as they do elsewhere but with the important difference that they deal in assets that are personal and lie within themselves rather than external assets of finance, equipment and so on. Their job is to create new meanings of their own assets which interest the market.

One of the businessmen I most admire is Nolan Bushnell, who founded Atari and developed the first mass-market video game. Atari was astonishingly successful, with profits of $300 million within a few years, becoming the fastest-growing company in American corporate history. Bushnell tells how:

> A guy wakes up in the morning and says, 'I'm going to become an entrepreneur.' So he goes to the best software programmer in the company where he is working and whispers, 'Would you like to join my company? Ten o'clock my place, Saturday. And bring some doughnuts.' Then he goes to the best finance guy and says, 'Bring some coffee.' And then he goes to the best patent lawyer and the best marketing guy with the same invitation. Ten o'clock Saturday rolls around. They ask, 'Hey, what is your company going to do?' You say, 'Build a new computer program'. Another hour, and you've all got an idea and a business plan. The finance guy says he knows where he can get some money [whenever I tell the story the Americans look bored at this point and the British look wistful]. Then they say to their host, 'So what have you done?' What, indeed? You've not provided the coffee. You've not provided the doughnuts. You've not provided the idea. You've been the entrepreneur. You made it happen.

These people share five characteristics:

- *vision*: A dream, and the desire to bring the dream to life. In *In Defence of Genius* entrepreneur-turned-pianist Ernest Hall said: 'Everyone must begin to trust their dreams. Out of that trust is born the artist who is the role model for the entrepreneur we now need.' Having made his money, Hall became famous not only for turning a vast old carpet factory, Dean Clough, into an arts-and-business centre but for discovering the delights of outrageous Japanese clothes at the age of 71.
- *focus*: Entrepreneurs are fixated on success. Austrian-born but Cambridge-resident Hermann Hauser is one of Britain's most successful venture capitalists and believes entrepreneurs should focus on only one thing. He says he distrusts anyone who says their company can do two things or even one-and-a-half things. Jeff Bezos would

agree: 'It's very hard to do even one thing in a truly excellent way and doing two things in a truly excellent way can get very tricky.' World chess champion Gary Kasparov says the difference between a good chess player and a great chess player is not really that the great chess player knows which moves to look at but that he knows which *not* to look at. Entrepreneurs know the dangers of what Ayelet Fishbach and other psychologists call 'goal dilution'. When someone has only one goal, and only one means of achieving it, the link between the means and the end is very strong, but each increase in the number of goals weakens the link and motivation falls.

- *finance*: I have known entrepreneurs who are inseparable from files of spreadsheets and others who make do with scraps of paper. They do not need to be financially astute so long as they realize that their success will be measured purely in financial terms, chiefly by their ability to generate cash. Financial skills assist one to avoid pitfalls, move faster and sleep at night. Entrepreneurs are comfortable with risk not in the sense of liking it but in the sense of not being afraid of it.

- *pride*: Trevor Bayliss, inventor of the clockwork radio, says, 'You need an ego the size of a truck to be an inventor.' Entrepreneurs believe not only that their idea will work but that they are the only one to make it work. They treat it as the centre of the universe which, for them, it is. They have pride in themselves and their idea and they are reluctant to give up. Their pride is seldom dented by failure and many serial entrepreneurs regard even failures as campaign medals.

- *urgency*: All the vision, focus and pride come to nothing if the entrepreneur is not in a hurry. Entrepreneurs always want to 'do it now' partly for competitive reasons but mostly because they cannot be bothered to think of anything else.

It is no secret that entrepreneurs can be difficult to work with. They have given themselves the job of head thinker and they only take advice when they want to. They have a low boredom threshold. There is good evidence that entrepreneurs have above-average levels of dyslexia and also that this does not handicap them. The known examples include Richard Branson, Steve Jobs and John Chambers, who founded Cisco, as well as the founders of Ford, General Electric, IBM and IKEA. Paul Orfalea, founder of Kinko's, who has both dyslexia and Attention Deficit Disorder, says, 'I think everyone should have dyslexia and ADD', which is one way of putting it. Cass Business School discovered that, compared to a national average of 10 per cent of the population, the incidence of dyslexia in entrepreneurs was as high as 35 per cent and in ordinary managers as low as 1 per cent. These are extraordinary disparities.

They can also disregard strategy in ways that frighten conventional managers. I remember a meeting with Art Barron, the former head of Paramount Pictures, when he was Chairman of Time Warner International. The Chairman of HBO had asked, 'What's our strategy?' Barron barked, 'We don't have a strategy. Strategies are for the little guys.' In one sentence, Barron consigned Michael Porter and his theories about the importance of corporate strategy to the past. In the creative economy, strategy emerges out of routine business.

Intuit founder Scott Cook, who is one of Silicon Valley's most imaginative entrepreneurs, as well as a director of conglomerate Procter & Gamble, estimates that 90 per cent of company strategies are irrelevant. He recounts with glee that when Google's two co-founders Larry Page and Sergey Brin compared the success rate of staff suggestions that fitted the company's strategy with ideas that someone thought were worth a try irrespective of the company's strategy, the latter had a higher success rate. He prefers 'emergent strategies' that just arise naturally from what people are doing right.

The Network Office

Creative people need offices for all the same reasons as other people: to go to in the morning, knowing one's colleagues will be going there too; to keep files; to hold meetings; to do 'office' work; and to demonstrate they work in a stable, solid kind of company. For many companies, this still holds true. But for many freelance people whose assets are in their head or in their smartphone and whose only files are electronic, the office itself is mobile.

Harlan Cleveland, whose accomplishments included being an American Ambassador and President of the University of Hawaii, and who was awarded the Prix de Tailloires for 'accomplished generalists', liked places built 'more around communities of *people* than communities of *place*'. Management consultant Arie de Geus says that 'A good decision is like an intelligent conversation.' Victoria Ward, banker-turned-entrepreneur and one of the founders of business adviser Spark Now, says they need areas for 'forced serendipity' ('encouraging' serendipity would sound better), spaces that provide 'knowledge shelters', and spaces where two people can meet on neutral ground. Everyone who has worked in an office, or been to a conference, will know what she means. People like to congregate in corners, around the water-cooler or the coffee-machine, and companies that fail to provide this environment are forced to have 'away days' out of the office.

These network structures tend to be flexible and flat, with short reporting lines, rather than rigid and hierarchical. America's W. L. Gore company has been flat since it was founded by husband-and-wife team Bill and Vieve Gore in 1958 to develop the innovative Gore-Tex fabric and now has annual sales around $3 billion. CEO Terry Kelly, who was chosen by staff, is delightfully upfront: 'It's a very chaotic environment. For some reason, management just never took hold . . . we don't like the "manager" word.'

For many young people, their work-based office and network is often a nicer and more convivial place than home. They are likely to spend more time, engage in more interesting activities and meet more friends there. Small groups emerge informally. Amazon has its 'pizza rule' that any team which, when working late, orders more than one pizza is too big and must split up. The St Luke's advertising agency in London encourages people to set up a new 'family' every time the core work-force exceeds 30 people. New York's Eye Image does the same. Gerard Fairtlough, the former chief executive of Celltech, believes the ideal size of a working group is about 70 which he calls a 'creative compartment'. People behave as if they are members of an extended family or tribe although, as anyone who is a member of a family or tribe knows, this does not imply undiluted happiness.

John Kao combines being an innovation expert and a jazz pianist.

His book *Jamming* takes jazz and jamming as a metaphor for the process of creativity. He once worked with legendary rock artist Frank Zappa and would appreciate London's Tomato advertising collective (with credits for campaigns for MTV, Nike and IBM), whose one-time CEO, Steve Baker, says that he used to run the company 'like I'd manage a band'.

A network space is a base camp for further exploration because a network company needs to extend far beyond its physical location. Creative people need the freedom to go talk to anyone they want, whether inside or outside the office. Procter & Gamble has more graduate scientists than do Harvard and Yale but reckons to get 20 per cent of ideas from outside. The Italian company Alessi, which is renowned for its striking, innovative designs, doesn't employ any designers but buys in ideas from elsewhere and provides skilled technicians who act as intermediaries between its staff and outside designers.

The attractions of these companies has stimulated an even greater growth in the numbers of people who have an office at home or who don't have an office at all and either lodge temporarily for an hour or a day in someone else's office (as a just-in-time person) or sit in cafes and tea-rooms. The demand for temporary lodging with coffee and Wi-Fi has driven the growth in city centres of business clubs, cafes and short-term office rentals as well as co-working spaces where anyone can rent a workspace or a room for multiples of an hour, like the Hub in London and XinDanWei in Shanghai.

A well-known management expert liked to ask his audiences where they would go for advice about a new idea. Who would you discuss it with first: your boss, your colleagues, or the people who report to you? It is a trick question. The right answer is, I'll discuss it with anyone who might know what to do, whether they are inside or outside the company.

The Temporary Company

Network companies use temporary companies for specific, short-term tasks and projects so people can focus on the raw ingredients of work such as its purpose, people and jobs-as-things-to-be-done. They are well-suited to the post-industrial, post-employment job, partly because people can more easily retain ownership of their skills and intellectual capital.

A temporary company provides a social, intellectual and managerial framework for managing a creative process. It is fit-for-purpose and tightly drawn. Hermann Hauser's plea for entrepreneurs to focus on only one thing at a time is easier in a temporary company as it has no baggage from the past. It may be hard, even for those inside, to tell who is central and who is peripheral, who is being paid a fee and who is earning a share of the revenues, who is likely to be there next month and who is not.

A project team often functions as a temporary company. Ashridge Business School surveyed 600 companies across the world and found that 75 per cent of their project teams were dispersed geographically and as many as 30 per cent were dispersed across different time zones. About half were virtual and never met. The project leader identifies the people best qualified to carry out each function and brings them together for a specific task over a specific period of time. In this way, costs can be tightly controlled. Ask the managers of a conventional company how much it costs to keep the business going and they may not know, but ask the heads of a temporary company and they will know.

Their function is to generate ideas such as prototypes, Beta versions and business plans rather than produce a profit. Any excess of revenues over costs is likely to be removed by increasing the payments made to the people involved in terms of fees and royalties so the individual makes a profit but not the company. Temporary companies prefer to increase their costs and make a loss to decreasing their costs and making a profit. They do not need profits as the company is only temporary and any profits would be taxed.

Clusters

These network and temporary companies function best in a large, diverse group of specialized and like-minded businesses which work in related stages of the same value chain so knowledge is shared more quickly, collaboration is easier and inter-company transaction costs are lower. As a result, creativity and innovation are sharpened. The most fruitful clusters consist of a variety of companies of different sizes and shapes all looking at problems and opportunities from a slightly different perspective rather than a few large companies on their own, however large they might be. It is the combination of multiple, specialized competitive viewpoints that does the trick.

They develop in four stages: one, a natural asset or nearby market draws companies in. Two, the resulting concentration and competition encourages specialization, which attracts workers who have specialist skills and companies that want to hire them. Three, these specialisms split into separate companies and become ever more specialist and competitive, knowing their neighbours are doing the same. If there is a gap, it is rapidly filled. Four, the proximity increases spillover. Clusters have high 'multiplier' effects and any inputs from outside the cluster are quickly disseminated.

Creative people need creative people next door to hasten success on the current project and to test ideas for the next one. Their conversations and negotiations, both competitive and collaborative, help people to generate a common sense of what is wanted and what could be done. Best practice is seen as a bare minimum because the aim is not to be as good as others but better than others.

Clustering takes place not only in the office during office hours but also with one's colleagues in the evening and at weekends with whoever happens to be around – who, of course, are usually people in the cluster. This group intimacy is another reason why someone's choice to work in a sector is as much a personal matter as a commercial one.

The theories of clusters started with Alfred Marshall, the father of modern economics, who wrote that when a number of like-minded companies engaged in similar tasks cluster together 'the mysteries of trade become no mysteries, and are available to all'. He said proximity created 'something in the air' (Charles Leadbeater's book on the knowledge economy is titled *Living on Thin Air*). Whenever anyone has a new idea it is taken up by others and combined with suggestions of their own to become a source of further ideas.

Designer and engineer James Dyson was the kind of man Marshall had in mind. When Dyson was developing his new cleaners he bene-fited from being within an hour's drive of Birmingham's many small engineering and machine tool firms. When he moved his manufactur-ing from Britain to Malaysia in 2002 it was not, he said, only to take advantage of Malaysia's lower costs but because he realized that Bir-mingham's older, experienced men were retiring and fewer young people wanted to be apprentices or graduate engineers, and the clus-ters were breaking up. He could no longer drive to the city and talk to a few people about what he wanted and together with them work out a solution. He said nobody seemed interested.

It is the people who make a cluster succeed, to start with, rather than the companies. The story of Hollywood's cluster began when a few European film-makers landed in New York in the 1920s, kept on travelling to escape New York's uptight Protestant establishment and came to the West Coast, where the sun shone brightly. Hollywood is a classic cluster in that it includes every stage of the value chain and is ruthlessly competitive at every stage. It has an insider mentality. The verdict of the *Wall Street Journal* on outsiders is damning: 'Even legendary businessmen who are breathtakingly successful everywhere else usually go down in utter miserable defeat in Hollywood. What-ever they tried, most have lost their shirts.' For Barry Diller, who has made serial fortunes in TV, film and home-shopping, 'The issue of corporate ownership is irrelevant. What is important is the energy, character and entrepreneurship of the individuals who run the stu-dios. The rest is noise.' Having expanded from being the world's biggest film cluster to its biggest TV cluster, Hollywood now has more professional YouTube video-makers than any other city.

YouTube's headquarters are based 350 miles to the north, on the edge of Silicon Valley. The founders of this cluster were the students and staff at the universities along Highway 101, south of the San Francisco Bay area. Like Hollywood, it has benefited from being far away from both the East Coast (and East Coast universities) and Washington DC establishments. Its extraordinarily rich ecology of university students and staff, inventors, developers, financiers and lawyers has generated not only new ideas but the financial capital to start the businesses to sell them.

The obvious success of Hollywood and Silicon Valley has led many cities to attempt to mimic them. Mumbai's film industry likes to be known as Bollywood (after its old name, Bombay) and Nigeria's Lagos calls itself Nollywood. With typical English humour, London has named a road interchange in East London as Silicon Roundabout and Scotland has Silicon Glen. Beijing uses the Silicon Valley label to describe its Zhongguancun electronics district.

There are thousands of smaller clusters that are as important to their inhabitants and serve the same purpose. Artists and writers were the first to congregate in special places to meet each other, to be close to galleries and to take advantage of cheap rents and hospitable cafes. With the increase in flexible working, just-in-time people and temporary companies, all sectors have one or two favoured places in every city. London's garment district lies north of Oxford Street, which is close to the retailers in Mayfair but has much lower rents. Music stores set up shop in Denmark Street to be close to the nightclubs in Soho. London's TV production companies based themselves in Fitzrovia to be close to the new Channel Four, which was required to buy in all programming from outside producers. When Channel Four moved its offices, the companies stayed put to benefit from the cluster and also because Fitzrovia, by then, had London's best broadband network.

Most clusters are invisible to outsiders. Visitors could walk north of Oxford Street and not notice the garment businesses or stroll through Soho and not notice Britain's film industry. They could spend the weekend in Poole, a quiet seaside resort tucked away on the south coast, without knowing it is home to the world's two largest manufacturers of the electric motors called air spindles that are essential to make printed circuits. They could drive through the Oxfordshire countryside and not notice the hundreds of companies that make up the world's leading cluster for the design of Formula One racing cars. Vroom Valley emerged when Britain's motor manufacturers lost touch with the consumer and had to sell out to foreign competitors, leaving behind hundreds of skilled designers and engineers who re-grouped in new companies operating at frantic pace, with workers driven as much by enthusiasm as by pay, relentless innovation, imaginative design and flexible working time.

The downside of clusters is a me-too quality, since everyone knows what everyone else is doing and the temptation to copy someone without thinking can be strong. The best antidote to mindless copying is the cluster's ability to attract newcomers from outside who bring new ideas. Hollywood is notorious for mindless copying but it is also extremely competitive and loves novelty. It is the favoured destination of every new generation of investors and film-makers not only from within America but elsewhere.

Clusters that are sponsored by government have mixed fortunes. They flourish in countries which have a history of government intervention and where previously creativity was discouraged and people need government approval to get going again. Governments in China, Singapore and the Gulf are using clusters in this way. Shanghai built over 70 creative clusters between 2005 and 2010 as symbols of its determination to promote creative industries. Few had roots in the local creative community, or managers with the right experience, and many dwindled away or became conventional offices. The owners of the city's second generation of clusters such as Anken and Jinggong have a better understanding of creative business and a brisk commercial strategy.

Financing Ideas

When they start, people need imagination, talent and spare time more than money, and many people have these, especially the spare time. I am impressed by the number of ideas that arise while someone is working on or thinking about something else. At this stage, there is little need for financial capital and few barriers to entry. Success can come quickly although the failure rate is high, mostly because supply exceeds demand and, as a result, incomes, whether wages, fees or royalties, may be insufficient to keep going.

The main sources of money are what the person already has and what the business itself produces less the costs, called the internal or organic cash-flow. One way to increase this net cash-flow is to reduce expenditure and every entrepreneur does this to some extent, both to increase the available cash and to justify later claims for a share of any equity if that is part of their plan. To this can be added money from family and friends as well as government grants.

This may be sufficient. The creative economy is notable for the number of ideas and companies that started with little money and made enough from sales to the public or to clients to stay in business and grow handsomely. Artists and art dealers, advertising agencies, architects, software developers, dotcoms, film-makers, designers, composers, games developers and more; it's a long list.

If not, the business needs external finance. The most hard-to-get money is seed money when the idea is not much more than an idea, the assets are personal and subjective, and the sums are too low to interest a bank or a private investor. At this point, a few thousand pounds from friends and family may make all the difference between going on and giving up, as much by giving confidence as paying the rent.

One way to raise initial money is crowd-funding, which can increase the number of family and friends to Facebook-like proportions. Crowd-funding involves raising a relatively small amount of money from a large number of people each of whom contributes a small proportion of the whole. Most crowd-funding is provided in return for a non-monetary reward, such as an invitation to a special event or an advance pre-release delivery, and is therefore outside the scope of mainstream financial regulations. If it is used to raise conventional debt and equity it becomes liable to regulations.

The entrepreneur uses an existing website or a special crowd-funding platform to say how much money they want and offers a range of rewards. Most platforms charge around 5 per cent for a listing and 3–4 per cent commission on donations. Kickstarter, one of the world's largest platforms, vets proposed projects but others are more open.

It works best for new films, games, performances and music albums as well as apps and products which have a definite output in a short timescale. Typical sums range from a few thousand up to hundreds of thousands of dollars. By 2012 the 500 largest crowd-funding websites were raising an estimated $1.5 billion annually (not including donations to non-profit companies like Wikipedia). It was reported that about 10 per cent of the films shown at the 2012

Cannes and Sundance Film Festivals were crowd-funded. The British games association, UKIE, says that $50 million has been raised for games and films, with smaller amounts raised for design, music and technology. It is not unknown for projects to raise more than they asked for. Zombies Run asked for $12,500 but raised $73,000 and America's DoubleFine asked for $400,000 and got $3,336,000 (one of the pleasures of crowd-funding is that observers know exactly how much people ask for and how much they receive).

The four founders of the Pebble, a clever watch that wearers can sync via Bluetooth with an iPhone or Android smartphone, decided to ask for $100,000. They had a powerful enticement because supporters would get an advance copy of the Pebble before it went on sale and could customize designs and colours. The response was amazing and Pebble received pledges of over $10 million before stopping.

Crowd-funding was boosted when Barack Obama's Jumpstart Our Business Start-ups Act (JOBS), part of America's deficit-reduction package, included crowd-funding as a way to boost the economy (Obama had used crowd-funding successfully in his 2008 and 2012 campaigns). According to Duncan Niederauer, head of the New York Stock Exchange's EuroNext, crowd-funding 'will be the future of how most small businesses are going to be financed'. America's Securities and Exchange Commission (SEC) has developed crowd-funding regulations to balance the need to keep proposals as open as possible, so attracting small donations with minimum paperwork, with the need to monitor a company's offers and expenditures against abuse (Pebble was criticized for missing deadlines). In 2012, a British start-up company called Seedrs became the country's first crowd-funding agent to win approval within existing financial regulations and the games agency UKIE has proposed a whole new regulatory framework specifically for crowd-funding.

Scientists use crowd-funding to raise research funds, especially for projects with environmental or social benefits. The University of California, San Francisco, crowd-funded a conservation project in Madagascar and offered to name a new species after any donor who gave $5,000 or more. Science-based crowd-funding platforms like Indiegogo and Petridish offer the same services as arts-based sites with the added attraction, if the university is a registered charity, of offering tax breaks on donations.

The next level of funding, although Pebble's success did up the stakes considerably, is borrowing from a bank or anyone else (debt) or selling shares for cash (equity). Debt is simpler because it involves the loan of a fixed sum over a fixed period and lenders do not become involved in the company's operations. Equity involves a more complicated calculation of the value of the company, the price of a share in the company and an estimate of the company's growth over years so that the investor can reasonably expect to sell their shares for a decent profit in a relatively short time-scale (known as the return on investment, or RoI). As shareholders, investors have some say in the company's business, ranging from hardly anything if they hold a small minority to influence or outright control if they have a majority. The permutations of value, price and influence may not be infinite but can seem so on occasion.

The choice depends on the company's current financial situation, the degree of future risk and the nature of future rewards and, of course, on the willingness of bankers or investors to play their part. Debt allows the company to keep control but requires it to have some assets as security and collateral. Selling equity allows the borrower to get cash at no financial cost but involves relinquishing a degree of control. If something is routine and safe, then the better option is debt. If something is risky, the better option is either a loan from family and friends on a non-commercial and possibly interest-free basis, or equity.

It can be relatively straightforward to value assets to one's own satisfaction but harder to meet the criteria of banks, investors, collaborators and other outsiders. There are several methods, ranging from estimating the cost of replacement, which might be sensible for valuable physical assets like property and equipment but is not much help in valuing something that is unique, to estimating an asset's value in future years and then deducing its net present value. These methods are not readily available when an asset is new and unique but valuations become more robust as an asset acquires a history.

David Bowie was able to point to his sales history and turn his copyrights into a bankable asset when he raised $55 million from Prudential by capitalizing his future song royalties as 10-year bonds at 7.9 per cent, which was a useful premium above the American 10-year Treasury rate at the time of 6.37 per cent. Banker David Pullman, who devised the Bowie bonds, later sold similar bonds for James Brown and the Isley Brothers. Rod Stewart issued a $15.4 million securitized loan and Bruce Dickinson's Iron Maiden, one of music's most business-like bands, raised $30 million. These bonds did well initially but their value dropped as online sales rose.

In asset terms, Bowie, Stewart and the others had kept their copyrights and therefore had a balance sheet, whereas most artists live off fees and only have income. In economic terms, Bowie is a capitalist while others remain employees. Many creative people are forced to sell their rights at the beginning of their career in order to get much-needed cash. This means giving up their best opportunity to change from being a freelance-for-hire to building up a company with capital assets.

America recycles investors and money as fast as it does ideas, and each generation of American entrepreneurs funds its successors, so the biggest source of start-up investment is the people who got start-up equity a generation back and want to invest in a new business. They have the advantages of having the cash and understanding the nature of risk. In Europe, after exhausting the much smaller sources of private investment, would-be entrepreneurs are obliged to turn supplicant in front of banks with little experience of running a successful business or government officials with no experience at all and are in danger of working to other people's political agendas and paternalism (Britain's most successful film producer, David Puttnam, has criticized British entrepreneurs for their too-high dependence on government and a 'soup kitchen' mentality.)

What happens when the money runs out? People who are paid a regular wage in the ordinary economy seldom run into trouble so long as they ensure their income exceeds their costs; and since their wages, which make up the larger part of their income, are known in advance, this should not be a demanding task. They cannot do much about their income so their priority is costs. People living off their wits in the deal economy have the opposite concern. Their priority is their income and they should focus on new ideas and projects. Many get into difficulties because they bring the attitudes of the ordinary, job-as-employment economy to the business of the creative economy and try to reduce their costs.

Once started, Americans are better at keeping their companies going. Their attitude to a business in trouble is to save the company as a 'going concern' even if the creditors who are owed money are not paid. Britain takes a different approach and tries to protect the company's assets in order to pay off the creditors (usually headed by the tax authorities, so the money leaves the private sector).

The result is that America tries to protect the company from a creditor who might wish to close it down and sell the assets while Britain tries to protect the creditors from the company. In a word, America is debtor-friendly and Britain is creditor-friendly. This has led the *Economist* to suggest that 'Europe's inability to create a rival to Silicon Valley owes much to its tougher bankruptcy laws.'

Hits and Misses

The factors that make an idea successful, such as self-expression, meaning and novelty, result in high-gearing and skewed financial rewards. Success is rare but when it comes it brings a higher proportion of a buyer's attention and cash than it would in the ordinary economy.

One possible response is to try to make every idea a hit. This is fine as a means of motivating oneself but gives no guidance as to how much effort to put behind each idea; nor how to balance quality with the need for quantity; nor how to squeeze as much as possible out of the occasional success while mitigating the impact of the many failures. And it does rather ignore reality. Hits are rare.

A better tactic is to generate a portfolio of different ways of monetizing one's own knowledge and abilities, which has the side-effect of freeing up each output to settle at its own level of content and cost. Instead of producing everything at an equilibrium price, which would be sensible if each product were identical and marginal costs and revenues could be maintained over a long run, these people produce a bundle of differentiated products.

They know from experience that only a small number of works will be a hit and manage the output on the assumption that the few hits will compensate for the larger number of misses. Absolute costs and prices are not so relevant, which is why a marginal change in costs such as interest rates has less impact on a business that lives off hits than it does on a conventional company.

Maintaining a portfolio is even more important in a niche where money flows abundantly regardless of whether a particular product is a hit or a miss. A Time Warner friend once advised me 'to get close to the trees when the apples start falling'. He meant, keep close to businesses which generate high levels of cash and avoid sectors with low margins and too many people chasing too few projects.

Choose your orchard wisely. In its boom years, pop music was renowned as the easiest way for anyone to make money without needing to think or work much. By 2010, being a label manager had gone from being fun and profitable to being a badly paid dead-end. Radio Top 40 presenters have been replaced by club DJs and online platforms. Magazine journalists who rose on the back of the advertising surge, when money was easy, now find they are competing much harder to write more words for smaller fees. Professional photographers face competition from amateurs with smartphones. Book publishers used to rely on book reviews in upmarket publications and on their negotiating influence over small booksellers. Now they need to negotiate with e-book platforms and write their own blogs.

Negotiating Deals and Contracts

When I was a Director of HandMade, one of Britain's biggest film production companies, I would have been surprised to see a film in the office. We owned the master copies of our films but they were locked away in a closely guarded, air-conditioned, humidity-controlled vault about 50 miles away deep in the countryside. We did not really make films. We made deals. We lived off ideas and we made money out of deals.

Deals are agreements to reconcile two people's 'ideas about ideas' at a specific moment in time. Sellers want to protect their work while increasing revenue, and buyers' desire, for as low a cost as possible, to increase their opportunities for future revenue. A deal reflects each party's knowledge of present values (which may differ) and their forecast of future values (almost certain to differ).

The scope for deal-making is immense because ideas, assets and rights can be easily merged or divided. Physical matter can be varied only within the laws of physics and, if taken apart, can be impossible to put back together again, but intangible matter can be varied merely by thinking it or saying it and consolidations and splits can be fast and numerous.

The only constraint is the inventiveness of the people making the deal. In other words, an intellectual constraint on an intellectual thing.

Inventiveness in deal-making is a basic and much-admired skill. When IBM was looking for a new operating system, it talked to several companies including Microsoft. Bill Gates swiftly bought a licence to what became MS-DOS and licensed it on to IBM but kept ownership of the underlying copyright. Every company that wanted to develop software for IBM had to buy a multi-use licence from Microsoft. That single clause, almost unnoticed by IBM, made Gates's fortune.

When word got out that the veteran Johnny Carson was leaving *Saturday Night Live*, most of the contenders to replace him signed up to a 'most favoured nation' agreement that they would not work for less than $25,000 an episode. Jay Leno refused to sign up and offered to work for the union minimum, known as 'scale'. He got the job.

George Lucas became a billionaire because of quick thinking when he was facing a negotiator who was feeling generous and didn't know the value of what he had. He and Alan Ladd at Twentieth Century Fox had already agreed most of the terms for Lucas's fee for the first *Star Wars* film when the director's success with *American Graffiti* prompted him to ask for a little more money. Ladd said no but, wanting to make a gesture, casually gave him all rights to the merchandise. He thought the extra rights were worth little and anyway his Fox colleagues, who were sceptical of the film, did not want to be involved in what they called 'toys'. They were wrong. Since 1977, *Star Wars* merchandise has earned $20 billion, which is more than twice as much as the films have made. To manage this business Lucas had a staff of only 30 people and revenues were running at $3 billion a year when he sold the company in 2012 for $4.05 billion.

Deals are usually between two people (adding a third increases the complexity exponentially). The relationship between the two sides is different to that between a senior and a junior or between a manager and an employee. It is a relationship between, if not equals, then two people equally free to assert their views and to say yes or no.

The priority given to deal-making affects a company's structure, management, working hours and remuneration. It puts a premium on managers who are skilled at negotiating with outsiders and can do so under conditions of mutual trust. Managers need to be good with people; expert at judging value or, at least, knowing the market's current estimation of value; and competent at legal terms. They need to know how they will make money from a deal in ways that the other side will accept as reasonable or will not know about. As a result, companies are changing from being a block of workers to a market-place of deals.

The process develops in stages. With assets as vague as ideas, the ability to state convincingly what they are and what they are worth is highly prized. At best, it is an honest calculation of market value. At worst, it's hype. Usually, it is a forgivable mix of the two. The hype is not only on the seller's side because buyers may be overly optimistic that they will make money too.

As each new deal is negotiated so more people gain an opportunity to put forward their own estimate of its meaning and value. Someone who says convincingly why an idea is interesting and valuable gains the right to take it to the next stage. Saying what an idea could be is just as influential as having the idea in the first place, as the new meaning can spur people to action in a new direction and unlock more value.

Richard Caves, the Harvard professor who pioneered the study of contracts in the arts, criticized the tendency of artists to indulge in 'arts for arts' sake' but they may be doing so not because they are not interested in financial gain but because they believe their own vision is the surer way to win it. In my experience, creative people and business people are united by a desire to cajole their project to the next stage and to make money from it.

But it can be hard to pin down what a new project is and what it means. It is tricky to value a new idea that is personal and subjective. The more novel and the more full of meaning something is, the more its value can change. People will change their minds, and even two presentations of the same work can elicit different responses. As a result, estimating demand is chancy. Past history is no guide to the future, as banks are obliged to say.

Negotiators do their best to look back at what something cost and forward to its value to the next person in the value chain but the cost of past inputs, however important at the time the money was paid over, becomes less important at the next stage in the value chain. A good idea and a bad idea (say, a script or a prototype) may have cost the same but only a good one will be able to move further along. A higher cost does not ensure higher revenues nor more certain revenues. Anyway sellers are more likely to be thinking about future revenues than past costs.

A deal will turn upon how much a seller wants to gain the other person's resources and how much the buyer values the asset at that moment. They have to both calculate their fixed costs and marginal income, which involves quantifying their own risk–reward profile, and try to estimate the other's profile so they can decide whether the risks are worth the rewards. At worst, they expect to recover their share of marginal cost. At best, they maintain their own value, gain extra resources and enhance the likelihood of future income.

Each side will be wondering how much income they can gain in the future. One side may want a stronger asset, or more control over the asset, while another may want cash. Sellers want to increase the value of their assets so buyers can add further value. Sellers put their perceptions up against the buyer's perceptions. In practice, people try to cover their costs and seek a share of future revenue. The outcome depends on two people's views of future income, which will be based on a mix of knowledge, ambition and negotiating skills.

All these uncertainties cast doubt on the usefulness of case studies, benchmarks and so-called 'best practice'. A case study is a highly selective description of something that, in hindsight, proved to be correct. It will skirt over, because the truth cannot be known, how people actually made decisions. Apple's designer Jonathan Ive remarked years later that 'There were multiple times when we almost shelved the iPhone' – but even he could not quite remember the to-and-fro of the arguments. Case studies and schemes that reduce past experience to a set of rules are missing the point.

The purpose of many contracts is to confirm a deal on copyright, patents or trademarks. The seller wants to keep as much of the rights as possible while allowing the buyer to license enough rights to make money. The seller wants to retain or increase each right's absolute value while the buyer wants to lower it and create new rights, new values, for themselves.

Sellers start by deciding which rights to sell and which to exclude. This, by itself, usually constitutes the larger part of a contract. Rights contracts are superficially about what a licensor allows a licensee to do (stream a film, use a design) but they are also about what the licensor *prevents* a licensee from doing. When I was involved in licensing Universal Studios films, the Universal management made it clear that their purpose was not so much to allow people to do things but to stop them doing other things.

Rights-owners are nervous about allowing access to their back catalogues because they fear they might cut into audiences for their new releases. One reason why film studios, music labels and book publishers fight for the extension of copyright is not so they can license material themselves but to stop anyone else from doing so. A company's contracts are the best way to protect its assets as well as a source of future revenue.

10 RULES FOR SUCCESS

These rules have been collected by people making their own way in the creative economy in both small and large companies.

1. *Invent yourself.* Create a unique cluster of personal talents. Own your image. Manage it. Build momentum. Leave school early, if you want, but never stop learning. Learn the rules. Manage the rules. Break the rules. Scavenge for new ideas. It does not matter where you get ideas from; what does matter is what you do with them. If you're bored, do something else. Be clear about your own assets and talents. They are unique and they are all you have.

2. *Put the priority on ideas, not on data.* Train your own imagination. Build a personal balance sheet of intellectual capital. Understand patents, copyright, trademarks and other ways to protect and also to allow access to ideas. Hire the best lawyers. People in the creative economy are more worried if they lose their ability to think than if their company loses money. Think about it.

3. *Be nomadic.* Nomads are at home in every country. You can choose your own path and means of travel, and choose how long you stay. Being nomadic does not mean being alone; most nomads travel in groups, especially at night. Nomads appreciate both the desert and the oasis. Writer Charles Handy says leaders must combine 'a love of people' and a 'capacity for aloofness'. Likewise, creatives need both solitude and the crowd, thinking alone and working together.

4. *Define yourself by your own (thinking) activities*, not by the (job) title somebody else has given you. If you are working for company X on project Y, it is more interesting to say you are working on project Y at company X. Computer companies try to sell 'business solutions' to their clients; in the creative economy we exchange creative solutions with each other.

5. *Learn endlessly.* Be curious. Borrow. Innovate. Remember the US Electric Power ad: 'A new idea is often two old ideas meeting for the first time'. Use retro, reinvention, revival – be a magpie. Use networks. If you cannot find the right network, start it. Take risks and do unnecessary things. Ignore Frederick Winslow Taylor's famous instruction to the Ford Motor Company's workers that they should 'eliminate all false movements, slow movements and useless movements'.

Wayward movements can lead to amazing discoveries. Sleep with one eye open.

6. *Exploit fame and celebrity*. The production costs are small (fame is a sunk cost) and the rewards are virtually unlimited in terms of the ability to charge more for one's services and revitalize a life that is momentarily stuck. Being well known (even slightly known) is as important in the creative economy of the 21st century as being a good engineer was in the 20th. The essence of being a star, according to David Bowie, is 'The ability to make yourself as fascinating to others as you are to yourself.' This is not about being famous for 15 minutes, which is how Andy Warhol summed up media attention, but being famous for being creative, which was Warhol's own achievement long after he had stopped painting or indeed working at all.

7. *Treat the virtual as real* and vice versa. Online life is merely another dimension of everyday life. Do not judge reality by whether it is based on technology but by more important and eternal matters such as humanity and truth. Bandwidth is useless without a message, without communication. At all times, use the RIDER process: review, incubation, dreams, excitement and reality checks. Mix dreams and reality to create your own future.

8. *Be kind*. Kindness is a mark of success. Data never say 'please'. Humans can and should say 'please' and mean it. People treat each other as they themselves are treated; exactly as a fast computer produces data more quickly so will a kind person be invited to more networks and receive more knowledge.

9. *Admire success openly*. Martina Navratilova, who won Wimbledon nine times and the US Open four times, believed that the person who said, 'It's not whether you win or lose that counts', probably lost. Equally, do not be fixated on success: be curious about failure. Creative people are the strictest judge of their own successes and failures because they want to learn from them (see Rule 5). The worst is depression, not recession. You will never win if you cannot lose.

10. *Be very ambitious*. Boldly go.

11. *Have fun*. Dance as if no one is looking. Stop testing and start experimenting. Albert Einstein said: 'If a is success in life then $a = x + y + z$, when x is hard work, y is fun and z is keeping your mouth shut.' This often irritates other people. But do not worry. Tom Wehr of the National Institutes of Health, Maryland, says the sleeping brain sorts out the previous day's affairs as 'a creative worry factory'. Feed it.

And when writing the ten rules for success in the creative economy, don't worry if you end up with 11. You can break your own rules (see Rule 1).

6
Owning Ideas

THE RIGHTS MARKET

What is the point of intellectual property? How should we balance the right to own and the right to use? What is the right balance between paying money to the makers and owners of ideas and having access to their ideas? What is the balance between paying authors more and enabling the rest of us to have better access to books? Or between paying the heirs of long-dead artists more and being able to copy their paintings? Or between higher profits and cheaper drugs? Why do some activities depend on copyright (films) while others seem to thrive without it (fast fashion)?

It is a contentious topic. Some people take the view that copyright should be stricter and last for ever. A few take the opposite view: that it should be weaker and shorter or even abolished altogether. Patents are subject to similar arguments. Should the same rules that apply to gadgets apply to human genes and crop seeds?

The argument over copyright went all the way to the American Supreme Court in 2003 when Congress tried to extend the term of copyright from the life of the author plus 50 years to life plus 70 years. The proposal was called the Sonny Bono Copyright Term Extension Act, because it was promoted as providing royalties for Mary Bono, widow of the singer, but it soon became known as the Mickey Mouse Act after Walt Disney realized the Mouse would soon be out of copyright and wanted to own him for ever. An internet publisher called Eric Eldred said longer copyright terms would damage his constitutional freedom to digitize old books and lodged a case at the Supreme Court.

Eldred and his team, which included the constitutional lawyer and copyright activist Lawrence Lessig, co-chair of Creative Commons, argued that life plus 50 was more than enough. Lessig said that Disney's suggestion that an extension was an incentive to produce more works was clearly preposterous (Sonny Bono was dead). An analysis by 17 eminent economists showed than even the anticipation of an extended reward would have no measurable impact. But Disney won.

Copyright brings forth a bewildering mix of emotions about freedom, property, money and the law. It is hard to be rational about such a heady cocktail. An earlier infighter described copyright as a 'subtle and esoteric area of law'. He was not a despondent plaintiff in one of Charles Dickens's more tortuous courtroom sagas but Bruce Lehman, Commissioner of the US Patents and Trademarks Office (PTO), and the author of a Green Paper on the country's information infrastructure. He was echoing Supreme Court Justice Story, who had said 150 years earlier that copyright and patent cases come nearer than any other kind of law 'to what may be called the metaphysics of the law where the discussions are, or at least may be, very subtle and refined and sometimes almost evanescent'. He was in good company. Mark Twain, who believed writers should be allowed to own their literature as securely as their house, wrote: 'Only one thing is impossible to God: to find any sense in any copyright law on this planet.'

Governments like to talk about promoting broadband but find it difficult to adapt copyright to cope with the resulting hike in digital media. America tried with a Digital Millennium Copyright Act (DMCA) and more recently with proposals for a Stop Online Piracy Act (SOPA) and a Protect IP Act (PIPA), which provoked a broad coalition of opposition as it became clear that many legal sites would suffer collateral damage. President Obama was pushed to say that he would oppose any bill that 'reduces freedom of expression or undermines the dynamic, innovative, global internet' and both bills were withdrawn. Britain had a stab by appointing Andrew Gowers and then Ian Hargreaves to carry out reviews. Hargreaves said: 'If the law does not change the creative economy will underperform. We need to get the right balance between privacy and protection and public domain, and that balance is not in the right place.'

A dozen governments including America, Japan and the European Union but excluding China and Brazil badly failed to get the right balance when they signed an Anti-Counterfeiting Trade Agreement (ACTA) in 2011. Two of the European Parliament's official investigators resigned in protest and three committees voted against, saying ACTA over-reacted to piracy and did not address the opportunities of online media.

It is the single most complex business issue in the creative economy. While the possession of land and physical objects is enshrined in a thousand years of law and custom, owning and protecting ideas is fraught with complexity and confusion. Land-owners sleep comfortably because they know the law, which their ancestors probably wrote, protects them, but the market-place of intellectual property is a more crowded and confusing place.

In one corner are millions of people who want to publicize their ideas and inventions almost regardless of whether or not they make any money. They want to share their ideas with anyone who wants to listen and, while they might want to claim what lawyers call 'moral rights', such as the right to be known as the author, are happy to waive their economic rights, which would bring in money. In another corner are a milling crowd who want to make money but do not know how. They may be excellent creators but they are amateurs at the law and business and cannot afford legal advice. In a third we can see a smaller group of people who are professional at both creating products and protecting their rights. In a fourth corner, a fortunate few sit atop their archives of intellectual property like prosperous bankers.

In the middle is a crowd of agents and intermediaries negotiating with lawyers, investors, government policy-makers, accountants and publicists. It is a volatile mix of legal nicety and skippy negotiation. They are buying and selling words, music, pictures; gadgets, computer software, genes; copyrights, trademarks, patents; proposals, contents, formats, fame, faces, reputations, brands, colours. The goods on sale in this noisy market-place are the rights to use or, in the lawyer's phrase, to exploit, intellectual property.

The problem is only partly *whether* rights-holders should be paid. A bigger issue in practice is the *how*: the hassle of finding out who owns the rights, negotiating how much they want for a licence and then making the payment. Companies which license rights as part of their normal business know who to call and how to negotiate, but many individuals who want to make a small one-off deal with trivial financial implications often do not know what to do. Rights-holders are monopolists and have no obligation to license their property or charge a fair price and if the likely income is small they are even less willing to bother. In an increasing number of cases, the rights market is so dysfunctional that the cost of negotiating a licence outweighs the income.

THREE QUESTIONS

I begin with three questions about intellectual property and then look at the three main systems of copyright, patents and trademarks. I describe how online networks are reinventing copyright, and how the American Patent and Trademark Office is widening the scope of what can be patented, and suggest the 'rights contract' between rights-owners and the public needs to be rewritten. The three questions are:

Why property and property rights?
Why law and licensing?
Why international agreements?

Why Property?

The principle that someone who makes something should have the right to charge for it has worked well with physical property and so people who have ideas claim that their work is property, too, as a justification for protecting its use and being paid. In general, the analogy works well and is the basis for the arguments made by Mary Bono and then Disney. But charging for ideas is not straightforward, as

Eldred pointed out, because of the difficulty in defining ideas, the weak boundary between one idea and another, and our variety of attitudes to the ownership of ideas. It leaves wide open the question of how big the reward should be: the nature of the rights, how long they should last (called the 'term') and the scope for limitations and exceptions such as the right to quote extracts.

Disney and other rights-owners make a separate claim for incentives, saying that a person's expectation that they will own whatever they create will encourage them to do the work. This is often true but individuals are creative for many different reasons. Money comes into it sometimes, but not always. It is hard to justify ownership so long after an author's death as being much of an incentive (and I have never known a company make plans so far ahead). The talk of incentives is really a variant of the much stronger point about rewards.

There is a separate point that people have a natural right to own whatever they create, based on the writings of George Hegel, Thomas Hobbes and John Locke on the rights of man. These natural rights are strongest in the kinds of personal expression that qualify for copyright (so when singing 'I've Got You Babe', it is as important for the singer to acknowledge Sonny Bono as the composer as to pay his estate a royalty) and weakest in the more business-oriented ideas that qualify for patents and trademarks. These rights are protected by a class of so-called moral rights which sit alongside copyright (see page 116) and there is a view that as economic rights decline in efficacy so moral rights may step in.

The result is private property but it is property with a difference. It delivers ownership but it seldom guarantees or even offers possession. With physical property we can say that 'possession is nine-tenths of the law', but with intellectual property 'relationship is nine-tenths of the law' (this is why my Rule 2 for success says, 'Hire the best lawyers', page 75).

Why Law?

Intellectual property depends much more on statute and regulation than does physical property. Indeed, it exists only insofar as a government passes a law to say so. No law, no property. We need laws to define the kinds of ideas and works that qualify as property, spell out the owner's rights, set the terms and enable courts to punish offenders. It is a peculiar attribute of rights that they are mainly negative; they stop somebody from doing something. Copyright prevents others from copying and a patent prevents others from making.

Laws also state the term for how long a right lasts. The reason why an author's copyright in a book lasts for 70 years after the author's death is not inherent in the nature of writing or publishing but because governments have decided that is the proper balance between ownership and access. The reason why a patent lasts 20 years is not inherent in the nature of inventions or their market or their cost but because governments say it should.

Because intellectual property is so dependent on law, without having any external reality, it is liable to continuous amendment, especially by those with the best lawyers. As we saw with Sonny Bono, rights-holders are pressuring governments to make terms longer. England's original copyright term was 14 years but now copyright extends far beyond the author's death and usually beyond a work's commercial lifetime. Patents used to last around 15 years (American patents lasted for 17 years) but nowadays almost all countries have a standard term of 20 years. Even so, patents run out, as does copyright eventually, and right-holders are increasingly turning to trademarks, which last as long as the right-holder is in business.

The Grimm brothers published their first version of the well-known German folk-tale 'Snow White' in 1812 and, in spite of this and later editions qualifying for copyright, all their copyrights ran out in 1893. Disney used the Grimms' version to make its film, which was released in 1937 and whose copyright ran out in 2008, although it also made a 1993 digital version which is still in copyright. But Disney knows that all copyright eventually runs out and in 2008 it applied to the Patent and Trademark Office for a *trademark* for Snow White which, it said, would cover not only film and TV but 'current events, news and entertainment information via communication and computer networks'. If successful, Disney will own the Snow White trademark for as long as the company stays in business and will be able to stop rivals from using the name for their own versions in the same way as it used the Grimms story.

Why International?

The ease with which ideas travel internationally requires international conventions to protect rights-holders that are much stronger than those for physical property. The first global convention covered patents, trademarks and designs and was signed in Paris in 1883, and the Berne convention on copyright followed three years later. Since then there have been numerous conventions on matters from folk customs to plant varieties and biotech.

These conventions are under constant review (criticism might be more accurate a word) to take account of technological change. The copyright conventions have proved the most troublesome because of the ease with which art, designs, books, music and video can be copied. France was long the most friendly towards other nationals' works and America the most xenophobic. It is ironic, now, when America is so opposed to piracy, to remember that America did not sign the Berne Convention until 1989, a hundred years after European governments had signed up. Until then, American law only protected books 'manufactured' in America. This clever ruse allowed New York publishers to copy foreign books without paying royalties. The most successful British author of the 19th century, Charles Dickens, travelled to America to protest and then had to give live performances in order to earn a penny from American readers.

Patents still need to be registered country-by-country. Someone who registers a patent in country A gains protection only in that country and must register it separately in countries B, C, etc., for protection there. As the patent-holder in country A, they are the only person allowed to register it elsewhere because they are the only person who can claim it is novel. So a competitor can make and sell a rival product in countries B, C, etc., but cannot claim patent protection and, once the original inventor sees what is happening, a patent can be claimed to try to stop the competitor.

Every international treaty needs a secretariat to make sure its members behave themselves. The World Intellectual Property Organization (WIPO), which is now part of the United Nations, administers the Berne and Paris Conventions. The newer World Trade Organization (WTO) operates a regulatory system for Trade-Related Intellectual Property Rights (TRIPS). Both are based in Geneva. In Europe, the European Commission believes a Europe-wide system is necessary to Europe's internal market and so coordinates member countries' laws.

THE TOP THREE

The vast majority of creative ideas are covered by copyright, patents or trademarks. A text falls within copyright law, an industrial process falls within patent law and a company name falls within trademark law. However, a right-holder knows there is much to gain by bundling as many different rights together, like double-locking a door. An innovation which qualifies for a patent may also qualify for design rights and a trademark too. A film which qualifies for its own copyright will include many other qualifying works with their own rights; and any music in the film, even if only heard for a few seconds, will have its own bundle of composition, publishing, performance and recording rights. The last, by the way, are called 'mechanical' rights. Subtle it is.

The most common of the other varieties are design rights. Britain introduced design rights in 1787, almost 100 years before it extended copyright to art, showing the greater importance of design and manufacturing at the time. Today most countries offer several options for protecting designs, including automatic rights like copyright and registered rights like a patent, but the difficulty of defining a design makes these rights rather feeble mechanisms. There is strong evidence that fashion's commercial success depends on a rather loose attitude to copying. The British IPO reported in 2011 that most product designers did not bother to use design rights at all.

There is a global register of Geographical Indicators to protect region-specific foods and drinks, such as Champagne and Stilton, and a register for micro-organisms such as cells used in food and drugs.

Although internet domain names (URLs) were not conceived as trademarks, international law increasingly treats them as such, and so a prior registration of a trademark invalidates a rival claim to use the same name for a website address. There are global negotiations to extend IP protection to genetic information, traditional knowledge and folklore. Europe has a one-off law to protect databases.

America has special rules for trade secrets, which allow people to own information and to stop others from using it. A trade secret is a 'formula, pattern, device or compilation of information which is used in a business and which gives the business an opportunity to obtain an advantage over competitors who do not know it or use it'. It is a wide-ranging definition and can lead to bitter disputes and huge compensation. The American company Dupont suspected for years that South Korea's Kolon was stealing trade secrets of its popular strong-but-light Kevlar fibres. It went to court and in 2011 was awarded damages of $919 million. For a long time the most valuable trade secret was believed to be Coca-Cola's recipe but Google's PageRank algorithm is a strong contender.

COPYRIGHT

There is no copyright in creativity or in ideas but only in the expression of an idea. Creativity is the fuel of the process but it is not itself protected. As I mull over the writing of this next sentence, the various phrases in my head are not copyright works and have no protection but, once written, the sentence is protected. In law, all writing is protected, even my notes.

There are two problems with this. One, open democratic societies assume individual expressions of a literary and artistic nature should be freely shared. We do not own our contribution to a conversation. We do not own wit or insight. Thomas Jefferson wrote elegantly: 'He who receives an idea from me, receives instruction himself without lessening mine, as he who lights his taper at mine receives light himself without darkening me.' So why should people own their literary and artistic expressions merely because they write them down or perform them? Two, what harm can there be in quoting a sentence? What's more, the majority of works that qualify for copyright have needed no or very little monetary investment.

Creative people reasonably protest that their works are as valuable as any invention – if not more so, they think privately. While many works arise freely, in both senses of the word, a small but important minority require very large investments over a long period of time. Their creators have worked hard and long and must eat, and not only eat, but have the chance to be as rich as anyone else.

This tension has been evident throughout history and still affects attitudes today. Many early societies treated writing, painting and music as belonging to the community rather than the individual. Concepts of individual authorship and individually owned expression began to emerge in classical Greece but withered away in the early Christian period and the Middle Ages and never really took hold anywhere else until recently. Writers and artists believed themselves to be vehicles for divine inspiration and not entitled to benefit personally from their work. 'Freely have I received,' Martin Luther said, quoting the Bible, 'freely given, and want nothing in return.'

The ideas of individual inspiration and authors' rights emerged again in Europe as part of secular humanism. English case law recognized some authors' rights from the 15th century onwards but the Stationers' Company, which licensed printers and publishers, benefited more than the writers. Many writers were content with these arrangements because they were more concerned with publishing their work than with protecting it and received the bulk of their income not from sales but from state or private patronage. The mood changed during the Civil War when the royalist Stationers lost their privileges and authors began to assert their rights. Most of the writers lived in London and knew each other (an early example of a cultural cluster becoming a successful business cluster) and when the printers' increasingly intemperate demands for new work exceeded the writers' willingness to write, they found themselves in a strong negotiating position.

They lobbied Parliament to stop printers and publishers who 'have of late taken the liberty of printing, reprinting and publishing books without the consent of Authors'. Writer Daniel Defoe argued splendidly that 'A book is the author's property, 'tis the child of his inventions, the brat of his brain.' Queen Anne's Parliament duly passed the world's first Copyright Act in 1710. It laid down the fundamental principle that an author has 'the sole right and liberty of printing books', and anyone else has to ask permission, and Defoe, whose *Robinson Crusoe* was published in 1719, was able to say proudly that 'Writing is become a very considerable branch of English Commerce.' (Fifty years later, a group of London publishers paid Samuel Johnson 1,500 guineas, equivalent to $370,000 today, to write his *Dictionary*.)

In America, the technology of printing was protected by patents before the contents were protected by copyright and the States did not pass a federal law on copyright until 1783. Thomas Paine, Noah Webster and other writers grounded their demands for copyright on the natural law of Hobbes and Locke, given a twist by their own political independence and belief in free speech. As copyright historian Ronald Bettig puts it, the laws assumed 'an inherent connection between creativity, profit and social welfare'. In spite of the States' anti-colonial rebellion, they modelled their laws on the English Act.

Meanwhile the British widened the number of qualifying works. Engravings won protection in 1734, textile designs in 1787, sculpture in 1814, music performances in 1833 and paintings, drawings and photographs in 1862. It might seem odd that paintings had to wait so long but copyright is exactly what it says: a right to copy. Paintings had always been protected as private property and they merited copyright protection only when new technology was capable of producing copies that were attractive to buyers.

Copyright is unusual among the Big Three because every work that qualifies is automatically protected without the need to tell anyone, register it or put a © sign on it. America does maintain a vestigial registration system but American law protects works that qualify even if they are not registered. Qualifying works are not limited to what might be assumed. They are grouped into three main categories: one, literary, dramatic, musical and artistic works; two, sound recordings, films, broadcasts and cable programmes; and, three, the typographical arrangement of published works. To qualify, a work must fit the category, be original and involve skill and labour. The British Intellectual Property Office (IPO) goes so far as to say that a qualifying work does not need to have 'novelty or aesthetic value' so long as it is the result of 'independent intellectual effort', which, for example, enables the IPO to treat a written line of computer code as a literary work so long as it results from skill and labour.

The standard term for authors in the 1710 Act was 14 years, which was renewable once for a total of 28 years (the early American laws had even shorter terms of five or seven years). It is now the author's lifetime plus 70 years with variations for performances, broadcasts and films and other collaborative works. A new typographical arrangement of an existing book qualifies for 25 years.

The laws also specify the 'limitations and exceptions' that allow others to use a work without breaking the law or being liable to pay. The most common exceptions are 'fair dealing' (Europe) and 'fair use' (America), which allow people to use copyright material for education and research and to quote small extracts for review. The quotes in this book are permissible because they are brief; but more substantial quotes that were more essential to the work might have problems. The laws do not specify exactly how much can be copied and rely on words like 'substantial proportion'. Teachers who want to use copyright material in a class need to consider whether a licence is necessary, as do students who copy textbooks. In 1991, a New York district court fined Kinko's copy-shops $510,000 for copying 12 books and ordered them to pay the plaintiff's fees of $1,365,000.

Copyright law touches the creative economy at five points. The *author* comes first, a term which includes not only writers but other creators such as designers and film-makers. Second, the author's *action* on an idea by means of skill and effort creates a work. Third is the *work* itself, such as a text, image, performance, publication or broadcast. Fourth, the *right* to copy, specified by the law, which can be subdivided into an almost infinite variety of rights that may be sold or licensed in different media, territories, languages and time periods. Fifth, a *transaction* takes place in which the right-holder allows, or prevents, others from making copies. A transaction may be an agreement between author and intermediary, intermediary and intermediary, or intermediary and user.

These five stages have an internal logic. I create something; and I let you copy it, or not. The twin poles are what I do and what I let you do.

The Digital Flip

Digital ignores this logic. In a report on the internet and copyright, the American Department of Commerce said, 'The distinctions between authors, producers and performers are becoming irrelevant.' The basic definitions of original and copy imply a hierarchical master/servant relationship between the original and a copy. Digital flips this assumption on its head. The essence of digital coding is to reduce media to data, manipulate them and then reproduce them as perfectly as the original. The essence of the internet is to move these data around the world and reproduce them with scant regard for national laws. Together, these two processes are redefining the nature of media.

John Perry Barlow, a former Grateful Dead lyricist who is a co-founder of the Electronic Frontier Foundation, an internet body committed to free speech, argues the case for the flip vividly: 'We're going to have to look at information as if we've never seen the stuff before . . . The protections that we will develop will rely far more on ethics and technology than on law. The economy of the future will be based more on relationship than possession.' He welcomes this: 'Most of the folks who presently make their living by their wits do so not under the protection of legally instantiated methods of owning their own intelligence or expertise but by defining value on the basis of a continued and deepening interaction with an audience or client base.'

The first industry to flip was music, which takes to digital technology like a duck to water. Music tracks are short and require little bandwidth or storage space. The quality on a smartphone may be patchy but we accept scratchy sound more readily than we do indistinctly printed words or murky pictures.

The result has been a steady twenty-year-long increase in the number of musicians, the number of new tracks and albums and number of old tracks made available. Listeners are more willing to sample new kinds of music and more able to do so. The 'like' and 'follow' buttons on Facebook, QQ and other networks lead people to a much wider range of sounds than did radio or the local record store.

As digital copying became routine there was confusion over what was legal to copy. Screen technologies treat music and pictures as they treat words by reducing all formats to files that look alike on a screen whether on a desktop or a smartphone. Someone accustomed to copying a text file for free sees little reason why they cannot copy a music file for free, and someone brought up on listening to radio for free sees little reason not to listen to a music file delivered to a smartphone for free.

The music labels played along, to start with, seeing the internet as a marketing opportunity and encouraging artists to upload music promos with a maximum of 30 seconds. Then a few artists began to break the 30-second rule and the Beastie Boys, licensed to Capitol, put some of their out-of-print songs on the internet against Capitol's policy. David Bowie launched an album on the internet before selling the CD, Elvis Costello started to put all his work online so it could be downloaded and Metallica allowed audiences to record performances and trade the tapes.

The tide turned when a student drop-out called Shawn Fanning developed Napster's file-sharing program to enable people to search for MP3 files held by all other users and transfer files to their own hard disc. The deal was that in return for being allowed to search other people's computers you allowed them to search yours. It was possible to type in the name of a track and Napster searched not only websites but the hard discs of all connected users for that track. If a music executive had put a demo recording of a new unpublished track on to a hard disc, Napster found it, copied it and delivered it home. These search-and-find services became so popular that several universities' networks were clogged and the authorities banned their students from using them. The students responded with a nation-wide campaign for free speech.

The realization that anyone can exchange music on the internet began to terrify the major music labels. The Recording Industry Association of America (RIAA) took legal action against Napster, as did Metallica's singer Lars Ulrich when he discovered fans had uploaded the band's work-in-progress, and also sued individuals who downloaded music without paying for it. Napster's defence was that it merely provided a system for copying files which is no different from the use of a tape or disc to record a broadcast. It said it did not itself infringe any copyright and said rights-holders cannot blame it any more than they could blame the manufacturer of a ladder which a burglar uses to gain access to an upstairs window. But in 2000 a US district court decided that the sheer scale of Napster file-sharing undercut its defence of 'private copying' and Napster was found guilty of 'wholesale infringement'. Napster relaunched itself as a legal service and later became part of Rhapsody.

In the 10 or so years since downloading became widespread there has been extensive infringement of music copyright as well as, more recently, of TV and films. By 2010, illegal copies of Hollywood films were available in Asia a few days after their American release. Some of the illegal companies operate massive server farms. The FBI's 2012 arrest warrant of German-born Kim Dotcom, who ran his website Megaupload from Hong Kong, said it had over a billion visitors, over 150 million registered users and 50 million users every day. The FBI estimated it had revenues of $175 million from selling advertising and premium services.

There is little agreement about the size of the loss in terms of the number of units or their value. The recording labels estimate their losses to be $20–30 billion a year, the games industry claims losses of about $3 billion a year and book publishers claim about $1 billion a year. The Business Software Alliance reckons half the world's software users are infringing copyright and that rights-holders lose $7 billion a year. The Hollywood studios claim America's 'content theft' of film, TV, music, games and software is $58 billion a year although this figure, which is the highest of all estimates, is hotly contested.

In the early days, industry estimates assumed that every stolen or infringed copy was equivalent to a lost sale and so if a $10 album or video was stolen then the rights-holders lost $10. Their recent estimates are more conservative, suggesting that only one in five or ten infringed copies is a lost sale, which seems closer to reality. Many people who use material illegally would not have bought their own copy, either because it was not available locally or because they could not afford it. Prices of legal copies in some countries are exceptionally high. When a DVD of Christopher Nolan's Batman movie *The Dark Knight* costs $75 to buy in Russia, compared to $10 to buy and $2 to rent in America, the temptation to steal is high. The real choice is between an illegal copy or no copy at all.

The broader impact on people's attitudes and behaviour is also more complex than was initially assumed. There is evidence in both directions: that people use free downloads instead of paying, which is a lost sale, and that they also use them to discover new tracks and videos, which leads them to buy more.

Music and other entertainment products, and increasingly all products, depend on being recommended by those who have already seen, heard or otherwise experienced them and so a degree of copying is endemic to the business. The success of many modern brands, from software to shoes, depends upon their rapid dissemination to create a network effect, a buzz of 'street cred'. So, it is said, copying, and that includes theft, helps the company rather than harms it. David Petrarca, director of 2011 HBO hit series *Game of Thrones*, which was reputedly the most illegally downloaded TV series ever, believes 'illegal downloads don't matter because such shows thrive on cultural buzz and the social commentary they generate.' Computer software depends even more on these network benefits than do media and entertainment. Someone who infringes a computer software licence (for instance, by installing software with a single-user licence in a second computer) perceives little damage is done and, indeed, little may be done. Software companies want their software to be as widely networked as possible, and often give it away. There is more than a shred of common sense in all these attitudes but companies still need to cover their cost and make a profit.

Alternatives

The internet would be a barren place if the early developers had claimed private property rights. Briton Donald Davies and American Paul Baran, who separately invented the packet switching technologies that virtually all digital networks, including the internet, now depend upon, claimed no copyright. Tim Berners-Lee at CERN, the European Laboratory for Particle Physics in Geneva, did not assert copyright or claim a patent for the World Wide Web. Nor did the inventors of Apache software, which operates the majority of servers; SendMail, which runs over 70 per cent of e-mail programs; Bind, which was written by four University of South California students and is still the most popular DNS software for turning numerical e-mail addresses into plain English; and Larry Wall's Perl, which facilitates hypertext links.

Meanwhile, the mainstream entertainment companies were so locked into copyright that they did not grasp what was happening. They could not understand how anything could prosper without copyright. By the time they realized what was going on, the basic principles of open access had become established and the game was over.

The standard bearer of open access is free and open source software (FOSS), which means anyone can write and edit software code on condition they allow others the same right to re-write what they have done, on the principle of share-and-share-alike. The pioneer of FOSS was Richard Stallman, who began to develop a new operating system, GNU, on share-and-share-alike principles in the early 1980s. Computer hackers love verbal puns and GNU is a recursive acronym, an acronym that includes itself, for 'GNU's Not Unix'. It refers to AT&T's Unix language, now owned by Novell, which many users dislike for its strict licensing conditions and high costs. Stallman wanted GNU and Unix to be the opposite in terms of ownership and licensing conditions. Stallman joined forces with a Finnish software engineering student called Linus Torvalds who had written a share-and-share-alike kernel, the system's central processing unit, which he called Linux. Stallman's operating system with Torvalds's kernel became one of the most famous examples of FOSS where the source code is free and open.

The proponents of FOSS give away source code on two grounds. First, they uphold the moral absolute that nobody should own something so basic as computer code for the same reason that no one should own the letters of an alphabet or indeed a language. Second, they believe private ownership inhibits development (in ecological terms, it constrains learning and adaptation).

Torvalds says a person who wants to own source code is like a man who, having invented a printing press, requires everyone who wants to rearrange letters into words to seek his permission. Richard Stallman argues with evangelical fervour that most forms of human expression must never be privatized and has devised a General Public Licence (GPL) which functions as a copyright licence under the Berne Convention and puts a program permanently in the public domain. He wants to replace copyright, which supports rights-owners, with a system of 'copyleft' which supports users.

By the industry's own standards, Linux and GNU are outstanding successes. Linux provides the kernel of Android's operating system and had 60 per cent of the server market in 2010 compared to Microsoft's 30 per cent. It dominates the supercomputer market, running on over 90 per cent of the world's 500 fastest computers, because their highly specialized users want to be able to rewrite the source code continually without negotiating any copyright or patent licence with the original manufacturer.

It has a deserved reputation for being up-to-date and user-friendly. In 2012, the former head of Microsoft Research, Europe, said Microsoft had only four people working on Windows R&D. In contrast, Linux has thousands of programmers, and they are probably smarter, too. Microsoft has admitted that 'Linux and other OS advocates are making a progressively more credible argument that OS is at least as reliable, if not more, than commercial alternatives. The ability of the OS process to collect and harness the collective IQ of thousands of individuals across the internet is simply amazing.' Computer expert Eric Raymond puts the case forcefully: 'The Open Source world behaves in many respects like a free market or an ecology, a collection of selfish agents attempting to maximize utility which in the process produces a self-correcting spontaneous order more elaborate and efficient than any amount of central planning could have achieved.'

A remarkable example of this spontaneous ecology is the Creative Commons systems of licences, which promote a default culture of permission rather than of restriction for arts, culture and video. It grew out of the desire of many people to license photographs, videos, writing and other media so that others could be confident that they were free to use them when previously they would have been uncertain because of the vagueness of fair dealing rules. Sensibly, it offers three versions of each licence: one for humans, one for lawyers and one in computer language.

FOSS and Creative Commons have had a positive impact on the development of creative economies and their underlying principles of share-and-share-alike have become a moral code for how people should behave both online and offline. This acceptance came grudgingly. When FOSS emerged, the software companies were hostile and when Creative Commons started the film companies attacked its licences as not being proper copyright, which was incorrect, and tried to stop its representatives from attending industry meetings. It is now clear that both systems have been helpful rather than destructive and they have provided a sensible user-friendly service for a small but significant number of people.

This was demonstrated at a conference on Co-operation and Ownership in the Digital Economy (CODE), organized by Arts Council England and Bronac Ferran, which discussed art, anthropology, broadcasting, astronomy and genome sequencing. The speaker on genetics, Tim Hubbard, later became the only British member of the Advisory Board of the global Encyclopedia of DNA Elements (ENCODE), which has suggested a new definition of genes which would take account of epigenetic regulation. Like the American/British map of the genome, ENCODE operates on FOSS principles.

Open Access

The FOSS principles are now being applied to the huge amounts of data that governments pay for with tax-payers' money and which the public feels it still owns, in some way, and has rights over. This so-called 'public data' includes maps and postal addresses, which are essential for geo-location apps, as well as tidal and navigational data and weather data. Government agencies often lack the skills to use public data and they almost certainly lack the money but, worse, they often prevent anybody else from using it. The Swedish statistician Hans Rosling, inventor of GapMinder, who describes himself as the Robin Hood of public data, says the worst culprits are international organizations like the United Nations, World Bank and IMF, which get data from member countries and then 'sell it in inefficient and stupid ways'. This dog-in-the-manger attitude is opposite to the spirit of FOSS, which holds that public benefits increase in proportion to the number of people who get their hands on raw data.

The American federal government excels at opening public data for public re-use, opening the door to America's lead in Global Positioning Services (GPS) and geo-location apps, but most governments mismanage or waste it. President Obama has ordered all publicly funded research to be freely available. In Britain, the Open Rights Group and Tim Berners-Lee are working with government to persuade public agencies to open the doors to public data. It is not easy because many agencies face financial pressures and, if they do make data available, want to do so for the highest price. There are also issues of privacy. It took a long campaign to obtain Ordnance Survey map data for public re-use and even postcodes are privately owned.

The market in government-funded research is similarly inefficient because researchers sell the results to commercial publishers which charge high prices for making them available so the public is either unable to see them or has to pay a fee, which means they pay twice. The publishers say the cost of checking the articles, called 'peer review', is expensive, which it may be, but they make large profits and prevent anyone not attached to a university from accessing the results. America's small Public Library of Science and, much later, the world's biggest source of research funds, America's National Institute of Health, led a campaign for government-funded research results to be made 'open access'. In 2012, over 10,000 academics boycotted Elsevier, one of the biggest publishers alongside Wiley and Springer, and the tide turned. The British and French governments have given support in principle and the world's two largest private foundations, the Bill and Melinda Gates Foundation and the Wellcome Foundation, require their research results to be open access.

Open access has travelled from a geek idea to a moral principle to a mass movement, from the first stirrings of FOSS through to Creative Commons and now the demand to free public data. A broad coalition of hackers, researchers and now governments are committed to share-and-share-alike as the first principle for regulating the use of information and media. Rights-holders need to re-think the rules on commercial, proprietorial copyright to match.

For a long time copyright material was protected by a mix of good law and bad technology. By good law, I mean law that was fair and effective, and whose penalties were proportionate to infringement. By bad technology, I mean technology's inability to make good copies. The best protection of copyright is a legal copy that is cheaper or more easily available or better quality than an illegal one.

The challenge of digital is that excellent *technology* for creating and copying (or re-creating) material is now cheaply and widely available and the public are taking what they can. That puts more pressure on the *laws*, which are not coping. The technology is leading the race, with the users close behind, and the laws a distant third. It is much easier and more fun to make new software and media content than to make new law.

PATENTS

Patents are a straightforward example of ideas as property as they give a monopoly almost as robust as ownership of a physical thing. Thomas Jefferson's fine words about the impossibility of owning ideas did not stop him from being one of the three people who set up America's first patent office. He was Secretary of State at the time and his fellow examiners were Henry Knox, Secretary of War, and Edmund Randolph, Attorney General, whose eminent status indicated the seriousness with which the government took its new role. In the whole of their first year, Jefferson and his colleagues gave out three patents.

Now, the US Patent and Trademark Office (PTO) gives out three patents every 10 minutes. In international league tables, patents have replaced agricultural output and miles of railway track as an indicator of economic development.

The stakes are high. Each smartphone depends on as many as 10–20,000 patents. Their brand-owners and the manufacturers of operating systems (such as Windows, Apple's iOS and Google's Android) are engaged in contentious negotiations which frequently spill over into litigation and sometimes go to court. Judges and juries are faced with difficult decisions over whether a patent is valid, which is complex enough, and then even more difficult decisions about the effect of any infringement on competition and the level of any compensation. In 2012, a British judge tried to reduce these complexities to a matter of taste when he ruled that Samsung's Galaxy tablets did not copy Apple's iPad because 'They are not as cool.' American courts try to be more objective but it isn't easy.

The complexity of global supply chains means the original inventor might have registered one kind of use, a licensee might want to do something different, and a sub-licensee want to use it in a different way again. The original patent-holder might have been acquired by another company. Android had only four employees when it started to develop its operating system and could not have foreseen how it might be used. Later, other patent-owners began to ask Android to pay licence fees for what they said was the use of their components but Android refused.

Each patent must be correctly licensed in the country where it is made and where it is put into a component as well as in the country where it is assembled and sold. Part of the long-running saga between Apple and Samsung turned on where Apple's Intel chips, which use a Samsung patent, were really sold. Apple says they were sold in America and waved a receipt that gave the address of Apple's Cupertino headquarters. But Samsung waved a delivery note which said they had been sold in Germany and then shipped to China. If Apple was right, it was free to use them under American law. If Samsung was right, American law did not apply.

The sums at stake are massive. The amount of money that changed hands for smartphone licences in 2000–12 is estimated to be about $40 billion. When American Judge Posner cancelled a hearing between Apple and Google because he thought it trivial, he said: 'It's a constant struggle for survival. As in any jungle, the animals will use all the means at their disposal, all the teeth and claws that are permitted by the ecosystem.'

It is inevitable that these sums attract companies which buy patents purely to start litigation rather than to trade, known as trolls. America has more trolls than anywhere else but Chinese companies are catching up. They rely on the high costs of court cases, and the delays, to persuade rights-holders to pay up. A small British company, Serverside, which supplies credit-cards worldwide, was sued by an American company based in Marshall, Texas, where patent laws are notoriously vexatious. Serverside discovered the likely cost of defending its patents was $2–4 million and settled out of court.

In the same way as the origins of copyright still resonate today so the origins of patents as industrial property help to explain how they function today. The word 'patent' comes from the Latin word for 'open' because the early written permissions were sealed in such a way that they could be easily opened and checked. The first recorded patent was awarded by the City Council of Florence in 1421 for glass-making and patents soon became a valuable business asset. In the 1460s, when John of Speyer crossed the Alps to bring one of Germany's new printing presses to Venice, he was given patent letters to protect his business. The local writers had no such protection because copyright was not yet thought of.

A few years later, another European trader, William Caxton, brought a printing press to London and asked King Edward IV for a patent monopoly. Both Caxton and king did well out of the deal and for the next few centuries monarchs and guilds sold patents as a source of revenue and as a means of political and religious censorship. Slowly, as trade developed, inventors won the right to patents regardless of royal whim and in 1624 Britain passed a Statute of Monopolies, which stopped politicians awarding patents to suit their own interests. It was the beginning of the rights contract between an inventor and the public.

America passed its first patent registration system in 1790 and started a formal system of testing in 1836. The first Japanese patent law was not passed until 1885, at the beginning of the Meiji period of modernization, after an American had told his Japanese interpreter that Japan was a nation of copiers. The interpreter Korekiyo Takahashi said later he did not have the 'slightest idea' what his visitor was talking about but he was determined to find out and then helped to set up the Japan Patent Office and became its first Commissioner. China's patent law, introduced in 1984, is stronger than its copyright and trademark laws and more rigorously applied.

Three Steps

The registration of a patent varies in different countries from a simple application which is automatically accepted to a detailed application which is critically examined to prevent a patent office from being in the embarrassing position of granting two monopolies for the same idea. This external burden of proof is a major difference between patents and copyright. Inventors have to prove their new invention really is new.

A patent is given to the first person to file an application rather than the first to invent (although America only adopted such a first-to-file system in 2013). It is a condition of filing that applications are published. Knowledge that is available before the filing date is known as 'prior art' and used to evaluate whether an idea is novel.

The cost of applying for a patent in most countries is negligible in terms of the patent office's own charges but can be high if complications arise. The British Intellectual Property Office (IPO) charges $45 for an initial application but almost every further step incurs extra fees. America's PTO charges $380 for a basic filing, an extra $870 for obligatory checks and $1,000 for renewal. China charges $150 for filing. Many private inventors and small businesses are reluctant to pay these costs or unable to do so (every Dyson cleaner comes with a leaflet complaining about 'outrageous' patent fees). The European Patent Office and the Patent Cooperation Treaty have helped to cut costs and speed the vetting process, but litigation costs remain substantial. The British Gowers Review reported that the costs of defending a patent could be as much as £750,000 and they can be much more.

To qualify, the idea must pass the rules on patentable matter similar to copyright's rules on qualifying works. America's criteria say: 'The laws of nature, physical phenomenon and abstract ideas are not patentable.' The British have four kinds of exclusions: 'a discovery, scientific theory or mathematical model; a literary, dramatic, musical or artistic work or any other aesthetic creation whatsoever; a scheme, rule or method for performing a mental act, playing a game or doing business, or a program for a computer; the presentation of information'. It also rules out ideas that are 'against public policy or morality', which has been used to exclude stem cells and some other micro-organisms.

If judged patentable, an idea then has to pass three tests. The first is novelty. The second is the inventive step. The invention must be truly inventive in the sense of being 'non-obvious' to a person 'skilled in the art', who is defined as a normally educated person who has some knowledge and experience of the subject. The need for an 'inventive step' is used to reject ideas that are obvious as well as any that are happenstance or meaningless. It is akin to copyright's requirement that a work must involve skill and expertise and confirms meaning as an essential requirement of creativity.

Third, the idea must have a practical impact, usually defined as a technical effect, or the capability of being made and used in industry. It is relatively easy to evaluate impact when inventions are mechanical, physical things but much harder when they are intangible and examiners have to test an idea of an idea. The definition of 'technical effect', especially in relationship to software, is the biggest controversy in patenting today.

The bare bones of patenting are being put under severe stress by technological change and commercial ingenuity. I have selected two areas of pressure: business software and genetics. I show how America approved the patenting of biotechnology in 1980, computer programs in 1981 and business methods in 1998. Europe and Japan are not so generous. We have come a long way from John of Speyer and his printing press.

Mr Bezos's Shopping Basket

The early computer programs were not treated as intellectual property and received no protection. Then America's 1976 Copyright Act and the European Union's 1991 Directive on computer programs categorized software code as a literary work and gave copyright protection. Most other countries followed suit.

The protection is not worth as much as it might seem. It stops an end-user from copying a program in its entirety but it is powerless to stop another developer from copying its main features, tweaking the code and producing another program. When Microsoft 'copied' Apple's desktop, and when Borland 'copied' Lotus's spreadsheet in the early 1990s, Apple and Lotus sued and expected to win. But they lost.

The courts found in favour of the copiers. They said Microsoft had not copied Apple's code line-by-line but had only picked up Apple's 'look and feel'; and that Borland had not slavishly copied Lotus's entire code but only some of its principles. Under copyright law, a qualifying work has to be new but it does not have to be unique. Microsoft and Borland were able to claim that far from copying someone else's work they had actually produced their own and could claim their own copyright. The courts' decisions alerted industry to the weakness of copyright law in protecting computer programs and the need for something stronger.

Could a patent be the answer? Companies as diverse as banker Merrill Lynch and retailer Wal-Mart argued that their computer programs qualified for a patent. Merrill Lynch had a system for managing share transactions and Wal-Mart had one for controlling its inventory and they and many others wanted to protect their systems as securely as they protected their buildings and equipment. They locked their warehouses at night and wanted to put patent locks on the intellectual processes inside.

The Supreme Court's decision in *Diamond v. Diehr* (1981) had already found in favour of patenting a computer program so long as it fulfilled the three criteria of novelty, non-obviousness and impact. The case arose because the PTO had refused an application for a computer-based device to develop synthetic rubber on the grounds that patent laws exclude a mathematical formula. The Court decided that, although a computer program by itself, 'as such', cannot be patented, a computer program that delivers a separate inventive function could be. It distinguished between the underlying code, which could not be patented, and its technical effect on a business process.

This extension of patenting from a computer program to a business method was confirmed in 1998 when the US Court of Appeals decided in *State Street Bank & Trust Co. v. Signature Financial Group Inc.* that a computer-based business method does fulfil the criteria for a patent. The Court said the three criteria worked the same way here as elsewhere. It was aware that it is difficult if not impossible to distinguish between the mathematical code of a business method and the business method itself. In e-commerce, the software is the method. There is no external, physical, bricks-and-mortar reality.

The State Street case marked a watershed in American patenting policy and since then the PTO has given patents to thousands of business methods. Dell's success as the largest computer seller in the world depends on personalizing each computer to a customer's specification and delivering it more quickly than its competitors. It protects its business by over 70 patents including one for the way it packs computers into a shipping box.

The name of Peri Hartmann is not well known in publishing but he has a patent for a 'method and system for placing a purchase order via a communication network' which enables a customer to click once to confirm an order and is a factor in the success of Amazon (US patent no. 5,960,411). Amazon CEO Jeff Bezos, whose name appears after Peri Hartmann, refers to it as his 1-Click system. It is hardly non-obvious and, according to James Gleick in *The New York Times*, the patent examiner had some doubts before she was convinced. Amazon then sued its largest competitor, Barnes & Noble, and forced it to change its online ordering system into a two-click process.

Jeff Bezos has ambitions for his baby. His application stated: 'Although the present invention has been described in terms of various embodiments [based on Amazon.com as it then was] it is not intended that the invention be limited to these embodiments. Modifications within the spirit of the invention will be apparent to those skilled in the art.'

He was cleverly exploiting the legitimate scope for a patent to cover unspecified and as-yet-unknown applications if they could be imagined by a person skilled in the art. In other words, if someone familiar with online sales could imagine a subsequent use, even if they could not quite work out how to do it, then the Hartmann/Bezos patent would cover it. The intent is to excuse a patent-holder from having to apply for a new patent for every (minor) variation. In Amazon's case, Hartmann and Bezos said that people who were 'skilled in the art' and likely to see future modifications could expect to see Amazon's 'No Trespassing' sign. These signs last 20 years, which is almost a lifetime in dotcom terms.

The result is a ballooning increase in the patenting of ideas that are in existence and commonplace but carried out, for the first time, by a computer. The PTO has awarded patents for club buying (enabling a group of buyers to get a discount), offering professional advice, and generating footnotes in a text. It has awarded a patent for a system that 'lowers your price if your customer asks about a competitor's lower price'. In his advice to the federal government in its anti-trust case against Microsoft, lawyer Lawrence Lessig said: 'This is a disaster, a major change that occurred without anybody thinking through the consequences. In my view, it is the single greatest threat to innovation in cyberspace, and I'm extremely sceptical that anyone is going to get it in time.'

Google Chairman Eric Schmidt expects the litigation battles to slow down innovation. Asked by the *Wall Street Journal* about the likely endgame, he said future start-ups would have a tougher battle and might not get off the ground. 'Google is doing fine. Apple is doing fine. Let me tell you the loser here. Imagine a young [Android co-founder] Andy Rubin trying to form a new version of Danger [the smartphone company Rubin co-founded before Android]. How is he or she going to be able to get the patent necessary to offer version 1.0? That's the real consequence of this.' A patent system that is supposed to encourage innovation is actually slowing it down.

But the PTO shows little sign of wanting to 'get it', in Lessig's words. Its description of suitable candidates for patenting in the relevant business classification, Class 705, includes such routine activities as '(1) Determining who your customers are, and the products/services they need/want; and (2) Informing customers you exist, showing them your products and services, and getting them to purchase'. It admits Class 705 is 'transitioning away from technology towards the end result the inventor is attempting to achieve with that technology.' It quotes approvingly a patent for a sales team (no. 6,070,149): 'The present invention relates to virtual sales personnel, and more particularly, to software which is capable of assisting a computer user to complete an on-line sales transaction in a substantially similar manner as a human sales representative.'

The American courts have belatedly begun to wake up to the possibility that a patent for something that is 'substantially similar' to what humans are already doing is on the verge of losing any distinctiveness and likely to block later, genuine inventions. In 2010 the Supreme Court ruled against a controversial patent claim lodged by two inventors, Bernie Bilski and Rand Warsaw, who had written a software program for an investment strategy for hedging investments in energy companies. The court agreed that the program used a machine (a computer) and also that it transformed the process and that it therefore passed what had become known as the PTO's 'machine-or-transformation' test which would normally make it a strong contender for a patent. But the court concluded that it was essentially an abstract process, rather than a practical one, and therefore not patentable. It was a temporary halt to the onward march.

The world's patent offices outside America have been reluctant to award these kinds of patents. The European Patent Office says the difference between America and Europe is that 'in Europe the invention has to be of a technical character whilst in America the fact that an invention uses a computer in any way is enough to qualify'. It does not award a patent for software that solves a business problem but whose 'technical difference' is solely due to using software instead of mechanical means and it has turned down Amazon's application (although Amazon continues to appeal). It says using software does not itself constitute a technical difference. The German, British and other European patent offices follow suit, as does China.

Computer software is now so integral to every business process that patenting a program gets close to patenting a company's heart and soul. America's policy opens the door to the patenting of every computerized business process which has severe implications for innovation and social equity.

Private Genes

The patenting of biological matter is even more controversial. Some people say it is close to patenting life itself, though we should be careful what we mean by life. Many governments have allowed people to own and register plant varieties for decades. The Finnish patent office gave its third-ever patent to a novel method of producing live yeast as far back as 1843 and a few years later Louis Pasteur got a French patent for his yeast culture. America took the lead in plant patents, starting with the 1930 Plant Patent Act, followed by Germany and other European countries. Britain passed its Plant Varieties and Seeds Act in 1964 and awarded a monopoly right to the owner of any plant variety that could be shown to be novel, distinct, uniform and stable. A plant qualifies for protection even if it has a history of growing wild so long as it has not been sold commercially.

At the time, patenting a seed or a plant for agricultural purposes was regarded as little different from patenting a chemical or biological recipe for pharmaceutical purposes. Western farmers and horticulturists were eager to increase yields as their costs grew and they had to compete with imports from low-wage countries. The huge investments in faster-growing and more disease-resistant seeds over the past 40 years would not have been possible if the seed companies had not been able to protect their investments. Home gardeners, faced with too many weeds and the modern curse of too little time, enjoyed the benefits of buying huge quantities of glyphosate in Round-Up and other patented weed-killers.

Almost every plant is now being analysed for its genetic value. The biological make-up of maize, potato, rice, wheat, sorghum, cassava, millet, soybean and wheat has been or is being privatized. L'Oréal has patented the use of the kava shrub to reduce hair loss. An American company, RiceTec, obtained a patent for the gene sequence of basmati rice, although the PTO later withdrew the patent under international pressure. Nestlé India applied to patent a process for parboiling rice. Other companies have applied for patents on tea, coffee, cotton and pepper seeds.

My favourite example is the Gentian. For centuries, Indians used a species of Gentian, Dogbane, as a tranquillizer. In the 1950s, a company began to sell a patented version in Europe where it became so popular that the Indian government had to ban its export because prices locally were rising beyond what Indians could afford. Over in Africa, the chemical properties of another Gentian, the Madagascan rosy periwinkle, which has pretty pink flowers with a deep red centre, were highly sought after because its genetic properties seem to limit diabetes. Eli Lilly Inc. discovered it was more powerful as a treatment for cancer and earned about $100 million a year while the Madagascans receive nothing. Lilly justifies its claim by saying it alone identified the anti-cancer qualities and the manufacturing process is expensive. To the Madagascans, Lilly's actions increased the price and restricted the supply to those who assumed either they owned it or that it was in the public domain.

According to Dr Pennapa Subcharoen of Thailand's Ministry of Public Health, 'Drug companies come here, collect samples, take them away and say it is for the collective heritage of mankind. Then they study the samples, develop them, claim intellectual property rights and come back and make us buy them.' His point is that drug companies do not invent these plants but exploit local knowledge of their therapeutic qualities although often, as Lilly showed, they discover something not known locally. The Rio Convention on Bio-Diversity put some constraints on whether such plants may be traded but it sets few rules on who should pay, or how much and the average royalty is only 1–2 per cent of revenues. The developing countries want 10 per cent, which may seem high, but the US Park Service charges that for bio-prospecting in the Yellowstone National Park.

There is a delicate balance between owning what one creates and protecting those who are too weak, ignorant or poor to protect themselves; between allowing the richest and quickest to claim ownership by means of patents without allowing the inarticulate to be pushed to the margins. As Mahatma Gandhi said, 'I do not want my house to be walled in or my windows blocked. I want the cultures of all lands to be blown about the house as freely as possible. But also I refuse to be blown off my feet by any.'

Gene Grabs

Should the human genome be in the public domain and freely available to all or should individuals be allowed to own the use of specific sequences in the same way as they do plant varieties? The question became urgent when developments in cell technology allowed scientists to identify, nurture and re-mix cells so that they can create micro-organisms.

The American Congress famously said in 1952 that 'Everything under the sun that is made by man is patentable', which implied that everything that was not made by man was not patentable. Since then, America's position has shifted radically. Thirty years later, in *Diamond v. Chakrabarty*, the Supreme Court ruled on a patent application by Anand Chakrabarty for a genetically modified bacterial micro-organism designed to gobble up oil spills at sea. It decided to shift the dividing line from between inanimate things and living things (the former patentable, the latter not) to between the product of nature, whether living or not, and human-made inventions which may, of course, be living. It patented the bacteria.

The PTO's current guidelines say all micro-organisms except humans can be patented and justifies the human exception by quoting the 13th Amendment to the Constitution, which prohibits slavery.

This shift from saying 'nothing, never' to 'everything but us if it means slavery' was a breathtaking expansion of private property and a massive shift in the PTO's attitude towards the ownership of life.

It has issued a patent to Harvard University for an experimental mouse known as Oncomouse into which an oncogene had been inserted for the purpose of cancer research. The European Patent Office (EPO), after initially demurring, finally agreed, saying Oncomouse was such a considerable manipulation of genetic material as to be new and unique. Others protested the mice suffer during the research but the EPO decided the benefit to society outweighed the loss to the mouse. It was a neat variation on the 'rights contract' that balances the creator's reward against the social gain.

Meanwhile, parts of the human body have come up for private grabs since an American court decided people do not own their body parts as exclusively as they might assume. The case arose when a Californian university medical centre managed to patent a cell line found in a spleen that had been taken from a man, John Moore, who had hairy-cell leukaemia. The doctors had discovered that Moore's T-lymphocytes were very rare and, without telling him why, they carried out intensive tests ending in the removal of his spleen. The cells were indeed as valuable as they had expected, generating products worth hundreds of millions of dollars. When Moore discovered the university had privatized his cells, and made a profit, he sued; but he lost. The Supreme Court of California decided that we do not own our cells after they have left our body.

The EPO gives patents to individual human, animal or plant genes and gene sequences, and their function, as long as the other patentability criteria are fulfilled. It draws the line explicitly at patenting 'an entire human body' but it would be foolish to bet against body parts being patented at some time. The door has been open since 1998 when a EU directive stated that 'An element isolated from the human body or otherwise produced by means of a technical process, including the sequence or partial sequence of a gene, may constitute a patentable invention even if the structure of that element is identical to that of a natural element.'

These two approaches came head to head when scientists mapped the human genome. The publicly funded $3 billion US–UK Human Genome Mapping Project (HGMP) published all its results so they became public property. Sir John Sulston, Wellcome Trust, which sponsored the British research, said: 'Our basic information, our software, should be free and open for everyone to play with, to compete with, to try and make products from.' In contrast, the commercially funded Celera privatized many sequences that might have a commercial value. Both the HGMP and Celera agreed in principle that any use of a gene may be patented but they disagreed strongly on the criteria, especially the 'what'.

Is the 'what' a discovery or an invention? The general meaning of both words is clear. A discovery is something that previously existed and an invention is something new. The European Patent Convention says discoveries cannot be patented at all (they are 'excluded matter') and Britain takes the same view. But the American PTO says with some bravado that 'invention means invention or discovery' and American companies use the two words interchangeably.

The HGMP said that the identification of a particular gene is a discovery rather than an invention and cannot be patented. Every half-qualified scientist knows it is there and must apply skill and intelligence before they can justify a claim for a non-obvious, practical use. By publishing its results as quickly as it could, and making them 'open access', the HGMP prevented anyone else from patenting them.

On the other hand, Celera and other companies argue that their techniques of identifying a raw gene sequence is so difficult and out-of-the-ordinary (in other words, so novel and non-obvious) that they constitute an invention as popularly understood and qualify for a patent. They also say that they have a large number of ideas for industrial applications. It is a reasonable approach. To get a patent you have to show that your idea has a practical application but you do not have to prove you can deliver all the practical applications yourself, as Amazon showed in its 1-Click application and as biotech companies claim for products based on DNA. The Supreme Court tightened the rules in 2013 when it invalidated some patents awarded to Myriad

Genetics for breast cancer tests, but the impact was slight. The gene grabs continue.

TRADEMARKS

Brands and other trademarks are the most noticeable hallmark of global consumerism, loved by some and scorned by others. They are more than symbols and have become a unique and valuable commercial asset in their own right with the benefits of being recognized regardless of people's language or indeed literacy. The Nike Corporation is not in the business of selling any particular shoes. It sells its brand; it sells itself.

Trademarks are the oldest kind of the three main types of intellectual property although they were the last to be enshrined in law. The first brands marked domestic animals by burning their hide or clipping an ear and some historians suggest the word 'brand' comes from the Anglo-Saxon word to 'burn'. Potters, carvers, furniture-makers and stone-masons signed their work by incising their names and leaving a mark. The growth of industrial manufacturing and international trade gave further impetus to corporate branding as manufacturers wanted to promote their goods worldwide and buyers wanted to know what they were getting. Brands also helped manufacturers and retailers to maintain fixed prices, which facilitated the growth of large retail stores with untrained assistants.

The aim of a modern brand is to instil itself in a consumer's mind so powerfully that they cannot imagine buying anything else and indeed will pay a premium to display it. When this happens, the consumer is paying the company to advertise its brand (the reverse of the normal relationship). Brand-owners select a brand that can be easily transferable and integrated as tightly as possible into their own products as well as licensed to connected products. Many companies make as much if not more money from licensing than from their own products.

A brand can be worth more than other company assets. The Nike swoosh is reckoned to be worth about $10 billion, according to brand specialist Interbrand, which rates the most valuable brands as follows ($ billion):

Table 1: The most valuable brands
(Interbrand, 2012)

Brand	Value ($ billion)
Coca-Cola	78
Apple	77
IBM	76
Google	70
Microsoft	58
General Electric	44
McDonald's	40
Intel	39
Samsung	33
Toyota	30

The list of Chinese brands is headed by China Mobile and consists mostly of banks, financial services and alcohol. According to Interbrand, the top software and dotcom Chinese brands are QQ ($6 billion), Baidu's search engine ($2 billion), Lenovo ($2 billion), Alibaba's e-commerce websites ($1 billion) and Netease games ($1 billion).

Like a patent, a trademark has to be registered. Any mark that identifies something and distinguishes it from other things can qualify, including names, images, signs, colours and even smells. There are some exceptions, such as a word that other companies might reasonably expect to use, or anything that indicates a product's quality, purpose or value.

A trademark does not require any unique inventiveness, as does a patent, nor any intellectual or artistic effort, as does a copyright work. As a result, some lawyers say trademarks do not merit the description of *intellectual* property.

A total of 4.2 million trademark applications were filed in 2011, twice as many as patent applications, and an increase of 13 per cent over 2010. Over half, 2.1 million, were filed in Germany followed by China (1.4 million), America (1.3 million) and France (1.2 million).

Today, trademarks can be protected in two ways which complement each other. The standard way is by registration. The process is broadly similar to that for a patent. An applicant has to show that the mark is in use, that it qualifies as a mark, and that it has not been previously registered. If successful, and so long as the holder continues to trade and pay renewal fees, a mark will stay in force for ever. Fees for applying and renewing are low but, as with patents, disputes can be expensive. America has a separate service-mark for services.

Whether registered or not, trademarks are usually defended by laws against 'passing off', which prevent someone from passing off their goods as someone else's. The courts ask a practical question: Is the public likely to mistake this product for that product? According to copyright expert Michael Flint, there are five tests. The passing off must (1) consist of a misrepresentation that is (2) made by a business in the course of trade (3) to prospective customers (4) which is calculated to injure the business or goodwill of another business and (5) which damages trade or goodwill.

'Passing off' laws can be used to defend any kind of intellectual property. A book publisher might lose a copyright action against another publisher over a book that was similar but not identical to its own if no copyright had been infringed but, if its case passed the five tests, it might win a 'passing off' action.

A NEW RIGHTS CONTRACT

The basis of intellectual property is a 'rights contract' between a right-owner and the public which balances two principles: one, people deserve to be rewarded for their creative efforts and therefore should be able to restrict access and copying and, two, society as a whole benefits if works and inventions are put into the public domain and made freely available. It is a balance between ownership/control and use/access. No country gets the balance completely right and it would be unrealistic to expect it. People have widely different assumptions about where the line should be drawn, and as technology changes so do owners' defences and the public's ability to get access. But the gap between what we need and what we have is too wide.

The rights contract has somehow to cope with the fact that the familiar concepts of ownership and possession that we know so well in terms of physical property are not so compelling when applied to intellectual property. There is a deep-seated feeling that the illegal use of intellectual property is not so injurious as stealing the 'real' thing.

There is still a feeling that a physical book (the design, the covers, the paper pages; the thickness of it) and the physical copy of a film (again, the heft of it) have more economic value than their contents, and that it is this physical value, not the intellectual value, which determines the offence. People feel more guilty stealing a hardback than a paperback. It gets worse (or better, according to one's view). People who feel guilty about stealing a paperback do not feel so guilty about stealing the same words printed out from a computer or down-loaded from the internet. It is true that the likelihood of being caught is less but the feeling of guilt is less, too.

If someone steals a chair from a neighbour, everyone (State, Church and neighbour) agrees they have committed an offence and should be punished. Make a habit of it, and they will go to prison. Steal a book or 'forget to return it' and that is still theft but no one is likely to go to prison. Steal what's in the book and who cares? Copy a video and the neighbour says, 'Can I watch, too?'

Each country draws up its own version of the contract. America is one of very few countries to include intellectual property in its Con-stitution, giving Congress the power to 'promote the progress of science and useful arts by securing for limited times to authors and inventors the exclusive right to their respective writing and discover-ies' (Eldred used the phrase 'for a limited time' in his failed attempt to stop copyright terms being extended). This utilitarian approach favours a right-holder's commercial interests.

In Europe, the Continental countries, led by France and Germany, give priority to a creator's personal rights over companies. Germany frequently blocks YouTube under pressure from music rights-holders who complain their licence fees have not been paid and its parliament has debated proposals to stop Google from listing newspaper articles without paying authors' royalties. Britain stands somewhat awk-wardly between these two approaches because it favours America's commercial approach, and the two countries share an Anglo-Saxon tradition of common law but, as a member of the European Union, it is obliged to harmonize its laws with its neighbours.

The difference between the Anglo-Saxon and Continental approaches is symbolized by their attitudes to moral rights. Moral rights spring from the belief that authors have a personal claim on their work irre-spective of what commercial deals may be done. Immanuel Kant wrote in *The Critique of Judgement* (1781) that 'Every artistic work consists of the creative spirit in a physical object. People can buy the physical object but the spirit, the soul, cannot be bought.' Moral rights give authors a right to be identified as the author ('paternity'), a right to prevent derogatory treatment ('integrity') and a right to pre-vent false attribution. In France these rights are everlasting and inalienable. If I mock a 19th-century French novel long out of copy-right the writer's heirs can sue me. Americans or British have little sympathy with such sensibilities and both countries adopted moral rights only under international pressure in the 1980s and with much shorter terms.

There is a wider gap between these industrial countries and the rest of the world. China resisted the private ownership of ideas and inven-tions until the nationalist governments from 1912 to the 1940s and then again when Deng Xiaoping began to liberalize the Communist Party in 1979. Today, intellectual property is seen as a symbol of the modernizing reform package and officials are given targets for patent applications which they vigorously pursue (the People's Liberation Army has taken action against street traders who sell unlicensed PLA memorabilia). China's new companies defend themselves against copy-ing and companies that want to export realize they have to operate within foreign laws. But the country was isolated for so long that the instinct for free copying is still strong and this, coupled with the fact that physical platforms like LPs, CDs and DVDs never caught hold, means that most young Chinese get their first taste of popular enter-tainment online where copyright is lax.

Other countries were also slow to adopt European and American ideas on private ownership. Japan did not introduce its first intellectual property law until 200 years after Europe had done so. In Muslim countries, Sharia law says the property of one's brain is the property of God. Hindu traditions say the imagination is shared with the Divine and cannot be independently owned.

There is also an age-old division between exporters and importers, between sellers and buyers and between 'commerce' and 'culture'. Sellers want their products to be protected in all countries, as I want my luggage to be mine everywhere, and the film, music and drug companies are reluctant to sell their products where they are likely to be copied or stolen. The importing countries, with little to protect in terms of their own intellectual property (which is why they are importers) seldom bother to have their own laws or, if they do, are slack to enforce them. Some of these countries treated Western rules on intellectual property as an unwarranted levy on the import of ideas, knowledge and technology but did not dare complain too loudly for fear of being shut out of Western markets in retaliation. America has made it clear to the governments of Australia, India, Mexico and Thailand that if they did not agree to its rules on intellectual property they would be shut out of America's markets for food.

There are two underlying trends in force, heading in opposite directions, a trend to privatization and a trend towards more open access. Both are getting stronger.

From a company's viewpoint, there are many arguments in favour of privatization and few against. No company would willingly give up the chance of a government-approved property licence. Claiming one's own copyright costs nothing and provides an efficient and globally accepted framework for deals and contracts, and enables companies to protect their investment. Patents protect the huge investments in pharmaceuticals and many other industries and have become a widely accepted (if flawed) indicator of innovation and business success. Trademarks have become an essential part of business and are appreciated by both brand-owners and consumers. As a result, an increasing number of creative works have a property tag attached, and the tag says 'private'.

The case against privatization also has powerful arguments. The links between incentives and rewards is weaker than it appears. Individuals create and innovate for many different reasons and many would do so even if their ideas were not protected. There is a tradition of science being freely available, which universities and public research companies uphold jealously. Tim O'Reilly, a computer publisher and activist, speculates about what would have happened if Isaac Newton had patented his laws of motion: 'No, I won't tell you what I know about parabolic trajectories but I'll calibrate your guns for a fee.'

As for claims of historical linkages between intellectual property and innovation, research by the United Nations and World Bank shows that many countries which flourished in the 18th and 19th centuries, including America, Britain, France, Germany and Switzerland, had minimal IP legislation. They all had patent offices but none actually tested applications to see if they were new and non-obvious. America, Britain and other European countries did not have systematic rules for registering a patent, including a proper search to see if the invention really was new, until the late 19th century. The first British Patent Office did not open for business until 1883 and, twenty years later, over 40 per cent of British patents were found to be invalid.

America and Japan Make a Move

Every few years the rights contract comes under fire from a new quarter. When peer-to-peer sharing became possible, and music was downloaded illegally on a massive scale, American rights-holders responded by taking legal action against teenagers, although with minimal impact, and they are still struggling with how to stop large-scale infringement. Two American copyright bills fell at an early stage and several European Parliament officials resigned in protest at the European Commission's proposals.

Google's bid to digitize out-of-print books on a non-profit basis was fiercely attacked by many authors as well as by several European governments. When commercial e-books arrived, the rights contract was found wanting again. Blind and partially sighted people wanted to use the Kindle's and other e-book devices' built-in print-to-speech facility so they could hear the words spoken. America, France and

Germany believed it would be difficult to stop fully sighted people abusing the exception but reluctantly gave way.

At the 2009 Copenhagen and 2012 Rio global conferences on sustainability the majority of delegates wanted to make energy-efficient technologies more widely available to developing countries but many technologies rely on patents that increase the price beyond what poor countries can afford. China was the only country to include an IP lawyer in its delegation and argue the case for patent exceptions for low-energy technology, but no agreement was reached. One proposal to use 3D printers to make spare parts for tractors in Africa failed over concerns over the copyright in the printers' software.

The framework within which these issues are being decided is skewed to commercial exploitation and private profit. It was set years ago when America, springboard of globalization, realized how greatly its exports and therefore its entire economy depended upon its trade in intellectual property. A Presidential Task Force said:

> Property concepts have been central to legal theory and social and economic activity in our society, but concepts of property were formulated to deal with tangibles, primarily land and chattels. When information, ways of dealing with information, or information products are treated as property, issues arise which differ from those resulting from the application of property theories to tangible matter.

The wording is awkward but the thinking is clear: we need a new foreign policy not only for information but for intellectual property, for the ownership of ideas and information.

The sub-text was also clear. America needs a policy that suits American interests. All exporters of creative products, whether selling a brand or licensing a copyright, need both a high level of protection everywhere and the same level everywhere. Help came from the Japanese who were as dominant in electronics as the Americans were in entertainment and wanted to ensure their patents in TV, video and music equipment were protected in all countries. Sony was also starting to invest in music and films. Japan sided with America, but it was not enough, and Washington wondered what to do.

America believed the global conventions on copyright and patents were too weak and anyway had little love for the United Nations agencies which monitor them. So it turned to the more business-oriented regime for trade and, after intense lobbying, over 100 governments met at Marrakech, Morocco, in 1994 to establish a new World Trade Organization (WTO) and sign a treaty on Trade-Related Intellectual Property Rights (TRIPS). The TRIPS agreement covers all creative products: copyright, patents, trademarks and service marks; geographical indicators; industrial designs; the protection of new plants; the layout of integrated circuits; and trade secrets.

The TRIPS agreement was the world's first global treaty to treat intellectual property as an economic issue. Till then, disputes had been private matters of contract which had to be resolved behind closed doors or in the courts and government had no role. Afterwards, governments could use the WTO to enforce IP rules and misbehaviour could lead to sanctions or even expulsion.

Some countries resented the enforcement of Western principles of private property in this way, whether to art, plants, medicines or aboriginal art. This critical view was put by economist Jeffrey Sachs of Harvard University:

> Just as knowledge is becoming the undisputed centrepiece of global prosperity (and the lack of it, the core of human impoverishment), the global regime on intellectual property requires a new look. America prevailed upon the world to toughen patent laws and cut down piracy. But now the transnational corporations and rich country institutions are patenting everything from the human genome to rain-forest diversity. The poor will be ripped off unless some sense and equity are introduced into this runaway process.

The main organizations facing this challenge are the national intellectual property offices, which I call, half-jokingly, the Central Banks of Intellectual Property. They run the world's registers of patents and trademarks and so issue the currencies that constitute the greater part of corporate wealth. They also devise the rules of copyright that govern the ownership of arts, culture, design, media and entertainment.

These national monopolies of valuable currencies can be highly profitable. The American PTO earned $2.2 billion in 2012 and its net profit, depending on how the federal government allocates the overhead, was about $88 million. The British IPO had revenues of $115 million and a surplus of $22 million. Their revenues come from registering patents and trademarks and not from copyright, although America's PTO stills sells a vestigial registration service. The Berne Convention on copyright prohibits registration from being compulsory in case it discriminates against authors.

There is now a call for the re-introduction of copyright registers in order to clarify who owns what and to assist in micro-licensing and micro-payments. In America, the Chicago Board Options Exchange and a private equity firm have launched an International Intellectual Property Exchange (IPXI) with board members from Philips and Microsoft. It allows people to buy, sell and hedge licences. The main traded asset is a 'unit licence right' (ULR), which is a non-exclusive licence that can be bought and sold like equities.

Several entrepreneurs in China have set up private city-based exchanges, such as the Beijing Copyright Trade Centre, and about 20 other cities were in the process of setting up exchanges until the government became nervous at the lack of regulation and called a halt. The British government has taken up Ian Hargreaves's recommendation for a copyright hub to facilitate the licensing of rights which have a large number of transactions but low values.

The Public Voice

What has been missing until recently is the public voice. In 2003 a group of Americans asked WIPO to hold a meeting to discuss how FOSS principles might be incorporated more extensively in its discussions, on the basis of the success of Linux, the Human Genome Mapping Project and the Global Positioning System and other 'share-and-share-alike' systems. WIPO was initially welcoming but changed its mind under American pressure. An American PTO official stated that 'Open Source software runs counter to the mission of WIPO, which is to promote intellectual property rights.' She was wrong about open source software, which is a copyright licence, and wrong about WIPO's mission, which is, in full, 'To promote innovation and creativity for the economic, social and cultural development of all countries through a balanced and effective international intellectual property system.'

A few years later I gathered together an international commission of 19 leading thinkers including Lawrence Lessig, John Sulston, Lynne Brindley, Jamie Boyle, Vandana Shiva and Cory Doctorow. Our Adelphi Charter on Creativity, Innovation and Intellectual Property laid out basic principles for the balance between private property and public access. One year later, when the British government asked Andrew Gowers to hold an inquiry into copyright, he said we had given him the best possible starting point. The Adelphi Charter's basic axiom is the balance between a creator's right to a private reward and society's right to public access (the rights contract).

Today's laws are out of balance. First, copyright. The principles of England's 1710 Act have held up remarkably well compared to other ancient laws, and still provide a workable set of principles, but the strains are showing. There is a widening gap between the software and dotcom sectors, where start-up costs are low and which can grow over time without much need of copyright, and the media and entertainment sectors, which have high upfront investment costs and need to break even in a relatively short time, and where copyright is more critical.

The first group of companies are doing well especially with the growth of share-and-share-alike, which has been shown to be an efficient way of sharing knowledge and speeding up business development not only by internet hackers but by companies as established as IBM and Google (whose Android operating system still uses a Linux kernel).

But the second group are suffering badly (and suffering partly at the hands of the first group, who control the gateways). These companies pinned their hopes on stricter copyright penalties, which is a small and shrinking part of the answer. They need to re-think their business models in the light of changing demographics and new technologies and then, but only then, to re-think their copyright licences. The precipitous fall in revenue of recorded music and newspapers is the result of companies' overall business methods rather than specific copyright issues. It is in everyone's interest that commercial rights-holders manage to loosen the shackles of their old thinking and take a new approach.

Few governments are being helpful. The most time-consuming global initiative of recent years has been the ACTA treaty, which was negotiated confidentially and roundly criticized. Governments spend too much time on celebrating the spread of broadband and not enough time on working out the necessary changes to intellectual property (as they also fail to re-think laws on competition policy and tax). There are signs this is changing. Britain's Gowers Review pleaded for 'rational' policy-making. But Britain and other governments are still too dependent on occasional reviews and still reluctant to bring these issues into mainstream policy-making.

In patenting, we need to consider whether or not a patent requires a technological invention (as in Europe, Japan and China) or not (as in America). America's fondness for giving patents to business processes that are conventional but happen to be expressed in computer code should cease. Patents in technology where innovation is cheap and fast, such as software, merit shorter terms than those in technology where R&D takes a long time and depends on market testing and clinical trials, such as pharmaceuticals. There is evidence that patent-driven R&D into healthcare focuses too much on marginal benefits for rich people and seldom bothers with drugs for the tropical diseases that affect over one billion poor people in developing countries. Other models are emerging such as UNITAID, which has raised $2.1 billion in five years for low-cost drugs, primarily through a tax on air travel.

We need to review registration, which lies at the heart of the process. The three patent tests of novelty, inventive step and technical effect are being stretched beyond what lawyers and examiners can agree on, let alone what the public or our elected representatives know about or, if they know, can understand. American examiners have an average of two days to write a 10–20 page report and too many applications are sloppily examined. An applicant who is turned down can re-submit in the hope their application will land on the desk of a sympathetic, or tired, examiner and get a more favourable response. Apple applied for a patent for Siri, its voice recognition software, eight or ten times (reports differ) before being successful. Nokia stated in 2012 that it had been the target of 150 lawsuits based on patents in the previous five years and said, not unreasonably, that those lawsuits were presumably based on the strongest cases its opponents could find. It reported that only one patent out of 150 was found to be valid. If there is a choice between giving fewer but more stringent patents, and making higher profits, patent offices should put the priority on higher standards.

The market-place is becoming noisy. Who is checking the balance between private ownership and public access? The national offices look after their customers. Who should look after the national offices? Who should examine the examiners? Justice Storey's description of copyright law as transcendently subtle does not encourage outsiders to become involved but they must or contracts will be one-sided.

7
Search, Learn, Mix and Share

THE DIY UNIVERSE

Jo Lusby is the CEO of Penguin Books in China. She said in 2006 that 'Every significant publishing development in China has its origins in the internet.' When I checked with her a few years later she said she had seen nothing to change her mind.

The global advisory firm PwC estimates that 25 per cent of all consumer expenditure on entertainment and media is spent on digital, divided about equally between money spent on getting access and searching and on content. But Jo Lusby is not talking only about money. She is saying the internet is where all the new ideas are, from new kinds of writing and reader involvement to new experiments in distribution and pricing. This is happening faster in China than elsewhere because the traditional book industries are relatively less developed there than elsewhere, but the trend is universal. The internet has its own ideas about publishing and reading and even its own language. People read books but use a Kindle.

In this new world, says Troy Carter, manager of Lady Gaga, it is death to a musician if their fans first hear what they are doing on one-way media like radio. Carter always makes sure the first news about his client Lady Gaga is released online to an insider network of fans and followers. He says Radio's Top 20, which was the ultimate achievement for decades, is now an also-ran. He lives as he speaks and has invested in a dozen online start-ups as well as Backplane, which he describes as a social corridor.

This chapter looks at how the internet has become the default ecology for text, music, TV and film and the default market-place for promoting and selling other products and, this being the creative economy, the dividing lines between making, promoting and selling are thin. It starts with the factors determining the internet ecology.

One, the internet is now the world's biggest market-place. In some markets, like media content, it is dominant, while in others it affects sensibilities, expectations and prices.

Two, it now generates unimaginable amounts of data on people's attitudes, likes, dislikes, behaviour and contacts and stores it on the cloud. This so-called 'big data' can be analysed, used and re-used without ageing. Companies use mathematical algorithms to refine their analysis and find new meanings. The future of the internet is tied up with the future of big data and algorithms.

Three, the internet is based on network relationships and these networks are user-led. They are invented, written and used by people wanting to make them smarter, if only by a little amount and only for their own satisfaction. They network to improve the network. This collaborative creativity has implications for creativity, ownership and compensation.

Four, integration. The internet has escaped from the shackles of the desktop and laptop and is now available on a range of devices from tablets to smartphones and, even more dramatically, tiny radio transmitters embedded in everyday objects that transmit data to the cloud so it is available worldwide. These trends to integration are partly helped and partly hindered by major gateway companies trying to create their own mini ecosystems.

The Mega Market

The online economy is the fastest growing economy in the world, far outpacing China's economy. This is happening for two reasons. It is becoming easier to get online wherever one is and to spend more time online.

Young Americans and Chinese also have an extraordinary ability to invent more attractive ways of using the internet and living digitally.

People in California and two or three other American states are producing a stream of innovations at a rate seldom seen before in history. The second largest source of dotcom innovation is China, especially in networks and e-commerce. Far more Chinese spend time online to search, shop, network and be entertained than people in any other country.

There is not much interchange between the two global cyberworlds. Very few Americans enter Chinese cyberspace. Many more Chinese enter American cyberspace and use American websites even though the Beijing government bans several foreign networks, including Facebook, YouTube and Twitter, and closely monitors search engines. In practice, Chinese people can get access via proxy servers.

A Chinese and an American coder will both be fluent in the same program languages, even if they cannot speak their respective analog languages, and both can create algorithms that both can read, but so far this commonality has not produced much interaction. It will surely do so in the future.

There is more overlap between investors. Yahoo originally owned 43 per cent of Alibaba, China's biggest e-commerce site, and still has a 10 per cent stake alongside Singapore's Temasek, Japan's Softbank and the Moscow-based Digital Sky Technologies (DST is also an investor in China's 360Buy.com, as well as Facebook). Several smaller American funds have offices in Beijing. South Africa's Naspers has about 30 per cent of Tencent, which is the world's third largest internet company after Google and Amazon. Tencent itself has a joint venture with Activision Blizzard. Wal-Mart has invested in Yihaodian. European companies are less active.

In 2012, 2.4 billion people, 34 per cent of the world's population, had their own access to the internet. This means well over two billion people and their family and friends had access to a network that is built on the three propositions of the creative ecology: universality, freedom and markets. The regions with the highest proportion of users are North America and Europe but the largest number of users, 45 per cent, is in Asia. China has 560 million users, more than twice as many as America's 245 million.

That year, several million people were searching Google every second. One hour of video was being uploaded to YouTube every second. Facebook has over a billion registered users and over 150 million are online at any time. Tencent's QQ has over 700 million accounts and usually over 100 million people online.

There were over six billion mobile phone subscriptions, which means quite a few people had more than one. Over one billion smartphones and over 55 billion apps had been sold, many developed by individuals very cheaply, but still generating $9 billion revenue for their developers. The largest categories are games (49%), social networking (30%), entertainment (7%) and news (6%). People who had a choice between being online or using a previously downloaded app were shifting to the latter. At the end of 2012, the average American spent more time using apps than being online not only on smartphones but on desktop computers as well. In China and India, the mobile web is more popular than desktop access.

Online shopping is increasing rapidly in countries where physical retail outlets are scarce or unattractive or people lack the time to go shopping. Young urban Chinese, Indians and Brazilians spend over 30 per cent of their disposable income online compared to national averages of 5 per cent in America and European countries. Alibaba's transactions topped $159 billion in 2012, more than Amazon and eBay combined.

All governments monitor access to the internet to identify crime or the possibility of crime. In general, more open access correlates to a higher level of creativity and innovation, as indicated by the Quad markers of change, diversity, learning and adaptation. America and Europe have the most freedom while Arab countries, Iran, African countries and Cuba score lowest. The exception is China where the government intervenes extensively but people's inventiveness in coding, applications, e-commerce and online media is exceptionally high.

The civil wars in North Africa and the Middle East known as the Arab Spring were fought out online as well as on the ground with Facebook, Twitter, Tumblr and other social networks being the favoured arenas. In Egypt, Facebook's April 6 Youth Movement had 70,000 members. In Syria, both government and opposition regularly uploaded videos to YouTube and Flickr. The government started an online Syrian Electronic Army (SEA) to combat the rebels' use of Facebook, Twitter and YouTube. In a report published by West Point's Combating Terrorism Center, analyst Chris Zambelis reported that many websites, videos and blogs had high professional standards as well as showing amateur footage of fighting, air strikes and prisoners.

Big Data

The internet is a self-replicating data machine with increasingly vast amounts of data and, instead of trying to remember what exabytes and zettabytes mean, sensible people now talk about 'big data' rather in the spirit of America's Big Country. When asked how big, they just say, big enough. The current threshold of a big data set is about an exabyte, or a quintillion bytes, but the criterion is not so much the number of bytes as the nature of the boundaries between different data classes and the number of possible relationships, and the need for new data tool-kits to manage them.

The need for new tools first became clear in astronomy and weather systems and then in financial markets, which not only depend on multi-dimensional relationships between a large number of variables but whose many users are not trained specialists and need simple tools and easily understood visual summaries. The next group of users were dotcoms, defined as companies that exist wholly online and have no bricks-and-mortar physical presence and so no traditions or inherited knowledge of physical trading. They are interested only in how people behave online.

Wherever we move in cyberspace we leave a data trail. Whenever we click, send an email, use a search engine, buy a ticket or check a social network, we leave our footprints. Wherever we turn on a smartphone we announce where we are. Added together, our trails make up a shadow economy that reflects what we do. In many ways, it is not really a shadow economy but another parallel economy, which is as real as the visible physical economy.

For years, online companies collected this data but did little with it beyond facilitating their primary purpose of networking or search or e-commerce. Then they began to explore ways of using their data more imaginatively. They hired bright young maths graduates, called 'quants' after their talents for 'quantitative analysis' and algorithms, to organize data into classes and show links between them.

They soon realized they were sitting on a gold mine with a difference. Instead of having to dig expensive mines in awkward places, they could stay home and sit back while their customers brought the gold to them for free.

The essence of big data is that everything is either data or mathematics. The gold is data and the picks and shovels are mathematics.

When we write in a search request, for example, the search engine reduces our words to data and adds the data to its stored database. Knowing what one person is looking for is not interesting by itself but if the quants can compare all searches, and sort them into categories, the results can be revealing.

In 2009 a Google engineer called Corrie Conrad realized that people's searches for medical information mapped the spread of flu outbreaks more accurately and much more quickly than did America's health service. She developed an algorithm that refined the information and delivered it to frontline healthcare services and drug manufacturers.

The company then started to look at how people actually write down their searches. It started to generate a massive amount of data on how people spell: the most common first attempts, the most common mistakes and misspellings and the most common corrections. It used this data to generate the world's most comprehensive spell-check service. It did not need to learn any languages with all their linguistic oddities and exceptions but simply compared each new spelling with all other spellings, including the mistakes and corrections, to calculate the odds and the likely routes to the desired result. All this was done for a trivial cost. It was normal business.

It developed an algorithm for translation by analysing hundreds of thousands of United Nations and European Union documents in the same way. The algorithm did not need to know the linguistic rules of grammar and vocabulary, as previous systems had tried to do but understandably failed. It only had to analyse what people did. It turned a socio-linguistic problem into a mathematical one.

Journalist Gary Wolf is interested in people who live their lives in numbers and use data to monitor what he calls the Quantified Self. He says:

> Sleep, exercise, sex, food, mood, location, alertness, productivity and even spiritual well-being are being tracked and measured, shared and displayed. Until a few years ago, although sociologists could survey us in aggregate and laboratory psychologists could do clever things with volunteers, the real way we ate, played, talked and loved left only the faintest measurable trace. Then four things changed. First, electronic sensors got smaller and better. Second, people started carrying powerful computing devices, typically disguised as mobile phones. Third, social media made it normal to share everything. And fourth, we began to get an inkling of the rise of a global super-intelligence known as the cloud.

This outflow of data can be used in unexpected ways. When natural disasters occur, as in the 2010 Haiti earthquake, the data being generated by victims' smartphones told rescue teams where they were and in what condition without the victims having to speak or move. The United Nations' Global Pulse measures social network usage in developing countries for signs of change and stress such as food shortages, flooding or civil war. The CIA-backed Palantir Technologies (incidentally, the name comes from Tolkien's *The Lord of the Rings*) analyses connections between people, places and events to locate terrorists after human-based methods fail.

There are dangers in this approach. Algorithms, like any rule-based device, can spin out of control. On one occasion two bookseller algorithms on Amazon, Profnath and Bordeebook went haywire over the same title, driving the offer price to $23,698,655.93, plus $3.99 shipping. The reasons remain unclear but it seems that Profnath's algorithm undercut competitors' prices while Bordeebook upped its price to make a bigger margin, possibly because it did not have the book in stock. Unsurprisingly no one bought the book and no damage was done.

Mistakes in financial transactions can cause more serious damage even if they are spotted more quickly. On 6 May 2010 a 'flash crash' caused the Dow Jones index to sink 800 points in a few minutes. But this was small beer compared to what might have happened.

Investment firms are now fighting what are known as 'algo wars' with algorithms with names like Stealth and Shark, which try to outwit each other at speeds measured in pico-seconds or trillionths of a second. Few of these firms' staff can keep up (that, after all, is the point) and still less the authorities that are supposed to regulate financial trades. New York traders still disagree as to why it happened. One reason the financial crises in Europe resist easy solution is the predominance of algo-based trading that is proprietorial, secret and outside regulatory understanding.

Privacy is more vulnerable, too. It is commonplace that dotcoms like Google and Facebook know much more about people than has any previous organization, private or public. They know where they are, what they are doing and how much they like to spend (according to Google, credit card companies have algorithms that tell them when a couple is likely to break up and affairs likely to start). Their commercial justification is that this information allows advertisements to be targeted not only at a particular person's demographics, which has been possible for years, but at their private habits.

Google usually knows when people become ill before their doctor does because their first act is to search online for medical information. Eric Schmidt, Google's CEO, supported by Microsoft's Craig Mundie, once offered his assistance to President Obama to help with America's floundering healthcare system which, he said, lacked up-to-date, relevant doctor–patient information but the authorities were nervous and turned him down.

People's love of smartphones ratchets up the stakes to another level. Britain's Blippar uses a smartphone app to create moving images from consumer packaging and enables Cadbury, Virgin and other brands to monitor customers' attention by location and time of day. The Nashville RedPepper company, which bills itself as an 'ad agency by night, invention lab by night', is working on a Facebook-based system that photographs a customer's face as they enter a store and then sends special offers to the customer's smartphone.

Does it matter? One of the lessons of retailers' loyalty schemes is that the majority of people are willing to supply information if they see a benefit although often, it must be said, they have no choice.

There was unease about Google's StreetView photographing of streets and the people in them, and also of its collection of the names of local Wi-Fi networks, but the benefits were generally felt to be worth it.

There are also questions about what happens if the personal data is wrong or stolen. European and American privacy laws enable people to identify and correct wrong data held in known databases. With big data, nobody really knows where the data is (or in which country or subject to which laws). Anyway, every byte is constantly being copied into new data sets.

Big data sets are expensive to maintain and quants demand high salaries. Large companies can afford the costs but smaller ones and non-profits can be excluded. University researchers worry about the added costs in their research budgets, even from renting a data set for a day, especially in America and Europe where public spending is being cut. Running big data favours large organizations over small ones.

Networks of Networks

The internet is best understood as a way of connecting users to networks by means of other networks. The inventor of Ethernet networking, Robert Metcalfe, was the first to sit down and do the maths when he was having trouble selling Ethernet to customers and needed to prove its benefits would increase exponentially. He calculated the value of a network is equivalent to the square of the number of nodes; in other words, of the number of people or computers attached to it. The smallest possible network consists of two people who talk to each other and, in this case, Metcalfe's law says the value is 2×2, or 4. If a third person joins, the number of connections is three; and Metcalfe's value is 9. If a fourth joins, it jumps to six; and the value is 16. The number of connections always increases faster than the number of people. With 200 million access points it is possible to connect with 200 million other people; and the network value is 40 million billion. With China's 600 million people connected the network value is 36×10^{16}. The number is too big to grasp. We are back with big data.

The internet has been designed by its users for its users. It is my network, it is your network, it is our network. This goes against the grain of telecoms thinking for decades. AT&T, British Telecom, Nippon Telecom and other operators were so focused on building their network infrastructure that they hardly noticed the internet, just as later the music labels and newspapers were slow to notice. Their business strategy was to forecast customer needs, offer premium services for business customers and carefully manage day-to-day operations. They called it the 'intelligent network'. They were so wrong.

Every time they made their network more 'intelligent', people wanted something else. The solution was explained by AT&T's David Isenberg, in a paper provocatively entitled, 'The Rise of the Stupid Network: why the Intelligent Network was once a good idea, but isn't anymore'. Isenberg had studied human consciousness under Nobel Laureate Albert Szent-Györgyi, who was a scientist and a political activist, and knew that a network's structure directly affects whether its users can communicate as they want. Isenberg wanted a democratic, user-led network with the user in control. He wanted to reduce network constraints to what he calls the 'insignificantly trivial'.

He realized the telecom companies were locked into four old assumptions: that infrastructure is scarce and commands a high price; that talk generates most traffic; that hard-wired circuit-switching is the key technology; and that the network company controls the network. He said that all these assumptions were crumbling. Bandwidth was becoming freely available; digital data was more popular than voice; hard switches was being replaced by more flexible routers; and intense competition means no single company owns the network, let alone controls it. Isenberg believed the user should be in control and 'networks should be guided by the needs of the data, not the design assumptions of the owner'. He puts the 'intelligent network' in the same category as the paper-less office, a fruitless attempt to organize people's needs which ignores what they really want to do.

His paper was described by AT&T's Tom Evslin as 'a glass of cold water in the face'. *Computer Telephony* magazine said it was 'potentially the most controversial paper to come out of the telephone industry, ever'. The choice between intelligent and stupid networks surfaced again in arguments between the PC industry and the online industry. Where do we want intelligence: in the network (or cloud) or in our hands? We can borrow Isenberg's phrase and call it the 'obedient' cloud because it does what we need. Clouds are living memories and they are becoming entire brains. They are organized to respond to inputs (more data, another algorithm) in an intelligent or at least an arithmetical manner, which, for them, is much the same thing.

When Peter Martin, former Deputy Editor of the *Financial Times*, set out to describe the internet's impact on business he caught this spirit of open, obedient service.

> The internet's ad hoc, flexible, consensual structure offers powerful lessons to everyone in business. It is, in some ways, a prototype of the way companies will have to operate in future. The consensus stems from a shared purpose: the creation of a network that allows easy communication. This is in part a technical vision, and it requires deep knowledge of computer science. But it is also an ideological one, requiring a humanistic commitment to freedom of expression and to a medium of communication that rises above the interests of government and commerce. An ethic of collaboration and open discussion around a common purpose is an extraordinarily powerful and creative force.

These principles of ideas held in the public domain, open and free collaboration, a refusal to rush into property rights, a constant revision leading to more elegant solutions, peer group rewards and consolation, and a moral sense of equity and integrity evoke many communal forms of creativity from the beginnings of science to the network office.

One of the attractions of social networks like Twitter, Tumblr and Pinterest, as well as China's QQ and Weibo, is the speed with which they broadcast likes and dislikes. Their 'follow' buttons encourage re-tweeting and re-blogging and re-pinning. The word 'curation' has emerged from its arts niche to describe what many people feel free to do as they select and re-present their favourite topics.

These network relationships allow people to bring in others (and to wave goodbye to them, too) at all stages of the creative process from the thinking of the original idea to its design and marketing. In turn, this has allowed them to act like editors and impresarios of other people's work; to be tenants, rather than owners, of property rights. Data is continually being geo-located, recycled and re-curated.

China's Douban is Facebook with a difference. People do not have to register, though many do, and there is one wall or pinboard for everyone. Users post comments on culture, design and media, mostly about music and stories, but anything goes and it is a prime source of information on foreign works, old and new. As I write, the home page features Han Han, a uniquely Chinese writer and blogger, and singer Li Yuchun as well as Aldous Huxley and Simone de Beauvoir. Its aim is to extend its users' circle beyond their own family and friends.

Integration

Everyday usage generates vast quantities of data that are stored on cloud servers. Data-owners use algorithms to make connections between data and generate new meanings. Each network opens doors to other networks, each with its own data and algorithms. The fourth trend, integration, follows these three.

It is being driven by the development of Operating Systems with standardized control panels on every device that give universal access to the cloud. Android was coded around 2003–4 but was not bought by Google until 2005 and not launched until 2007. It is now by far the most popular OS for smartphones. Apple's iOS was also launched in 2007 and Microsoft, for so long the Big Daddy of desktops, released Windows-8 in 2012. With the same OS and the same apps on all our devices we can use and extend our reach, our network, from wherever we are to practically everywhere else.

This is the theory. In practice, brand-owners fight to promote their ecosystem to their customers and erect patent-protected barriers to restrict access to others even if they are willing to pay. It is unclear whether this tactic will succeed. The immense rewards of universal access are likely to force them to let everyone in. If not, they are vulnerable to public indifference (as befell Compuserve, AOL, MySpace and Yahoo!) or anti-trust policy (which required Microsoft to licence its software to others).

One of the benefits of universality is a bundle of developments called ubiquitous computing or smart objects or the Internet of Things (IoT), which tracks the position and state-of-being of objects wherever they are. These systems use tiny radio frequency identification (RFID) chips that are put into, well, practically everything. The first users were Chinese home appliance and clothing manufacturers who wanted to track exports as they travelled from the factory to the truck to the container ship and the customer. The chips are small enough to be inserted into products without the user noticing but strong enough to transmit a continuous signal, which is picked up at threshold points. The early systems were little different from the electronic tickets used on urban transit, like London's Oyster Card, but so-called smart cities are now beginning to use similar systems to manage road traffic, waste disposal, street lighting and security.

They become more useful if the data is no longer restricted to a closed system, like Transport for London's network (TfL) but sent to a cloud so anyone can access it, at which point smart computing becomes the Internet of Things. Several cities already allow car-drivers to access their data on on-street parking so drivers can see the nearest free space. The combination of open data, public access and trivial user costs allows the location of almost everything to be known, whether things or information about things. Attaching a RFID tab to property, whether phones, pets or umbrellas, means Lost Property will be a thing of the past. Smart boarding passes will tell airplane passengers of flight delays as well as tell the airlines where late passengers are loitering. The main candidates are the home and office. In eHealth, for example, data can enable patients to have more control over their own care and medication. In developing countries it is being used for banking, energy control and water management. In Kenya the M-Pesa mobile network allows households to re-charge a fob attached to a bucket so they can get about 20 litres of fresh water for two Kenyan shillings, about two pennies. M-Pesa also tells farmers about the weather, crop prices and the location of the local delivery truck.

Smart computing and the Internet of Things is one of the few online innovations where China and Europe are in the forefront rather than America. China's interest is partly due to its increasingly profitable logistics sector and partly because the Internet of Things is concerned with management control and efficiency, rather than personal interaction. It is about things, not people, at least for now.

Whether about things or people these systems raise issues of transparency and privacy as well as the chronic internet challenges of competition policy, tax, consumer protection and copyright. The underlying issue is who controls the data and who decides to keep it private or allow access. It is easy to see how the Internet of Things could benefit healthcare in hospitals and at home but, as we saw from the White House's rebuff to Google, medical authorities are unused to sophisticated management systems and have an aversion to openness and collaboration. Health services are chronically reluctant to share medical information with patients. The success of smart eHealth depends on governments and doctors disrupting their institutions which, so far, they have been reluctant to do.

This part of the story is still being written. Whatever happens, it will be surprising. Internet expert John Naughton says the internet is a global machine for springing surprises, unstable and unregulated, and cannot stop mutating and adapting in unpredictable ways.

THE BATTLE OF THE QUANTS

Video games like Pet Society and FIFA Superstars are typical examples of how online companies use big data and smart algorithms. Their owner, the London-based Playfish, collects about one billion data points daily on players to track what they are doing second-by-second. If Playfish was tied to a proprietary console like PlayStation or Wii it could change a game only by changing the hardware and only in collaboration with the manufacturer but, being online, and owning its own data, it can update a game whenever it wants. It fights what it calls 'The Battle of the Quants', using algorithms as the only weapons, and did so well that the four founders were able to sell to Electronic Arts for $300 million and a further $100 million performance-related payments.

One of the founders, Kristian Segerstrale, makes this comparison between console games and online freemium games:

Old Physical Console	New Online Experience
Upfront high cost + then free	Free + then micro-payments (freemium)
Standalone	Collaborative, networked
2–3 year generations	4–6 week generations
Lots of IP (copyright)	Little IP (trademark)

Playfish's imaginative use of algorithms was one of many disruptive innovations that led a group of media executives who were members of the British Screen Advisory Council (BSAC) to set up a Blue Skies group to look into the future of online markets. As fast broadband spread, media businesses were finding themselves stuck with technologies, formats and price levels that prevented consumers from sampling and buying what they wanted.

Part of the challenge is that media are experiences rather than objects so potential buyers face a quandary. They cannot know if they will like something without experiencing it but they cannot experience it without buying it. If they buy it, which generally means paying for it, they may discover they don't like it after all. They therefore rely on recommendations much more than when buying objects which they can see and test. Sellers have to continually ask themselves: How much do I need to give away for free to persuade someone to buy or to recommend? There is one exception to this conundrum. Fans buy everything on trust, partly because they enjoyed previous experiences but also because being a fan means buying everything. So sellers also have to ask: How do I make someone a fan?

When the internet arrived, many rights-holders and producers tried to maintain their traditional ways of promoting experiences to would-be buyers by means of the existing hierarchies of promoters, critics and retailers. Music labels relied heavily on radio to promote new tracks. Film producers used festivals, cinema trailers and posters. Publishers used professional reviewers. But the internet bypasses these channels.

More and more people could upload, everyone could recommend and everyone could experience and often experience without paying. The old legacy companies believed that stronger copyright was the answer. It was part of the answer, but it was not enough. Revenues continued to decline, infringement to increase, and a new generation of young people found new ways to talk about and enjoy entertainment.

The Blue Skies group realized that people want to talk about, get access to and use online media with the same freedom as they do other consumer products. Their choices were no longer pre-programmed but picked up from social networks, blogs, friends, celebrities and the artists and performers themselves. It is cool to make one's own recommendation.

FOUR DEMANDS

This never-stopping stream of possibilities and recommendations led the Blue Skies group to identify four Golden Demands. One, people want to be able to choose *what to do*, first whether to watch a film, listen to music or go shopping and second to choose the specific film, track and so on. They know the range of what's available is virtually limitless and they want to take advantage. Two, they want to choose *when to do so*, whether in the morning or at midnight, this week or next week. They do not want to be told this film is no longer in the cinemas but is not yet available online, or that a hardback book has sold out but the e-book will not be published until next month.

Three, they want to be free to use media *wherever they are*. They do not want to be told they can download a film to a tablet but cannot display it on a TV set in the next room or transfer it to an MP3 player for their holiday, or that the video they downloaded in Europe cannot be played in Brazil. Or that the book their friend in New York is raving about is not available in London because of copyright or customs. It is worse if they can see it listed on Amazon but Amazon refuses to deliver to where they are.

Four, they want to *pay* in ways that they think are sensible. They see other businesses have worked out how to charge for their products and ask, with mounting frustration, Why do the media make it so difficult? There are many options (more than for most consumer products): a one-off 'turnstile' payment; a subscription for a period; advertising-supported so free to the consumer, like radio; 'freemium', where initial access is free but extras have to be paid for; or completely free.

'Free' can mean legally free or illegally free. If a seller fails to offer what a buyer thinks is a sensible price, the temptation to take without paying can be irresistible. A well-known music label bundles its music together in such a way that it charges $25 for 20 minutes of music that a buyer wants to hear but might listen to only once. Faced with such inflexibility, it is tempting to misbehave.

Of the four Golden Demands, those for *when*, *where* and *how to pay* feed back into the first one, the *what*. Make something more accessible and it has a better chance. It works in the other direction, too. If something is invisible or inaccessible or unreasonably expensive then it disappears.

The industries' failure to meet these four demands saw a decline in revenue in every sector. The desire for music is as high as ever. The market research company Nielsen reports more albums sold, more singles and more downloads. But revenues are down. It is the same with newspapers and magazines, books and films. The demographic and behavioural factors that drove up revenues for many years are as strong as ever, but revenues are down. The problem is that each unit of digital content brings in less revenue that did each of the old physical units.

Some kind of recovery occurred in 2011 when America's expenditure on digital music, which had been nil eight years previously, rose to the same level as its expenditure on physical sales. Of the digital expenditures, which totalled $3.4 billion, singles brought in $1.5 billion, albums brought $1.1 billion and royalties brought $0.8 billion. But the total revenue from both digital and physical experiences, $6.8 billion, was far short of what it had been. A few months later, the Long Tail, meaning the sale of older material, seemed to be happening at last. The sales of albums more than 18 months old, known as catalogue albums, reached 76.6 million, which exceeded the 73.9 million sales of current albums. But again the total was way down from its peak.

While the old labels struggle to understand the new world, new services like iTunes and Spotify found ways of meeting the Golden Demands. Their user-friendly online stores of old and new material, including rare, archive and supposedly unobtainable tracks, allow consumers to choose what they like and when and where. To begin with, musicians focused on the platforms' licence payments to rights-holders, which were very small. In the future we are likely to see a wider range of options mixing licence payments and uses in multiple combinations.

The generation of artists who have grown up in an online world rely much less on copyright than did their predecessors. They make money by ticket sales at gigs (not worrying if the audience records the music), direct CD sales, direct downloads from their websites, merchandising, movie and TV placements. Veteran industry observer Johnny Black says: 'That's where the cash is now and it can all be done without a record company.'

Erin McKeown, a 35-year-old American singer-songwriter who has released 10 albums, says traditional copyright-based revenues make up only 20 per cent of her earnings. She financed her 2012 album by an imaginative range of offers ranging from a cheque for Spotify royalties ('if I ever get one'), all her downloads, all her CDs, a discussion on baseball ('I'm really good at this') and a 'private concert in your home for you and your friends'.

Book publishers have been less affected so far than music labels and newspapers because the book's physical design is harder to copy and because online sellers moved quickly to develop legal e-book formats so piracy was minimal. But the gap between what print publishers know and what online sellers know is widening. The print publishers know how many copies are sold. The online sellers know each buyer's preferences and know the books they look at and don't buy as well as ones they do. Publishers could buy this data from the online sellers but it won't be cheap.

A book publisher could let me download one chapter for free as a promotion or I could pay for the download and then, if I want a physical copy, leverage the price of the download as a discount against a printed book. Retailers could reward loyal customers with one free download for every ten books bought. China's Shanda expanded from games to books and now owns several leading book websites. It sells e-novels for slightly under $1 compared to $5 for a physical copy and also sells subscriptions for $2–4 a month. It has to balance the opportunities for distributing material in whatever manner the market wishes against the perceived danger of devaluing the written text. Some people hope that print's physical format and exclusivity (design, cover, boards, binding, paper, typography and print quality) can retain a dominant position but it looks more likely that the two markets of print and digital will flourish in parallel, each focusing on its own strengths.

Amazon is starting to commission and promote its own books and YouTube and China's Tudou are commissioning new video series. YouTube makes most of its money from advertising and so tries to attract audiences that advertisers want to reach. With this in mind, it spends about $100 million a year on what it calls 'curated' channels supplied by leading producers ranging from the *Wall Street Journal* to producer Anthony E. Zuiker, who created *CSI*, skateboarder Tony Hawk, performer Madonna and TV producers such as Lionsgate (*Mad Men*) and Fremantle (*The X Factor*).

It also wants those weird home videos to keep coming. It invites bids from young Americans who have had one or two YouTube hits and are starting to get fans and sell merchandise and offers them studio facilities and Next Up grants of up to $35,000 to develop their skills. It has as many as 20,000 partners who upload videos on a regular basis and receive a share of advertising revenue.

What is happening to the traditional role of intermediaries? There are two views. The first is that the internet allows anyone to produce and distribute and intermediaries are redundant. Who needs an agent? The second is that cyberspace is more crowded than real space and people who may be good at creativity may not be good at, or interested in, the rest of the business.

The evidence suggests the latter view is likely to be right. The number of books, videos and music tracks increases remorselessly. In 2010 over 70,000 albums were released in America compared to 30,000 in the 1970s, but 94 per cent of those albums sold less than 1,000 units and 80 per cent sold less than 100 units. At the other end of the scale, an elite 350 titles, under 1 per cent, generated 70 per cent of the market's total revenue. Self-published e-books have the same profile. Amazon says nearly 20 per cent of its Kindle's best-selling e-books in 2012 were self-published, which sounds impressive, but the list of self-published books that fail to make any mark is very long.

The internet has been generating new kinds of market-places for many years. But the internet never advertises and its opportunities were not fully appreciated. There are three reasons. Code is an unusual kind of language because it is rule-based and mathematical. It does not need speech and has none of the accumulated oddities of ordinary languages. For these reasons, many companies tied to physical objects did not notice it or did not understand it and, by default, left the field open to different people with different attitudes.

Second, these attitudes are so unlike the mainstream industry's understanding of the world that, even when they did pay attention, they did not expect the newcomer to have much impact. The internet is unowned and unregulated and its commitment to open access and dislike of copyright baffled the establishment. Their standard-bearer was *Encyclopaedia Britannica*, which upheld strict editorial standards and paid experts to contribute. The share-and-share-alike community offered Wikipedia, which allows anyone to contribute, pays nothing and charges nothing. How could Wikipedia possibly survive? Wikipedia is now the seventh most popular website worldwide while *Britannica* ranks around 5,200th.

The third reason is management. People who write code, who live online, have a different mind-set from both conventional managers and conventional ideas people. They are both individualistic and collective, rule-based and playful. They combine a wacky imagination with arithmetical logic in ways that both creative people and corporate executives find hard to understand. The management of ideas is due for another shake-up.

8
Heartlands: Art, Design, Media and Innovation

THE IDEAS BUSINESS

The world economy generates a gross output of $71 trillion. The largest national economies are America ($15.7 trillion), China ($8.2 trillion), Japan ($6 trillion), Germany ($3.4 trillion), France ($2.6 trillion), Brazil ($2.3 trillion), Britain ($2.4 trillion) and Russia ($2.0 trillion). These rankings have changed dramatically in recent years due to the growth of China and Brazil and the relative decline of Europe.

The global creative economy is worth about $3,665 billion ($3.6 trillion), which is slightly over 5 per cent of the total. Ten years ago the creative economy was worth $2.3 trillion but made a higher proportion, 7 per cent, of global GDP. The reason for the divergence is that the global economy has grown most strongly in countries which proportionately have smaller creative economies. The ranking of creative economies is America, China, Britain, Germany, Japan, France and Brazil. If adjusted for population, the order is America, Britain, Japan, Germany, France and Brazil.

The underlying cause of expansion in both the supply and demand curves is the increase in the numbers of college-educated people and their desire to make and to buy creative products. The creative economy is as much about buying as selling. The second factor is the increase in internet reach and the power of search-and-share.

Both trends have been affected by a shift in the world's centre of gravity. In the past, the Middle East had a larger share of world trade than did Europe but around 1600 Europe became the best place to have new ideas and start a business. Over the centuries the Italians, Spanish, French, Portuguese, Dutch, English, Scottish, Germans, Poles and Czechs showed outstanding creative inspiration, technological imagination and management flair. In the 1870s, Britain had about 40 per cent of world trade, driven by vigorous creativity and innovation and benefiting from tied markets in the British Empire for obtaining raw materials and selling finished products. Since that high point, Europe has declined in economic power, though not in pure arts, and America has become the dominant cultural force and the largest economy.

Europe and America are still the dominant producers and users and their advantages will not dwindle quickly but their financial problems have reduced average wages and undercut investment. Their advertising expenditures dropped by around 20 per cent on average in 2009 and 2010 and consumer expenditures fell. Companies found themselves short of cash at the moment when they wanted to invest online and to expand into China.

The economic centre of gravity is shifting back to Asia especially Japan, China, Korea and India. Brazil, Russia and Indonesia are also developing fast. This shift is changing the global balance of trade as well as each country's soft power.

The Top Markets

America. Americans uphold strongly the three propositions of universality, freedom and markets, as evident in their constitutional commitment to free speech, their openness to novelty, their universities and research organizations and the rapid ascension of computer companies and dotcoms to world leadership.

Its creative economy is worth $1,043 billion. A report based on Federal Reserve Bank data found that American companies invest about $1 trillion a year in 'IP-related' intangibles and their accumulated IP asset base is as much as $6–7 trillion, which is more than the total GDP of all other countries except China. The Washington-based International Intellectual Property Alliance (IIPA) calculated that by 2010 media, information and entertainment contributed more to the American economy than almost any other sector: more than chemicals, aircraft and aircraft parts, primary and fabricated metals, electronic equipment, industrial machinery, and food and drink.

More people in America than in any other country have an intuitive understanding of turning an idea into a business and of company start-ups; more people take degrees in business or law and are competent, as managers must be, in mixing the two; more know how to prepare a business plan; more can handle a pitch to investors; more know how many shares to issue and at what price; and more feel comfortable in spending the cash raised and reporting back to the investors.

America dominates the global dotcom business. It has produced Amazon, Google, Facebook, eBay, Twitter, YouTube and Linked-In as well as Microsoft and Apple. No other country comes close to matching this array, and certainly not Japan or any European country. The main challenger to America is China.

It has a knack of taking ideas from anywhere and turning them into global ideas. The French invented film but the Americans invented the film industry and both the French and Americans seem to like it that way. A European invented the World Wide Web but the Americans turned it into a vast meeting-place and market-place.

Size counts. America has room for people to explore and pursue different lifestyles. People on the West Coast have different mind-sets from people on the East Coast and from Washington DC. It has a much bigger domestic market of 315 million people compared to Germany, Europe's biggest market, which has 82 million people, and to Britain and France, which have around 65 million each. It also has efficient nationwide systems for media, marketing, advertising and distribution.

At a Global Business Network meeting on 'The Future of Europe', analyst Peter Bennett asked this question: 'Why are there fewer big/ innovative information technology companies in Europe compared to America and Japan?' He pointed at Europe's fragmented markets; over-protected industries; lack of venture capital; lack of innovation; lower level of defence spending; and the 'brain drain' which is the other side of the coin of America's attractiveness.

All is not rosy. There are many Americans who feel their country is in decline, and threatened by the rise of China. It has never topped the global rankings for education but it excels at learning, which is more important. Median incomes have hardly risen since 2000. Its government is weak. Half its patents now go to foreigners. But these criticisms miss the larger picture, which is that America still has more spirit and more freedom to play with ideas than anywhere else.

Its main asset is its easy relationship between creativity, innovation and management, which are more integrated there than anywhere else. It has exported many of its national attributes but it has not exported this one, which implies that the reasons for the gap are more demographic and cultural than financial or industrial. The question is whether this will remain true.

Europe. Taken together, the 27 countries in the European Union (EU) have a total GDP of $15.6 trillion, slightly larger than America's, and a creative economy that is slightly smaller. Europeans in the big four countries of Germany, Britain, France and Italy, as well as in the Netherlands and Scandinavia, are now more likely to work in the creative industries than in manufacturing. Those who do so tend to be better educated than others, with almost half having a university degree compared to one-quarter of the total working population. They are also three times as likely to be self-employed.

Europe shares a prodigious cultural heritage from the ancient Greeks and Romans to the Renaissance, the Enlightenment and the industrial revolution, and it is tempting to treat it as a single unit. The European Commission urges us to do so and spends about $4.5 billion annually on European-wide networks to nudge our thinking. But Europeans' delight in their common heritage is tempered by pride in their distinct cultures, languages, aesthetics, industrial structures and international networks, which are by no means diminishing and remain strongest, naturally enough, in the cultural arenas of art, design and media.

Britain. Britain's creative economy is worth $171 billion as a result of its long-term stability, diversity and wealth and a good education system. It has a deserved reputation for oddball originality. The English language assists its exports but also offers easy access to American imports. Its art and culture sectors grew rapidly between 2000 and 2010, about twice as fast as the rest of the economy. Over 1.8 million Britons describe themselves as working in a creative job.

Its strengths in funky creativity are matched by its weaknesses in innovation. Manufacturing declined from 22 per cent of GDP in 1980 to 10 per cent in 2010, and the number of manufacturing jobs fell from 6.3 million to 2.2 million in the same period. This matters. London's design students like to talk about 3D printing to each other but they need to talk to manufacturers as well. By losing its manufacturers, Britain lost many potential re-users of its own good ideas, leaving the field to America, China, Japan and Germany.

Germany. Germany's market size is about $170 billion. It differs from Britain in still having several major international corporations in publishing, TV and music as well as many successful designers ranging from graphics to product design (cars, machine tools). Overall it has a slightly smaller output and its creative sectors make up a smaller proportion of the total than they do in Britain but this is due to its relative strengths in manufacturing. It has Europe's largest and most competitive manufacturing sector, which underpins its economy, provides a ready market for innovation, and leads to close links with China.

China. China's 1,350 million people have embraced the idea of creativity and innovation with enthusiasm, or perhaps one should say re-embraced it after a long hiatus as their innate creativity and ingenuity is not in doubt. It has a long history of creativity and innovation and in the 17th century was the world's richest country, about as wealthy as all Europe and much richer than America, but for several hundred years it has been too inward-looking, lacking in change and diversity, and too repetitive. It is once again rich as well as imaginative and ambitious and its creative economy is growing rapidly due to its encouragement of creativity, its huge domestic population and massive state investments.

On the Three Propositions, China scores high on universality but lacks the freedoms and open markets of America and Europe especially in media. It puts party unity and the national plan above management opportunism and contract law. It puts the ends above the means. This is not to say the Chinese are not interested in management. They are as skilled as anyone both personally and professionally but the risk/reward profile is different.

Its fastest-growing creative sectors are art, architecture, design, crafts and digital media, especially the mobile web. It has 560 million internet users, more than any other country, and Baidu, Tencent's QQ and Alibaba's Taobao are respectively the world's 5th, 9th and 10th most visited sites. In 2011 the Ministry of Culture estimated the cultural industries to contribute 2.7 per cent to GDP. We estimate its total creative economy to be 4–5 per cent nationally and higher in cities, reaching 12–13 per cent in Beijing and Shanghai. Many of China's 40 million university students want to travel to study, for a holiday or for a job and in 2011 the Chinese overtook Americans to become the highest spending global tourists, handing out $90 billion.

It became the world's third largest exporter of creative goods and services in 2005, which is quite an achievement for a country whose culture and language are unknown to most people.

However, many of these exports are financed and designed by others. China makes most of the world's clothes, including over 45 per cent of clothes bought in America, but they are all designed outside China. All iPhones are assembled in China but they are designed in America and the components are made in Korea, Switzerland and elsewhere. Foxconn, owned by Taiwanese but based in mainland China, charges only $8 to assemble each iPhone5, down from its $11 charge for an iPhone 4A.

Japan maintains its high reputation for cultural style in fashion, architecture and design. It has the world's highest per capita demand for newspapers and comics and its manga comics alone had sales of over $3.9 billion in 2010, including $1 billion exports, and accounted for almost half of all expenditure on consumer magazines. It is a world leader in home entertainment, cameras and toys. It spends more per capita on R&D than any other country and registers more patents. It seems unfazed by the rise of China. But Sony's Walkman dates back to 1975 and the company has lost its cherished pioneer status to Apple and Samsung. The country was late with the mobile internet and online media. Toyota's Prius hybrid car was a remarkable achievement but it was launched in 1997 and sales remain small.

What are the developing countries doing? They are trying to hitch a lift on the creativity express but many lack a sustainable creative ecology and business mind-set, let alone one attuned to foreign markets. Individual politicians often wish to be helpful but do not know what to do. As fast as they establish their own sectors (India's R&D, Thailand's film industry, South Korea's video games), America and Europe get even further ahead or simply move in to take control. In the 1990s, Brazil was the world's 6th largest music market; by 2012 it had fallen to 12th place.

Many turn inward to their traditional cultures and arts and want to promote these for reasons of national pride and hoped-for economic gain, but it is not easy. There is a widening gap between the rich countries' focus on digital media and the developing countries' focus on cultural heritage. America and Europe are forging ahead in coding, software, e-commerce and digital media but most developing countries lack the relevant skills and are shut out of these markets and pin their hopes on their heritage. It is a high-risk strategy. The evidence that a country's cultural heritage can provide a base for commercial expansion is very slight. We are seeing a new creative divide, not in people's wish to express themselves, but in their ability to make marketable products.

Sizing Up the Markets

The core sectors are divided into four groups: (1) Arts and Culture, (2) Design, (3) Media and (4) Innovation. The chief criterion is the source of revenue, whether from direct consumer expenditure (arts, books), clients (architects, designers) or advertising (media). I have also taken account of other criteria such as market structures and the role of online transactions. Each market overview has three sections: a snapshot of trends; the global market; and national markets in America, Europe, China and elsewhere. All data refer to 2012 unless stated.

The main indices are (i) market size and (ii) industry earnings. The *market size* is the amount spent annually in a specific market which shows what people are buying. For example, America's music market is the amount spent in America on buying music. *Industry earnings* gives company revenues; for example, the amount that American music companies earn from domestic sales and foreign exports.

The two global totals of markets and industries are the same but the figures for each country will differ. The major brand-owners and media companies earn substantial sums overseas so countries where they are based have larger industry earnings than domestic markets. Conversely, countries which import most of what they buy have a larger market than is shown by their own companies' earnings.

One of the changes in this edition of this book is a greater emphasis on retail. In many markets, the expansion of scope and scale depends more on distribution, logistics and retail than it does on production. The British Fashion Council says the British fashion market is worth £20.9 billion but acknowledges that consumer expenditure is about one-tenth as much.

Brand-owners have become more involved in retailing, sometimes willingly but often resenting the extra work. Fashion brands make as much money from licensing their signatures on accessories in other stores as designing new products, and a new line on the catwalk in New York may be a loss leader to pump up interest in accessories in the rest of the country or in South America. Advertising agencies offer advice on strategy and marketing. Architects offer advice on master plans, energy saving and project management. TV producers make money from audience voting and merchandise. By adding these new streams of revenue, it is possible to increase income at little extra cost.

The main sources of data are company reports, analysts' reports, national government statistics and trade data. I have given preference to data that is validated by both suppliers and recipients. The most robust data is supplied by companies, audited by an independent body and then sold back to the companies, such as data on box office admissions and broadcast audiences. Advisory firms with specialist experience can also provide good data, such as PwC's Global

Media and Entertainment Outlook and Battelle's review of R&D. The best data of all is compiled on an annual basis so errors can be corrected.

All governments have some way to go before they have an accurate picture of what is happening in their economies. America has the best information but it has gaps (the Bureau of Labor Statistics and a leading non-profit arts organization produce conflicting estimates of the number of artists that vary by a factor of eight). The Department of Commerce continually revises its treatment of America's investment and expenditure on intangibles and in 2013 it announced a new treatment of 'creative work undertaken on a systematic basis to increase the stock of knowledge' including R&D, and the creation of 'entertainment, literary and other artistic originals'. The result boosted the country's GDP by 3 per cent. Europe will similarly add R&D spending to its GDP as from 2014, which is expected to add 1.5–2 per cent to the total. Britain is also working hard to improve its data. In 2012 it deducted about $1.5 billion from its national accounts on design, fashion and software and then in 2013 added a 'hidden' $3–4.5 billion. It also adopted a new definition of creativity, based on five criteria, which enable it to rate all occupations according to their 'creative intensity', whether the job is in a so-called creative industry or not. These adjustments reflect the growing pains of a new economy that refuses to obey the rules of the old economy. The disparities do not affect the business actually being done but hamper governments as they struggle with unemployment and public deficits.

I include luxury products and brands in their own markets rather than as a separate sector. The luxury market has emerged as an increasingly separate market in recent years with its own super-rich demographics, but there is no clear dividing line between what is luxury and what is not. Market estimates vary widely, with many companies competing to give ever higher figures from around $300 billion to over $1 trillion if experiences such as holidays are included. The main markets have traditionally been Europe and America but China is said to have become the largest market in 2012 on the basis of foreign brands and strong growth in Chinese wine, tea, porcelain, fashion and silk. China's big spenders are nicknamed 'bao fa hu', which translates as 'explosively rich'. Having made a huge impact in their home market they are beginning to influence trends in Europe and America.

I exclude several sectors that are sometimes described as 'creative' and which use creative inputs but whose economic value depends more on repetition than creativity, such as tourism, theme parks and sport. It is true nonetheless that tourism and creative industries are complementary. Most visitors to New York say its cultural life is the main attraction; the same is true for London and Paris. The Indonesian minister Mari Elka Pangestu combines both tourism and the creative economy in her portfolio because foreign tourism is the best way to stimulate her country's creative markets. One of the biggest growth areas worldwide is the mix of tourism, international sporting events, culture and hospitality that is endearingly known as MICE – Meetings, Incentives, Conferences and Exhibitions.

ARTS AND CULTURE

Art

The art market consists of visual arts, associated art works and antiques. The main visual arts are painting, sculpture and 'works on paper' (such as drawings and original prints) but the market includes design, photography, jewellery, artists' books and ordinary books, furniture, fashion and musical instruments. Art today is anything which an auction house can sell or a museum put on show.

The art market is unusual in that it deals mostly in original works that are unique or rare. Artists and art dealers promote an object's scarcity whereas sellers in most other markets want to make as many copies as possible.

It is divided into the 'primary' market of new work coming fresh to the market and the 'secondary' market of older work. Here again it is unusual because the secondary, second-hand market is much bigger.

Artistic works qualify for copyright and artists normally retain the copyright in a work when they sell it. The purchaser buys only the object and not the copyright. Most artists do not encourage copying, even if they might gain financially, and use copyright to prevent anyone copying rather than licensing someone to do so. A quirk of the art market is a 'droit de suite' or re-sale tax under which an artist or heir qualifies for a percentage of the sale price, up to 4 per cent, each time a piece of work is sold, for 70 years after the artist's death. Originating in France, it is now law in over 60 countries.

Art exemplifies the deal economy because every work and every transaction is unique and by monitoring a work over many years it is possible to accumulate an accurate record of its price as it goes up and down. The Paris-based Artprice has a database of over 500,000 artists and 27 million auction results. Even two identical prints sold consecutively at auction constitute different transactions and may fetch different prices because the sale of the first will affect the market for the second.

The market's democratic nature as well as its low barriers to entry and low start-up costs make it open to new talent whether as an artist, a gallerist or a curator. It allows thousands of artists and dealers to operate and many individuals to buy, sell and give away privately but the competition for buyers is tough.

The art world is seldom interested in future trends. Designers talk endlessly about new trends. Artists and gallerists don't bother; they get on with the work.

Global. The global market was worth $56 billion in 2012, according to the annual report commissioned by the Maastricht Art Fair. This figure is short of the high of $66 billion achieved in 2007 before the financial crash but a significant upturn from the trough of $36 billion in 2009. It includes all varieties of art from antiquities to contemporary installations as well as jewellery, fine furniture and older objects which might originally have been categorized as crafts. Artprice gives a figure for Western fine art of $10 billion.

Art has a reputation of being the most often stolen in terms of objects, though not in terms of value (digital media take that title). Annual theft is estimated to be $4 billion of antiquities (Interpol) or $7.8 billion of art and antiquities (United Nations).

It is estimated by both the Maastricht report and the French government that China became the world's third largest market in 2009, the second largest in 2010 and overtook America to be the world's biggest market in 2011. But in 2012 it fell back to second place. In that year, America had a 33 per cent share followed by China (25%), Britain (23%) and France (6%). More new buyers are emerging in many places from Australia to South America, Russia and the Gulf.

This is part of a shift as radical as the emergence of American art buyers at the beginning of the 20th century. Unlike those Americans, however, who were offbeat pioneers buying on personal instinct, the new collectors are more conscious of investment values and how the market works. They are served by a worldwide network of gallerists, art fairs, art weeks and consultants.

Many art museums have switched priorities from their own permanent collections to negotiating one-off exhibitions which are co-curated and co-financed by museums and sponsors in several countries. This helps to overcome the newer museums' problem of having a big building but a small permanent collection (for example, the Guggenheim in Bilbao). The public is also more likely to visit a high-profile, one-off event. When the *Art Newspaper* started to review exhibitions in the 1990s, a museum needed 3,000 visitors to get into the top ten. Twenty years later, the threshold had more than doubled.

The top ten art museums in 2012 were the Louvre, Paris (9.7 million visitors), Metropolitan, New York (6.1 million), British Museum (5.6 million), Tate Modern (5.3 million), National Gallery, London (5.2 million), Vatican Museums (5.0 million), National Palace Museum, Taipei (4.4 million), National Gallery of Art, Washington, DC (4.2 million), Centre Pompidou, Paris (3.8 million), and Musée d'Orsay, Paris (3.6 million).

The top 10 exhibitions were: Masterpieces from the Mauritshuis, Tokyo Metropolitan Art Museum (10,573 daily visitors); The Amazon: Cycles of Modernity, Centro Cultural Banco do Brasil, CCBB (7,928 visitors*; an asterisk indicates entry was free); Nineteenth-Century Italian Painting, Hermitage Museum, St Petersburg (7,747 visitors); Ito Jakuchu, National Gallery of Art, Washington DC (7,611 visitors*); David Hockney, Royal Academy of Arts, London (7,512 visitors); Japanese Masterpieces from Boston, Tokyo National Museum

(7,374 visitors); Anthony Gormley, CCBB (6,909 visitors); Little Black Jacket, Saatchi Gallery, London (6,716 visitors); Golden Flashes, Uffizi, Florence (6,672 visitors); and Daniel Buren, Grand Palais, Paris (6,498 visitors). The list is notable for its eclectic mix of European art titans and fashion celebrities like Coco Chanel in Little Black Jacket. It also demonstrates the popularity of gallery loans and exchanges, as well as the invisibility of Chinese art at this level.

The two largest auction houses are Sotheby's and Christie's, both established in 18th-century London, which have revenues of $5.8 billion and $5.7 billion respectively. The next largest are Beijing's government-owned Poly and the private Guardian, with about $0.7 billion revenues apiece.

The list of the world's ten best-selling artists contains five Chinese, three Europeans and two Americans: Andy Warhol ($329 million), Zhang Daqian ($287 million), Pablo Picasso ($286 million), Qi Baishi ($270 million), Gerhard Richter ($263 million), Xu Beihong ($176 million), Mark Rothko ($167 million), Li Keran ($167 million), Francis Bacon ($153 million) and Fu Baoshi ($152 million).

The *American* market is worth about $18 billion. New York is still regarded as the world's largest, toughest and richest market and has the largest conglomeration of artists, dealers, critics, curators, museums and collectors. New York-based artists command the highest prices for contemporary art in painting, video, installations, photography and other areas. Among other cities, Los Angeles is the most prolific in both making and showing art while Palm Beach, Florida, hosts the country's largest contemporary art fair. Many cities have substantial art museums funded by the city government, foundations and local business.

Europe. The total market is worth $21 billion, 37 per cent of the world total. Britain and France are by far the largest markets, followed by Switzerland, Italy and Spain. London, Geneva and Paris are the main auction centres in terms of value and Paris has the world's largest number of sales. Europe is reckoned to have more artists, art colleges, art students, galleries and museums per capita than any other region.

Britain. The market is worth $13 billion. It is highly concentrated in London which has 1,300 museums and galleries. The largest markets are contemporary art, modern art, designer art, sculpture and photography. London has 48 per cent of the global market in Old Masters but another stalwart, antique furniture, has fallen sharply. Its contemporary art market was kick-started 25 years ago by Young British Artists (YBAs) such as Damien Hirst, Tracey Emin and Gary Hume.

China. The market is worth about $14 billion. The largest sectors are traditional Chinese calligraphy, landscapes and porcelain as well as contemporary work. Sales data provided by the government, auction houses, galleries and outside analysts often differ by 20–30 per cent because sometimes the Chinese bid high but don't pay and some pieces have been shown to be fakes or reproductions.

China has several high-profile clusters where artists work and show their output, such as 798 and Songzhuang in Beijing and M50 in Shanghai. It also has several art factories that produce copies of genre paintings, typically landscapes, portraits and animals in 18th- and 19th-century European styles. The most famous is in Dafen near Shenzhen.

Books

Publishing was the first industry to be able to copy on a large scale. The Chinese invented paper and some elements of the printing process but the Europeans were the first to bring together paper, re-usable moveable type, sticky ink and a press. It is now the largest media industry in the world and the pre-eminent copyright industry, having given us the two key words, author and copy.

In recent decades, the techniques of editing, design and illustration have changed dramatically, as have the commercial functions of finance, marketing and sales. The industry is undergoing a drastic transformation as the success of e-books and online sales (of both physical books and e-books) challenges the value chain from the author's original work through to retailing. In 2012 Amazon sold more e-books than physical books.

As a conveyor of human achievement from the awesome to the trivial, the book has no peer. People appreciate it not only as a packager of content but for its diversity of designs and for its solidity and convenience. The number of titles and of copies sold increases remorselessly, although the margins and profits on sales are ever tighter.

The traditional physical book has one attribute that distinguishes it from other creative products. It is the most given of all creative products, as its visual appeal, size, price range and cultural respectability make it a welcome gift in all circumstances and a new or best-selling book comes with the cachet of novelty and cultural approval. It is unclear whether the book as a gift will survive the popularity of e-books, which lack these tactile attractions and have their own problems of inter-platform compatibility, but it seems unlikely.

Publishers are negotiating new terms of trade with online platforms, although that usually means reacting with various degrees of politeness to what online distributors offer. Traditionally, publishers sold books to retailers at about 50 per cent of the retail price. But Amazon promoted its Kindle by selling e-books at around $9.99, even if it had paid a higher wholesale price to the publisher. This annoyed publishers because they lost control over their margins and could no longer use prices to differentiate between editions. When Apple introduced its iPad in 2010, it offered an alternative in the form of an 'agency model' by which publishers set their own retail prices and Apple as agent takes 30 per cent.

Amazon's willingness to deal directly with authors and give them a revenue-sharing 70 per cent royalty opened the door to self-published books (Bowker estimates about 200,000 titles were self-published in America in 2012). The huge sales of the *Fifty Shades of Grey* trilogy are extraordinary but its gestation was typical of publishing's eclectic and international market. Its author is British, it grew out of America's Twilight fan fiction and it was first published on an Australian website, the Writer's Coffee Shop. It was then professionally published by Germany's Random House.

Global. The total market for consumer (so-called 'trade' books), education books and professional books is $134.9 billion.

Table 2: Books: The biggest national markets (2012 ($ billion))

	Consumer and educational books	Business and professional books	Total
America	30.5	6.5	37.0
Germany	9.8	4.0	13.8
China	10.6	2.5	13.1
Japan	11.4	2.1	13.5
France	7.9	1.1	9.0
Britain	5.1	0.8	5.9
Spain	3.7	0.6	4.3
Italy	4.1	0.2	4.3
India	2.7	0.2	2.9
Brazil	2.0	0.3	2.3
Rest of the world	24.4	4.4	28.8
Total	112.2	22.7	134.9

Another measure is the number of new titles published:

Table 3: Books: new trade titles (2012)

Countries	Books
America	320,000
China	170,000
Britain	150,000
Russia	117,000
Germany	93,000
Spain	70,000
France	55,000

The world's largest book publishers, according to *Publishers Weekly* and *Livres Hebdo*, are Pearson, Reed Elsevier, Thomson/Reuters, Wolters/Kluwer, Hachette, Grupo Planeta and Random House. China has few large publishers. According to Bowker, the largest is China Education Publishing and Media, which had $680 million sales in 2012 and ranked about number 30 worldwide.

America. The market is worth $37 billion. Physical books still dominate but consumer e-books brought in $4.5 billion and educational e-books $1.0 billion. The figure for educational e-books masks a bigger shift away from book-based education to online learning as students bring the same attitudes to learning as they brought to music and video, and look for quick, easy and often free sources of information that bypass formal texts. PwC estimates trade e-book revenues will be worth $9 billion in 2015. In the business/professional market, physical revenues were $5.5 billion and digital revenues were $1.1 billion.

Europe. The consumer market is worth $27 billion, including $600 million on e-books; the educational market is worth $13 billion, including $600 million on e-books; and the business/professional market is worth $8 billion. Germany is easily the biggest national market, with $10 billion, followed by France's $7 billion and Britain's $5 billion. Europe's total of 270,000 public libraries (European Commission, 2009) is reckoned to be more than in the rest of the world combined.

Britain. The total market is steady at $5–6 billion consisting of consumer ($3.3 billion), educational ($1.8 billion) and professional books ($0.8 billion). The number of e-book titles overtook hardback titles in 2011 but e-book revenues are still much lower and bring in only $623 million, of which $250 came from educational e-books. The total number of new titles rose from 104,000 in 2000 to 157,000 in 2009 and then fell to 149,000 in 2011 (excluding self-published books available only on Amazon). Most sales are made by Amazon and other online sellers (40%) followed by chains (30%), supermarkets (20%), and independents (10%). Britain has many small publishers but, following the Random House–Penguin merger in 2013, wholly British-owned publishers have less than 10 per cent of the market.

China. China's large population means its book market is the world's third largest in terms of titles and turnover and Chinese books make up the second-largest language group after English books. The market is worth $13 billion, consisting of $4.6 billion expenditure on consumer books, $6.0 billion on education books and $2.5 billion on professional books. Its e-book market is still small, only $130 million, although the country's online-only books, texts and blogs are more popular than anywhere else. It publishes 252,000 titles a year and prints over 7 billion copies, but average prices are low and bookshops are often unattractive and this vast number brings in relatively low revenues.

Crafts

Crafts are hand-made, hand-crafted objects with both functional and aesthetic qualities. Some individual pieces are so well made and beautiful as to qualify purely as design or art and there is a tendency, at the top end, to use words like 'design' and 'designer-makers' and to reserve the term 'craft' for cheaper and functional pieces.

Some cultures regard art more highly than craft but the majority revere crafts more highly. Europeans are ambivalent and may treat a Sung bowl of the 12th century as a work of art but a contemporary bowl as craft. An English gallerist who asked Tobias Kaye, a wood-turner, whether he was making art or craft, got this response: 'Well, the process is art but the result is craft.' The gallery-owner was amused because the week before Richard Raffan, another leading wood-turner, had said the exact opposite: 'The process is craft but the result is art.'

Crafts therefore flourish in two separate markets. High-end designer crafts are part of the art market and exhibited in art galleries and sold at auction. These designer-makers work in the same way as other artists and with the same imaginative skill (in 2003 the artist Grayson Perry won Britain's prestigious Turner Prize for his pottery though, as a well-known transvestite, he is far from an average craft-worker). Crafts also flourish in the much larger fashion, tourism and leisure markets where people make and buy crafts with little regard for authorship or formal aesthetic, and value them by price and utility as much as quality. All craft works qualify for copyright if they fulfil the artistic criteria of being novel and contain an element of skill but the majority of craft-makers do not bother to claim their rights.

The *global* market is large and varied. The high-end market of crafts whose authorship and provenance adds value is worth about $3 billion and the mass market about $42 billion but both figures should be treated with caution because they include work that could be categorized as art or small-scale manufacturing.

America. The craft associations estimate the high-end sector to be worth about $1 billion and the total $6 billion. Total sales of craft materials to craft-workers are worth $12 billion, and grew at the rapid rate of 6 per cent a year between 2006 and 2011, but most of this is used for hobbies and not intended for sale.

Europe. The high-end, designer-maker market is worth $1 billion and the total market about $6 billon. There is a close correlation between the former market and other design and fashion markets, and so the main markets are Italy, the Nordic countries, the Netherlands and Germany. Craft markets, which are more extensive, are largest in Germany and Mediterranean countries.

Britain. The high-end market is worth around $0.4 billion and we estimate the total market is worth $1 billion. According to the Craft Council, 30,000 people work professionally, mostly in textiles and ceramics, followed by wood, metal, jewellery, glass, toys and musical instruments.

China's high-end market is estimated to be worth $2 billion and the total about $8 billion. The major sectors are jade, calligraphy, paper, woodwork, cloisonné, lacquer and pottery. The tradition of giving gifts to friends and business contacts keeps demand high. The industry makes and exports more crafts in the widest sense than does any other country, as much as $15 billion. At its peak around 2005, the Yiwu market in Zhejiang had 60,000 stalls, although electronic devices now outcell crafts.

Many popular tourist destinations have large craft industries in the wider sense of the word. *Thailand's* crafts sector is estimated to be

$10.4 billion, as much as 3 per cent of GDP, and *India*, *Indonesia*, *Brazil*, *Japan* and *Russia* also have large markets.

Film

No craft-worker can survive on one work but a film-maker can do very well from one film. This is partly because a successful film can achieve very high revenues. Joss Whedon's *The Avengers* sold $1 billion worth of tickets in its first 19 days, including $200 million in its first weekend in America, and earned over $200 million in merchandising. The biggest selling film ever is *Avatar*, which grossed $2.7 billion in cinemas within a few years. The three films in the *Lord of the Rings* trilogy took $2.9 billion at the cinema.

But the chief reason why the industry is so rich is that its business model enables almost everyone involved to earn a high level of fees and royalties and to do so even from a film that loses money. Producers and distributors take the largest shares but many others benefit even if profits are negligible. The lure of such riches attracts millions of people to be a player in the film-making game or to be close to those who are.

The industry has four main sectors: (1) American production by both Hollywood studios and independents; (2) other countries' national production; (3) global distribution companies which buy and sell other people's rights; and (4) thousands of local companies in production, distribution, cinemas and services.

The main trend in production is the growth of Hollywood's franchise and animation series, which are less risky than live action and play well in almost all countries. Hollywood's production output is level at 90–100 films a year but the number of independent low-budget films continues to expand, although they find it hard to get distribution in cinemas or on video.

The main distribution trends are cinemas with digital and 3D screens and, at home, the increase in the number of large, flat, 3D and HD digital sets which can display broadcast TV, pay-TV, DVDs, Blu-Ray and online media. The industry's marketing strategy is to optimize the balance between the cinema release, which gets most publicity, and the physical home video release, which brings in most revenues, and then to license the film for downloading and streaming direct to homes.

A film is a qualifying work and protected by copyright. Most national laws interpret the 'author' to include the screenwriter, producer, director and others, as well as giving separate protection to costumes, design and so on. Once made, a film's rights will be sold or licensed to distributors within each territory, in each medium (cinema, broadcast, etc.) and in each language. There is a trend towards registering film titles as trademarks and registering merchandise as designs.

Global. The world market for full-length features is worth $90 billion in terms of consumer purchases at the cinema box office, for home video and for TV. The cinema market is worth $34.7 billion, of which American cinemas earned $10.8 billion, followed by China ($2.75 billion), Japan ($2.4 billion), France ($1.7 billion), Britain ($1.7 billion), India (1.4 billion), Germany ($1.3 billion) and Korea ($1.3 billion).

American films still dominate the global box office and usually take the top 20 slots and about 30 per cent of the revenue. Most countries protect their national films through import restrictions, tax credits and subsidies. Japan and India are the only large markets where the audience prefers local films in the absence of government restrictions.

The global market in home video sales and rentals is worth $48 billion. Packaged video on DVD and Blu-Ray still dominate but digital licensing to sites like Wal-Mart's Vudu, Netflix, iTunes, Hulu and Amazon's LoveFilm is growing steadily as they move from lending DVDs to streaming direct to home TV displays. It is estimated Netflix spent $3.5 billion on licences for 2012.

The global industry produces about 3,500 films a year. India produces the largest number (1,100), followed by Japan (650), America (611), China (300), France (272), Italy, Spain and Britain. Other notable production centres are Hong Kong and Tehran.

In *America* the film market is worth about $33 billion. Box office receipts were $10.8 billion in 2012 from 1.4 billion admissions. In addition, home video brought in $22 billion, of which physical platforms

(DVD, Blu-Ray) brought in a declining $16 billion and online a rapidly increasing $3 billion. People spent another $3 billion on movie channel subscriptions.

The six Hollywood studios, known as majors, are Universal (owned by Comcast and GE), Paramount (Viacom), Walt Disney, Columbia (Sony), Fox (21st Century Fox) and Warner Bros (Time Warner). They have dominated the global business for a long time but their profits have declined each year 2007–2011 (in contrast, their owners' TV subsidiaries increased profits). They produced 94 films in 2012, which may seem surprisingly few, but each studio limits its output to what it can release effectively given the competition for cinema slots and media coverage. American independents, many of them tied into a studio, produced an additional 550 films. Hollywood's average production budgets are about $90 million and its average prints-and-advertising (P&A) budgets are about $40 million. Independent budgets average one-tenth smaller.

In *Europe* the total market is worth about $25 billion, of which cinemas earn $11 billion from one billion tickets (and $1 billion from advertising). Home video earns $14.5 billion, of which physical units earn $12.5 billion and digital earns $2 billion. American films take 70 per cent of European box office revenues.

The biggest cinema markets are France ($1.7 billion from 205 million admissions), Britain ($1.7 billion from 173 million admissions), Germany ($1.3 billion from 135 million admissions) and Italy ($0.84 billion from 101 million admissions). Most markets showed an increase in 2011 over previous years, due to better cinema management and the introduction of digital and 3D, except Italy.

European companies produced 1,280 feature-length films, of which 370 were documentaries. One of the main strengths of Europe is the high level of state funding, about $3 billion, which is spent mostly on production (69%) and distribution (8%).

Britain. The market is worth $6 billion, of which the consumer spent $1.9 billion at the cinema, $3.8 billion on home video and $400 million on pay-TV movie channels. The BBC, ITV and other free-to-air channels spend an additional $150 million to buy broadcast rights.

In 2012 the industry produced 223 films, of which about 50 were pure British, 10 were pure American and the rest were co-productions. Industry expenditure was $1.5 billion, down from a record $2 billion in 2011, consisting mostly of foreign investment, almost entirely from America, and $353 million of domestic expenditure. Exports total $2.3 billion, of which royalties bring in $1.5 billion and production services $0.9 billion. Of recent hits, *The King's Speech* cost $15 million, took $72 million in Britain and grossed $520 million worldwide. Sam Mendes's James Bond film *Skyfall* cost about $150 million, of which about $45 million came from product placement, and earned $151 million in its first 40 days to become Britain's highest-grossing film ever.

The *China* film market is worth about $2.9 billion, of which cinema contributes as much as $2.75 billion, up 40 per cent from 2010. It is possible that the total is higher as some cinemas deduct (skim) income before passing the net to the distributor. Home video revenues are negligible due to the high level of piracy. The State Administration of Radio, Film and TV (SARFT) restricts the number of foreign films that may be shown in cinemas to only 20 a year on a commercial, royalty-sharing basis, with an additional 14 films in 3D or Imax formats. The box office is split evenly between Chinese and foreign films.

The industry produced about 600 films in 2012, although only 300 were released in cinemas. Recent hits include Zhang Yimou's *The Flowers of War*, which cost an estimated $90 million and grossed $93 million within six weeks, and the low-budget films Teng Huatao's comedy *Love is Not Blind*, which cost $1.4 million and grossed $55 million and Xu Zheng's *Lost in Thailand*, which cost $4.8 million and took over $200 million to become the country's highest-grossing film ever.

Few Chinese films travel well. *Let the Bullets Fly* was successful domestically but took only $61,000 in America, and the big-budget *The Flowers of War*, starring Christian Bale, topped the charts in China and took $95 million but flopped in America, taking only $311,000. The exceptions are Taiwanese Ang Lee's *Crouching Tiger, Hidden Dragon*, which was the most successful ever foreign film in America, and his *Life of Pi*, which earned almost as much.

Japan. Japan is the third largest market after America and is worth $7.4 billion. The cinema market is worth $2.3 billion and the home video market is worth $5.1 billion (both figures were down by over 15 per cent from 2010 because of the tsunami). Japanese films, mainly action and fantasy, take over half the national box office but seldom travel.

India. The market is worth about $4.2 billion. Cinema accounts for $1.4 billion, as much as 55 per cent of revenues, one of the highest proportions in the world, the result of 2.7 billion admissions. Indian companies produced over 1,000 films in 2012, of which about 200 were Hindi-language Bollywood movies, with their distinctive mix of romance and music, and the remaining 800 more modest productions in other Indian languages. Industry revenues were $1.1 billion. The Mumbai studios are having difficulties in adapting to a digital market but new companies are stepping in. Anil Ambani's Mumbai-based Reliance Group, which owns BIG Cinemas, India's largest chain, invested $325 million in DreamWorks to acquire 50 per cent of the equity, and has investments in post-production labs in Los Angeles and London.

Nigeria claims to be the world's largest film producer on the basis of an upsurge in low-budget films made on location and distributed on DVD. The government says over 1,100 films were approved in 2012 and earned $600 million. Cinemas are rare (Lagos reportedly had only three working cinemas in 2011). The early so-called Nollywood films had budgets of around $10,000 but films are now more elaborate and more expensive. Popular themes are family relationships, life in the big city, moral dilemmas, witchcraft and religion.

Music

Music is the most intangible of all creative work as well as the most pervasive. Its creativity can be expressed in writing, performing and recording, and money can also be made from publishing and licensing. It is protected by a thicket of copyright at each stage. A composition is protected for the composer's life plus 70 years. Performing, recording and broadcasting are protected by what are called related rights or neighbouring rights, which range from 50 to 95 years. Musicians are adept at creating rights and at finding ways to charge for them. They have built up special collecting societies to manage their revenues, which monitor the playing of music on TV, film and radio; in bars, hotels and cafes; in offices, garages and warehouses; in shopping malls, hairdressers and airports. They levy a class or group licence on whoever is responsible and pass on the revenue to rights-holders (TV, radio and book rights-holders use these companies but to a smaller extent).

As labels have declined in importance so agents and managers have become the main deal-makers in all areas from live tours to fashion endorsements. American music has been transformed by promoters like Robert F. X. Sillerman, who founded SFX, and Irving Azoff, who founded Live Nation and whom *Billboard* listed as number one in its 2012 list of the Music Power 100.

Global. The global music market for recording and performing is worth $49 billion. After falling for 14 years, spending on recorded music grew for the first time in 2012 to $23 billion, which was split between physical sales of $15 billion, less than half their value in 2000, and digital sales of $8 billion. Spending on performance is $26 billion. The biggest markets are America ($15 billion), followed by Japan ($6 billion), Britain ($4 billion), Germany ($4 billion), France ($2 billion), Canada ($1 billion) and Italy ($1 billion).

Recorded music is one of the few entertainment markets whose revenues have plummeted. Having reached an all-time high of $39.5 billion in 1996, revenues fell to $33 billion in 2005 and $23 billion in 2011. Sales in the 1990s had been boosted by people buying CDs to replace older LPs and by a succession of new acts, but from the mid-1990s there was a dearth of new talent (for several years in the 1990s the lead singers with 10 of America's 20 highest-grossing live acts were over 60 years old). Meanwhile the internet was opening the doors to peer-to-peer sharing and slick new services like iTunes and Spotify, and piracy rose.

The country with the highest proportion of digital spending is China, where physical formats never really got a foothold, and digital now accounts for 75 per cent of expenditure. Outside China, the switch to digital is happening fastest in America, where digital revenues overtook physical revenues in 2012. Europe and Japan are moving more slowly.

The take-home revenues of artists and others depend on the deals between right-owners and online platforms, as it does in the text, film and TV markets. To their irritation, music labels have found themselves dependent on a bewildering and fast-changing range of devices, operating systems and licence conditions as their business moves from physical platforms to downloading and then to streaming.

The top three companies are Vivendi's Universal Music Group ($5.9 billion sales in 2012), Sony Music Entertainment ($5.6 billion) and Warner Music ($3.0 billion). These top three own about 80 per cent of the world's music publishing and recording rights. There has been a remorseless trend to concentration as the market shrinks. Vivendi started to buy Universal's music companies in the 1990s. Sony Music was jointly owned by Sony and the German BMG but Sony bought out BMG's 50 per cent. Warner Music has had no links with Time Warner since 2004 and is now owned by Access Industries, an American conglomerate. EMI ranked as the fourth major for many years until a private equity firm, Terra Firma, having bought the company with a loan from Citigroup, then became unable to pay the interest and control passed to the bank. In 2011, Citigroup broke up the company and sold its recording and publishing divisions separately.

The five highest-grossing tours in 2012 were by Madonna ($141 million), Bruce Springsteen ($123 million), Roger Waters ($115 million), Coldplay ($99 million) and Lady Gaga ($77 million).

America. The market is worth about $15 billion across all sectors. Recorded music brings in $6.5 billion, consisting of $3.4 billion from physical units and $3.1 billion from digital. Concerts and festivals are worth more at $8.7 billion. There are an estimated 185,000 working musicians, 90,000 aspiring musicians and an additional 300,000 people working in the industry, according to the National Endowment for the Arts. The NEA also reports that 20 million Americans say they sing weekly in a choir or chorus.

Europe. The market is worth $19 billion, consisting of $8 billion from recorded music ($6 billion physical units and $2 billion digital) and $11 billion from concerts and festivals. Outside the classical music repertoire, there is little exchange between countries, and national radio playlists and venues favour first their own national music and then American music.

Britain. The market is worth $4.3 billion. The market for recorded music is worth $1.9 billion, consisting of $1.3 billion from physical units and $0.6 billion from digital. PwC expects digital spending to overtake physical spending in 2015. The market for live performance is worth $2.4 billion.

British companies earned much more, about $6 billion annually, about 12 per cent of the global market, and five of the best-selling albums in America in 2012 were by British artists: Adele, One Direction (two albums), and Mumford and Sons. About 53,000 people call themselves musicians on their census forms, 29,000 people describe themselves as aspiring musicians and 43,000 people work in the industry in other ways, totalling 125,000.

China. Traditional music is a major part of Chinese culture but pop music by and for young people was slow to emerge. The total market is worth $300 million. Most music is listened to live or got free from the internet. The China Audio and Video Association valued the 2012 recordings market at $6.4 billion but said actual revenues were only $130 million. Some estimates are lower. Lu Jian, President of Ocean Butterflies and Secretary-General of the Recording Works Council, reported that members' label revenues have decreased from about $315 million in 2000 to only $120 million in 2012. There is a small but flourishing market in performances but these face government obstacles and ticket revenues are low ($150 million).

The local industry is small. Lu Jian says no label employs more than 100 people. For many years international labels collected only low revenues, around $60–70 million, until Baidu, China's largest search engine, agreed to pay a royalty for each download. Some domestic labels, such as China's largest independent label, Modern Sky, allow Baidu to download all tracks for free and make money from sponsorship, advertising and concerts.

Performance

The performing arts include theatre, musicals, comedy, opera, dance, ballet and circus. The core skills are writing, directing and performing and many more people work on financing, producing and casting; design, lighting and sound; costume; set-making; marketing; and administration.

The business is based on writers, directors and performers but impresarios, agents and managers play a key role. It also depends on buildings ranging from grand national institutions to thousands of local venues, big and small.

Dramatic works receive copyright protection when the original work is written down and when it is performed. Works and performances that are not written down or contain elements that are not in the script, such as design, sets and lighting, can be hard to protect and will not be protected unless someone (not necessarily the person who had the original idea) records them.

People's desire for live performance of all kinds is growing in spite of the development of broadcast TV and online media. The largest audiences are for musicals, drama and comedy and there is increasing interest in immersive, interactive performances that blend fiction and real life as well as an increasing number of site-specific events.

The *global* market is worth about $50–55 billion. It is not possible to give precise figures because of the variety of venues and activities and because many venues do not differentiate between performing arts and other events. The sector attracts a high level of private sponsorship and public funding, mainly for buildings but occasionally for performances.

New York's Broadway and London's West End are the twin centres of English-language plays and musicals. Some have an exceedingly long life – London's production of Agatha Christie's *The Mousetrap* is in its seventh decade. Cameron Mackintosh has produced or licensed over 53 major productions of *Les Misérables* in 42 countries, which have grossed $3 billion. The worldwide best-seller is composer Andrew Lloyd Webber's *Phantom of the Opera* ($5.6 billion), which can claim to be the single most successful entertainment venture of all time, surpassing the best-selling film, book, music album or game. Lloyd Webber also composed the music for *Cats* ($3 billion).

America is the world's largest market. Box office revenues are $13 billion, slightly more than the box office revenues for film and sports. New York has more theatres than any other city in the world. Broadway sold 12.3 million tickets and grossed $1.1 billion, and out-of-town performances sold 13.1 million tickets and earned $0.8 billion (notably, women buy 62 per cent of the tickets for out-of-town shows and occupy 70 per cent of the seats). Both Broadway and tour box offices have increased slightly year-on-year since 2000. Musicals account for 85 per cent of revenues. According to the Broadway League, Broadway contributes over $7 billion to New York's economy, made up by what theatre-owners spend on theatres ($15 million) and shows ($1 billion) and what visitors spend while they are in town ($6 billion).

Across the country, theatres receive about $4 billion private sponsorship (half the $8 billion worth of sponsorship given to the arts overall), as well as federal ($200 million), state ($200 million) and city ($500 million) funding. These 2012 figures show a decline of 20 per cent since 2008.

Europe. All European countries have a strong tradition of performing arts, especially in the capital cities, and many smaller cities have at least one theatre to provide a base for touring shows. We estimate the market to be worth $18 billion. The Eurozone financial crises led to cuts in government funding, but there is evidence that audiences have grown in France, Germany and Italy due to a stream of new productions, better marketing and lower seat prices.

Britain. The market is worth $2.6 billion. London's commercial and subsidized sectors combined sold 13.9 million tickets, earning $835 million, up 3 per cent from 2010. The number of tickets sold has stayed within a range of 10–14 million for the past 30 years but revenues have increased in line with inflation from $160 million in 1980 to $835 million in 2011. The West End sells more tickets than Broadway but Broadway's prices are about 50 per cent higher.

China. The performing arts range from traditional opera to drama, dance, comedy ('crosstalk') and acrobats. There is a strong theatrical tradition and some long-running musical and circus shows but there is a shortage of new writers and the market for contemporary work is small. As few as 20 per cent of people in the big cities go to the theatre once or more a year and as many as 40 per cent say they never go. The market size is $3.7 billion, excluding Hong Kong, consisting of $1.9 billion box office revenues and $1.8 billion from other sources.

The sector is developing modern skills as well as sustaining the traditional repertoire. The Shanghai Theatre Academy has established a School of Creativity and Shanghai's KunQu champion Zhang Jun is skilled in both his art and marketing. Many cities have built large theatres and promote large-scale, site-specific shows (such as Zhang Yimou's outdoor extravaganzas). Theatres favour ensemble shows of Chinese traditional musicians or dancers, or global imports, and there are fewer opportunities for small-scale experiments.

Video Games

There are two main markets: console-based games played on proprietary devices; and online games and apps that are downloaded or streamed to a much wider range of devices. The consoles were the largest market for many years but apps and online games are beginning to be more popular. The market for PC-only games is small and declining. Like other entertainment media, games are going online, especially in China and Japan, and using Facebook and Google Play to offer flexible freemium experiences financed by micro-transactions.

America's Atari was the first major producer but was soon trumped by Nintendo, a Japanese manufacturer of playing cards, which quickly became Japan's third most profitable company. By the early 1990s its 900 employees made more profits than did the 150,000 people working for Hitachi, then the world's biggest consumer electronics manufacturer. In turn Nintendo was outplayed by Sony's PlayStation, which has sold 400 million consoles and many hundreds of millions of games and has half the world market. At its peak it was responsible for 25 per cent of Sony's income and 30 per cent of its profits. The console industry is still dominated by the big three of PlayStation (PS4 and Vita), the re-emergence of Nintendo with its Wii and Wii U and Microsoft's Xbox.

The games themselves are mostly developed in America, France, Korea and Japan. Britain was ranked second or third but drifted downwards as developers and publishers failed to achieve international scale and preferred to sell out to America. Other governments were also quicker to provide tax credits to producers.

A successful game can outsell a major cinema release. In 2007, Infinity Ward's *Call of Duty: Modern Warfare 3* grossed $1 billion in 16 days. The following year, Rockstar's *Grand Theft Auto IV* which had 80,000 lines of dialogue and a cast of over 800 actors, and reportedly cost about $100 million; it earned $500 million in its first week.

The division between the Shoot 'Em Up and Kung Fu action games coming out of Asia and Britain and the more thoughtful games coming out of California's sci-fi and fantasy worlds is narrowing. Classic American games include Will Wright's *Sim City* (1985) and *The Sims* (2000), which sold 150 million units. Recent games include Sygma's *Farmville* about life on a farm, Valve's puzzle-solving *Portal 2* and Rockstar's *LA Noire*. The Entertainment Software Alliance says 69 per cent of American heads of households play games and the average age of a game player is now 33 years old.

A game consists of a bundle of literary, artistic, musical and dramatic copyright works and also qualifies as a film. Its software is likely to be patented and its name trademarked and in Europe its data set may be protected by the EU database law. This complexity and the constantly changing technology result in difficult and time-consuming rights negotiations.

The main trends are online games on Facebook, Google+ and other networks and as iOS or Android apps. There is a widening division between the fixed-location console games and what are called mobile/social games. A gamer playing with family and friends on a Wii is in a separate market from a gamer playing online with hundreds and thousands of other players, known as Massive Multiplayer Online Games, or MMOGs.

Global turnover in games is $60–61 billion. The major markets are console games ($27 billion and decreasing), online games ($17 billion and increasing), wireless games ($9 billion) and PC games ($3 billion). About $2 billion is earned from advertising. In addition, but not included in these figures, players spend about $3 billion on buying new consoles.

The largest markets are America ($15 billion), Japan ($7 billion), China ($8 billion), Korea ($6 billion) and Britain ($4 billion). The market grew by about 10 per cent a year during 2000–2010 because of increases in the prices of consoles and games, the frequency with which online games could be updated, more sophisticated pricing models (e.g. freemium) and the increase in 'serious' games, but the growth rate has since slowed.

The main companies in terms of revenue are Nintendo, followed by France's Vivendi, which bought Activision Blizzard in 2008 and sold it in 2013, and America's Electronic Arts. All these companies work closely with developers around the world through a variety of commissions, joint-ventures, first-look deals and investments. The growth of online games has seen new companies such as DeNA (Japan), Gree (Japan) and Nexon (Korea), all three of which are considerably more profitable than the older companies and also more profitable than Sony.

America. The market is worth $15 billion. Of this, console games take $9 billion, online games $3 billion and PC games $0.5 billion, and advertising brings in another $2 billion. Although the consoles are still dominant, the market is increasingly driven by online games and apps played on a freemium basis.

Europe. Consumer expenditure is $18 billion, consisting of $9 billion on console and handheld games, $6 billion on online and wireless games and $2 billion on PC games. Advertising brings in $600 million. The market has been steady for some years but its profile is changing as console revenues decline and online revenues increase. Online gaming is expected to overtake consoles in 2014. Britain is the largest market, followed by France and Germany. There are many small but world-class games developers in Britain, Ireland, Switzerland, the Netherlands, France and Germany but the only major company is France's Vivendi.

Britain. The market is worth $3.7 billion, up from $350 million in 1990. It is divided into consoles ($2.2 billion), online games ($0.8

billion), PC-based games ($0.3 billion) and wireless/smartphone/tablet games ($0.3 billion). Advertising expenditure is $0.1 billion.

The industry declined from 2009 to 2011 but recovered slightly in 2012. Few companies keep their independence as it is tempting to sell out to America. Richard Branson sold Virgin Interactive to America's Viacom, Bullfrog and Playfish went to Electronic Arts and Rockstar went to Take Two. The leading independent company is Mind Candy, whose Moshi Monsters sell to children aged six to 12, a kind of QQ for kids, with treats and pets, a 'rox' currency and Britain's best-selling children's magazine.

China. The market is worth about $6–8 billion and consists almost entirely of online games. The three major consoles have been banned since 2000 and would-be users have to get illegal imports or domestic clones or go online. Anyway, many Chinese enjoy being part of a group and prefer online networking and MMOGs. In 2011, China accounted for 35 per cent of global spending on online games.

The largest company is Tencent, which is bigger than Electronic Arts and Activision Blizzard combined. Other major companies are Shanda, whose founder Chen Tianqiao briefly became China's richest man; and NetEase, which operates 163.com and won the franchise for *World of Warcraft* from Zhu Jun's The9. There are only a few Chinese developers and Tencent and Shanda license most of their games from Korea, America and Japan.

DESIGN

Architecture

Architects design buildings and infrastructure for the construction industry. They are client-led and dependent on investors and developers raising finance and commissioning projects. Most firms operate as partnerships. There are trends towards large companies merging to bring in a wider range of professional and technical expertise, although, at the other end of the scale, an increasing number of architects are working in one- or two-partner firms.

The construction market is worth $5–7 trillion. The wide variation in estimates is due to uncertainties following the financial crisis in America and Europe, which caused many clients to postpone or cancel projects. China is the world's largest construction market ($1.25 trillion), followed by America and Japan, with European countries including Britain ($200 billion) far behind, although France has two of the world's top ten construction firms, Vinci and Bouygues. The 2011 report *Global Construction 2020* forecast that future growth would be greatest in China (almost doubling to $2.25 trillion by 2020, 25 per cent of the world total), steady in India, Brazil and America and negligible in Europe. It forecast Japan's expenditures would decline by 16 per cent.

An architect's sketches are protected by copyright, as are the scale drawings and models and all the artistic and literary works and designs up to and including the building itself. The person who commissions or buys a new building does not normally want or acquire copyright in it, just as someone who buys a painting does not get the copyright. Richard Rogers's firm once used copyright to prevent a client making last-minute changes but such occasions are very rare.

It is one of the most international sectors. It does not rely on words and its contemporary iconography is independent of any one nation or culture. There is nothing British about Tate Modern nor Chinese about Beijing's National Stadium (the Bird's Nest) which were both designed by the same Swiss firm Herzog & de Meuron. Governments that strictly limit cultural imports in other sectors frequently appoint foreign architects to design buildings of the greatest national and cultural sensitivity, such as when the German government asked Briton Norman Foster to design its new Reichstag parliament in Berlin.

Global. Architect firms have combined revenues of about $90–100 billion. Of the top 30 firms in terms of revenues, America and Japan have 20 between them, with British firms in third place. Data on company size and revenues should be treated with caution, however, because most large firms offer a wide range of advisory services, of which architecture is only one part.

There are about one million registered architects in the world.

Japan claims the largest number because it makes little distinction between architects and other kinds of designers (370,000), followed by Italy (111,000), America (80,000), Brazil (80,000), Germany (50,000) and Britain (30,000). China has 36,000 and the number is increasing rapidly.

America. The total design, building and construction market is worth $400 billion. To supply this, members of the American Institute of Architects have gross revenues of $26 billion, which is a 40 per cent fall from the $44 billion earned in 2008. Their net revenues, excluding sub-contracted work, were $15 billion. There are about 80,000 practising architects and 100,000 related professional people. Since 2000, there have been trends to mergers to enable firms to provide a wider range of skills but, in contrast, more than a quarter of AIA members in 2012 were working as sole traders.

Europe. Europe's construction sector was hard hit by the financial crisis and so large-scale commissions to architects became scarce. We estimate the market for architecture is worth about $15 billion, less than in 2000. The largest market is Germany ($4 billion), followed by Britain and France. The main sectors are urban regeneration, museums, commercial property and infrastructure.

Britain. The market is worth about $3 billion. Company revenues are $4.8 billion, which includes $2.5 billion domestic revenues and $2.3 billion from exports (the difference between the market total and British architects' revenues is accounted for by foreign firms). Britain now matches America in the number of its so-called starchitects, such as Norman Foster, Italian-born Richard Rogers, David Chipperfield, Tanzanian-born David Adjaye and Iranian-born Zaha Hadid.

China is the world's fastest growing construction market and has about 20 million people working in about 50,000 construction companies, which have revenues of $1.25 trillion. It is the biggest building boom in history. The work is divided about equally between buildings, where architects lead, and infrastructure, where they work alongside planners and engineers. The government reports market revenues of $24 billion.

For many years Chinese architects had little status and were poorly paid and new buildings were designed by in-house architects or occasionally by a local company working with a foreign architect with the Chinese partner in a secondary role. This is now changing, helped by many newly qualified Chinese architects as well as by Chinese architects returning from overseas. All global firms now have a Chinese presence and are hiring local architects. The first Chinese architect to win the prestigious Pritzker Prize, often described as architecture's Nobel Prize, was Wang Shu, who won the German Schelling Prize in 2010, the French Gold Medal in 2011 and the Pritzker Prize in 2012 at the relatively young age of 48. His small-scale minimalist aesthetics, always well integrated into the site, are beautifully evident in the Chinese Academy of Arts' Xiangshan campus.

Design

Design is the conscious improvement of something so it fulfils its function better, perhaps by being more elegant or more beautiful or just more fun. The successes like the Coca-Cola logo, the Nike swoosh and the 'No Entry' street sign are global icons, although few people could name their authors (respectively, Frank Robertson, Carolyn Davidson and a committee of Swiss bureaucrats, proving that committees can do good work if they try). Product design is intrinsic to manufacturing and as a country's manufacturing industry grows or declines so does its design sector. The market for industrial design is increasing in China, Japan, Brazil and Russia but declining in most European countries and America.

In the past, the 'something' described above was always a product and design was always product design. Modern designers are more ambitious. The Industrial Design Society of America (IDSA) defines design as the 'creation and development of concepts and specifications that optimize the function, value and appearance of products and systems for the mutual benefit of users and manufacturers'.

This catch-all mix symbolizes designers' belief that their conceptual skills are applicable to virtually all areas of human endeavour. They like to quote the Hungarian Bauhaus designer László Moholy-Nagy: 'Design is not a profession but an attitude.' America includes medical services as part of design, China includes planning and Britain includes the design of databases. Britain's Design Council says: 'Design is all around you, everything man-made has been designed, whether consciously or not', and uses design as a synonym for 'intelligent thinking' or 'innovation'. One admires the ambition but a 'concept' that optimizes the 'value' of a 'system' is so wide-ranging that it is almost meaningless. Every time designers make such claims they make their work less identifiable and harder to measure.

The evidence is inconclusive. Research by the London Business School shows that for every 1 per cent of sales devoted to new product design a company's sales and profits will rise on average by 3–4 per cent a year. The Design Council tracked a group of companies that used design intensively over a ten-year period between 1994 and 2004 and compared them to less active design-users. The design-intensive firms outperformed their peers by 200 per cent through both bull and bear equity markets. Yet even those companies ranked management and money as higher priorities. This raises the question as to whether design is an input which can be controlled and enhanced, as designers claim, or one of many outputs like style or convenience.

A design can qualify as an artistic work for copyright and for a separate design right, which is like copyright but lasts fewer years. It can also be registered and get a stronger level of protection. This is complicated enough but, in addition to these national rights, WIPO offers a global design right and the EU offers a European design right. There is strong evidence that this proliferation does not result in a higher level of protection but only leads to confusion. Many designers regard design rights as vague and weak and rely more on trademarks and brands.

The *global* market is worth about $165 billion, of which America, Germany and Japan account for as much as two-thirds. Some of the larger firms offer a wide range of skills from engineering design to architecture but size counts for little and even the largest corporate client is as likely to hire a small consultancy of 10 people as one of the giants. In this respect, design is like advertising and clients want to work with individually talented people who are in touch with new thinking.

America. The market is worth $41 billion. Turnover and fees grew between 1995 and 2000 by 15 per cent a year but have declined since then. The IDSA's research into recruitment and training suggest the four most sought-after skills for would-be designers are 'creative problem-solving; 2D concept sketching; verbal and written communication; and the processing of materials and manufactures'. Software skills rated fifth. The National Endowment for the Arts reckons there are 850,000 designers.

Europe's market is worth about $39 billion but revenues are declining as in America. National expenditures closely match per capita income, being highest in Germany, helped by its manufacturing sector, followed by Britain, Italy and France and the Nordic group of Sweden, Finland, Norway and Denmark. National approaches vary widely from France's highly structured industry, dominated by a few large companies, to the more diverse Swedish, Danish and British markets.

Britain. The industry is worth $8 billion a year, divided about equally between companies' in-house budgets and independent consultants. The word 'designer' is used as loosely as in America unless a prefix such as graphic or interior indicates a specific activity. As a result, it is difficult to estimate the number of people for whom design is a significant part of their work but most estimates range around 60,000 full-time designers.

China's market is worth about $25 billion. Given its isolation and its disdain for consumer choice or product aesthetics during most of the 20th century, its growth since 2000 has been impressive. The main sector is product design. Chinese design companies employ about 1.2 million people including support staff and Beijing alone claims 250,000 professional designers, generating $12 billion sales annually. Designers acknowledge their work is not yet competitive globally but the potential is huge because of the country's strong manufacturing base (it is the world's largest manufacturer of furniture, exporting $38 billion, one-quarter of world trade). Over 1,000 design schools were reportedly opened between 2000 and 2010 and Wang Min, Dean of the School of Design, Beijing, estimates one million students are currently studying design.

India matches China's growth in software and information technologies but lags behind in design. Darlie Koshy, Director-General of the Institute for Apparel Management, says: 'We have 800,000 technologists in the country but hardly 1,000 designers.'

Fashion

Fashion is an intensely competitive business which creates styles and brands for as many consumer products as possible. It is a volatile mix of art, craft, design, manufacturing, retailing and publicity. The designer fashion sector is the most public tip, with a fame and visibility disproportionate to its size, of the world's textile, garment, footwear and accessories sectors.

The old gap between couture and mass market has almost disappeared. Today, designers and brand-owners use high-end designs as one of many ways to drive high street sales, and not just in garments but in accessories, perfumes, watches and other lines. In the old model, designers created a few styles for a small clientele. Today, the world's two largest companies, Spain's Inditex, owner of Zara, and Sweden's Hennes & Mauritz, which also owns COS, manage what Inditex calls 'a non-stop flow of information from stores which conveys shoppers' desires to us'. As in other creative markets, fashion is increasingly dependent on logistics, retail and online networks.

A work of fashion is protected by copyright if it is made with 'individual skill and effort' and thus qualifies as an artistic work, so a handmade dress is protected by copyright but a mass-produced dress is not. In practice, manufacturers benefit from a degree of copying to help new trends to become widespread quickly while they are still in fashion. Fashion has worked out how to be wonderfully, endlessly inventive without needing strict copyright and relies more on trademarks, trade secrets and other forms of protection (including tight security) as well as company pride and peer pressure to inhibit people from copying too blatantly.

The trend to 'fast fashion' means many new clothes are cheap enough to be worn a few times and thrown away; seasons have shrunk from twice a year to a few weeks. Zara and H&M expect to get a new design from the catwalk into customers' hands within four weeks and they reckon to launch about 12,000 new items every year. For them, the design is only one starting point and manufacturing, logistics and marketing are more important. They seldom advertise individual items because each is in stock for such a short time.

Fashion events have begun to attract people in other sectors who are looking for new trends. Patrick Le Quément, the Renault designer who was responsible for its quirky reverse-angled hatchbacks, started going to Milan's fashion shows around 2000 and says he was then the only car designer present. Ten years later, many of the big car, electronics and media companies send their top designers to fashion shows, art shows and anywhere else they can get inside information on new ideas.

The *global* market for garments, children's clothes and accessories is about $1.2 trillion and the high-end designer market is worth $45 billion. The largest high-end markets are America, China, Germany, Japan, France, Italy and Britain. The major top-end companies are headquartered in New York, Paris or Milan and manage a variety of operations from design to direct sales, licensing and retail. In all countries except China, the sales of designers' accessories are growing faster than the sales of clothes.

The largest mass market company is Inditex ($20.7 billion), followed by H&M ($16.2 billion), Gap ($15.7 billion) and Fast Retailing's Uniqlo ($11 billion). The luxury sector is dominated by a few conglomerates such as Bernard Arnault's LVMH (with $29 billion revenues in 2011, of which $11 billion come from fashion) and François Pinault's Kering, formerly PPR ($12 billion).

America. The total market is worth $71 billion and designer fashion is worth $8 billion. Over 90 per cent of clothes bought are imports. The industry is based in New York, whose wholesale and retail businesses provided 175,000 jobs in 2010, 6 per cent of the city's private sector employment, and had a wage bill of $10 billion and a tax bill of $1.7 billion. Top American brand names include Gap, American Apparel, Ralph Lauren, Abercrombie & Fitch and Tommy Hilfiger as well as VF, which owns Lee, Wrangler and North Face.

Europe. The market is worth $84 billion and the high-end designer market is worth about $15 billion. Market size matches per capita spending and the largest markets are Germany, France and Italy. Of major companies, Inditex is based in Spain, as is Mango, and H&M is based in Sweden. The main designer brand-holders are centred in Paris and Milan, followed by London.

Britain. The total market is worth about $32 billion and the high-end designer market is worth about $4 billion. About one in three British people buy clothes online (Mintel) and online sales rose by 152 per cent from 2005 to 2010.

Britain has few brand leaders. Savile Row is the fashion equivalent of Rolls-Royce cars and West End theatre combined but sales are small. The largest company is Burberry, with revenues of $2.7 billion, of which about one quarter come from China. Other leading companies are Mulberry, Paul Smith (partly owned by Itochu, Japan) and Alexander McQueen and Stella McCartney (both owned by Kering). It excels in fashion colleges such as Central St Martins and Chelsea but many graduates go abroad to work.

China is by far the world's largest manufacturer of textiles and garments, mostly for export. Its markets range from international luxury brands in Asian-style malls to large stores with national and international brands and a spreading number of small boutiques where one or two designers sell their own output. We estimate a total market of $45 billion (cities only) and a high-end market of around $7 billion. Expenditure per capita is only about $100, one-tenth the amount in America, so there is room for expansion. Women's and men's expenditures are about the same, whereas in rich countries women outspend men by 3:1.

The leading casual brand is Metersbonwe which was founded by Zhou Chengjian in 1995 and now has over 3,000 stores in China and revenues of $1.4 billion (2012) of which about one-quarter are online. The name is Chinese but could be English and the company's stores give more prominence to the English version. Belle has about one quarter of the sportswear market and about the same of the shoe market and earns $5.6 billion revenues. Gao Dekang's Bosideng, the leading manufacturer of padded down clothing for over 15 years, has $1.3 billion revenues from its 7,000 stores in China and opened a $45 million store in London in 2012 which, like Metersbonwe, downplays the Chinese connection. Leading glamour designers include Masha Ma, Ma Ke and Uma Wang, who trained at Central St Martins, and Wanda Zhou. Some Chinese designers work with traditional designs but it is a small market.

Toys and Games

The design, manufacture and sale of toys and games are affected by the growth of film, TV and video games in two ways. On the one hand, the media provide a never-ending source of new products; on the other hand, children want to spend less time playing with physical toys and more time in front of a screen.

The name of a toy or a game can be trademarked, and its design and artistic elements, such as the printed design of a board game, can be protected by copyright, but the rules, even though they might be the heart of the game, cannot be protected. British patent legislation specifically excludes rules for 'playing a game'.

The industry consists of a large number of developers and a much smaller number of publishers. The publishers tend to employ their own developers since they now make most money out of redeveloping and updating old games and in licensing characters from books, TV and film. Apart from media spin-offs, new toys and games are rare.

The *global* market is worth about $60 billion, about the same as the more visible video games market, and continues to grow.

America. The market is worth $21.2 billion, about 40 per cent of the global market. After falling for several years, it increased by 2 per cent in 2011.

Europe. The market is worth $17 billion. The largest markets are Britain, France and Germany. Britain's purchases are driven by licences from American and Japanese media companies whereas other countries prefer local toys that reflect their own culture. Europe's own industry is concentrated in Germany, Italy, Spain and France and earns $5 billion, including $1 billion from exports.

Britain. The market is worth $4 billion and growing steadily as a result of British children's fascination with American TV and films. British parents are unusual in buying toys throughout the year whereas other countries restrict them to special occasions (leading UNICEF to criticize British parents for 'compulsive consumerism').

China. The market is worth $8.6 billion, an increase of 18 per cent over 2010, and focused on simple traditional games. China is also the world's major producer of games, exporting $20 billion and supplying 80 per cent of toys bought worldwide.

MEDIA

Advertising

Advertising has a love-hate relationship with creativity. In his revealing book *Confessions of an Advertising Man*, David Ogilvy, founder of Ogilvy & Mather, wrote: 'I tell new recruits that I will not allow them to use the word creative to describe the functions they are to perform in the agency.' Over 30 years later, Lee Clow, Chairman of TBWA Chiat/Day, gave the opposite and more modern view when he said: 'I am an artist who happens to be in the advertising business.'

Advertising agencies are widening their scope beyond the traditional outlets of press, TV and outdoor media and exploring new opportunities to promote their clients' logos, brand names and slogans. Agencies are beginning to make more money from the internet and sponsorship than from display advertising. To achieve this, they face a challenge. They need to learn new skills (new to them, at least) of marketing and merchandising and to compete with the many strategy and design companies, often younger and more nimble, which already have these skills.

It is moving from being a copyright business to both a copyright and a trademark business. Agencies use many copyright works as well as creating their own copyright, although ironically some of their most famous slogans, especially the simple ones, such as 'Go to Work on an Egg', were judged to lack the requisite skill and labour. As they move into marketing, so they become involved in the creation of trademarks and brands. As more websites develop algorithms to match advertisements to users, so it becomes a patent business.

There are two ways to measure advertising. The first is to give the figures for advertisers' expenditure on their agencies (the *agency market*) regardless of how much the advertisers also spend on media. The second is advertisers' expenditure on media (the *media market*). I give both sets of data: first, the amount spent on agencies; second, the amount spent on the media. In calculating market size, I use the former figure, since the latter payments appear as revenues of TV and other media and to include them here would be double-counting.

Agencies

The *global* agency market for the creation and development of advertising is worth $58 billion (*Advertising Age*). The market is dominated by agencies in New York and London, followed by Frankfurt and Paris and regional centres like São Paulo, Bangkok and Beijing. Most of the best-known agencies are part of global groups such as the newly merged Omnicom ($14 billion), and Publicis ($8 billion) followed by WPP ($10 billion) and Interpublic ($7 billion).

There are two exceptions to these groups' reach. Japan operates almost as a separate market in which the Dentsu agency ($3.6 billion) is dominant nationally, although it is weak in other countries. The other exception is China.

America. The agency market is worth $24 billion, including agency expenditures on marketing services ($4.7 billion) and public relations ($3.4 billion). American-owned agencies dominate the global business because American brand-owners are the major advertisers worldwide.

Europe. The agency market is worth $20 billion. The two main centres are London for English-language clients and Frankfurt for German-language clients. Other cities have lower levels of expenditure.

Britain. The agency market is worth $7 billion. This relatively high figure is due to the large number of global advertisers using London as their base for international campaigns. The core workforce, defined as those employed in member agencies of the IPA, is 15,000 people but the total workforce is about 250,000.

China. The agency market is relatively undeveloped. We estimate

$3 billion. Many advertisers, and all large state-owned enterprises, use their in-house creative teams and do not make a clear demarcation between strategy, marketing, branding and advertising; or indeed editorial.

Media Expenditure

These amounts are dwarfed by advertisers' expenditure on media, which includes all places where advertising can be displayed (the *media market*). Media budgets grew steadily from the 1970s to 2008 and provided most of the cash for the expansion of TV, radio, newspapers and magazines. The total amount spent on media worldwide in 2012 was $450–500 billion, depending on how much online media expenditure is included. According to Nielsen, the online market rose from $2.5 billion in 2000 to $72 billion in 2012.

Nearly half the world's advertising expenditure is spent on American and Japanese media and three-quarters is spent in ten markets:

Table 4: Advertising expenditure on media
worldwide (PwC, 2012)

Country	$ (billion)	Percentage of expenditure
America	172	35
Japan	51	10
China	36	7
Germany	25	5
Britain	20	4
France	14	3
Brazil	14	3
Australia	13	3
Canada	12	2
Korea	11	2
Rest of the world	128	26
Total	496	100

Another yardstick is the expenditure on different media: TV ($197 billion), newspapers ($93 billion), magazines ($43 billion), radio ($34 billion) and outdoor ($32 billion). As media move online so advertising follows, reaching an additional $95 billion in 2012, but the transition is difficult both for the media company and the advertiser.

America. Of its $172 billion total, TV advertising took $72 billion, by far the largest chunk, followed by newspapers ($26 billion), magazines ($20 billion) and radio ($18 billion). America's TV, radio and newspapers are city-based and more local than in other countries and so pick up a lot of local advertising. Online added $36 billion.

Europe. The European market for media advertising is $119 billion. The largest market is Germany ($25 billion), followed by Britain ($20 billion), France ($14 billion) and Italy ($12 billion). PwC expects seven years to pass before annual expenditures recover to match the $123 billion reached in 2007.

Britain. Britain's media expenditures are $22 billion. It is notable for having a higher proportion of advertising ($11 billion) spent online than any other country.

China. Media expenditures were $36 billion, up from $20 billion in 2007. The Chinese have fewer restrictions on locations where advertising can be placed, compared with other countries, and public tolerance is higher, offering more opportunities for growth.

Elsewhere, *Indian* and *Brazilian* expenditures grew at 12–13 per cent a year over the past three years and *Russian* expenditures grew at 30 per cent in the same period, though from a very low base. *Japan*'s long recession saw a further decline (−3 per cent in 2011). There is little growth in the rest of the world.

Press (*Newspapers and Magazines*)

Newspapers and magazines (press) share many elements with books (publishing). Both depend on words and both industries have publishers and publications. However, there are fundamental differences. First, newspapers and magazines are primarily funded by advertising whereas books are funded entirely by consumer sales. Second, the press is a brand business and people buy a brand rather than the specific content whereas few book publishers have a strong consumer brand and sales depend more on the writer and subject.

All newspapers and magazines are engaged in the difficult task of moving their content online. It is relatively easy to move the editorial online, although not as easy as it might seem, but much harder to replace the physical edition's advertising revenues or over-the-counter sales. A few newspapers with a business readership have moved to a pay-model, such as News Corp's London *The Times* and the *Wall Street Journal*, but the majority allows users to read everything for free and try to build up online advertising. In all cases, access fees and online advertising have not yet replaced the loss of print advertising, even though some online services are more popular than their print version.

The ease of starting an online news business has allowed many new publishers and bloggers to move in. One of the most successful is the *Huffington Post*, which was launched in 2005 and sold to AOL for $315 million in 2011. After the sale, many bloggers who had written for free launched a legal claim for a share of the proceeds but the courts said they had knowingly written for free and could not later seek to change that implicit agreement. It was an interesting insight in the economics of blogging.

Newspapers and magazines are treated in separate sections for the time being but as they move online their different formats and publication frequencies will become less distinctive and they will merge into one sector.

Newspapers

Global. The world's newspapers have revenues of $164 billion, consisting of advertising revenues of about $94 billion, down from $130 billion five years ago, and sales revenues of $70 billion. Global daily sales are about 520 million copies, led by India (110 million copies of an astonishing total of 65,000 titles), China (109 million), Japan (50 million), America (46 million), Germany (20 million) and Britain (14 million). Year by year, American and European readership and advertising revenues drop as readers move across to online services while in Asia, Africa and South America they are increasing.

Japan has five of the world's ten best-selling daily newspapers, headed by *Yomiuri Shimbun*, with 10 million daily sales, and followed by *Asahi Shimbun*, with 8 million. India has two titles in the top ten and China, Britain and Germany have one. In terms of readership, Icelanders read the most (96% of the adult population reads a paid newspaper every day), followed by Japan (92%), Norway, Sweden, Switzerland, Finland, Hong Kong, Singapore, Luxembourg and Austria. There is a strong correlation between high levels of political and cultural independence and high levels of newspaper readership.

America. It may seem surprising that America is not higher up the title rankings, since Americans are very news-conscious. The reason is that almost all American newspapers are city-based and so it has a large number of small-circulation local newspapers and few national papers. Another curiosity is that America's newspapers are primarily funded by bulky advertisement supplements, whereas other countries, especially Japan, rely mostly on sales. The country's 2,400 newspapers earned $32 billion in 2012, down from $60 billion in 2006. Their advertising revenue fell from $49 billion to $23 billion and sales revenue fell from $11 billion to $9 billion. These are huge drops, bigger than the fall in recorded music.

Europe. The market is worth $52 billion. The largest national markets are Germany (20 million sales), Britain (14 billion), France (7 billion) and Spain (4 billion). Germany's high sales and revenues of $12 billion are supported by its high levels of education and political awareness and its loyalties to local newspapers. Elsewhere revenues are falling. In France, all national newspapers lose money in spite of $1.54 billion annual subsidies.

Britain. Britain has a wide variety of titles and revenues of $9 billion coming about equally from advertising and unit sales. The *Daily Mail*'s Mailonline.com is the world's most-visited newspaper-based website, attracting 100 million unique visitors monthly. Its earnings were slow at first and only reached $30 million in 2012 but that was nearly enough to compensate its owner for the loss of print revenues.

China. The newspaper market is worth $18 billion, divided between $10 billion sales and $8 billion advertising. Newspapers are smaller and more restrained than elsewhere, with fewer pages and colour photographs. With a few exceptions, editorial is written according to Communist Party guidelines and it is easier to influence coverage for political as well as commercial reasons.

Magazines

The *global* market for consumer and business magazines is worth $98 billion. According to the International Federation of Periodical Publishers (FIPP), America publishes the most titles, followed by China, Britain, Germany, the Netherlands and Japan. The bulk of global revenues comes from advertising, which rises every year in absolute terms but falls as a proportion of total advertising expenditure. Publishers are experimenting with online versions and some are turning their printed edition into a free 'loss leader' to attract people to the website.

America. The magazine market is prolific, with both strong national titles and many regional and city-based titles, totalling 7,100 titles in all. Consumer titles earn $20 billion and business magazines earn $10 billion, but both sectors are declining.

Europe. The market is worth $29 billion, consisting of $10 billion consumer expenditure and $19 billion trade expenditure. The largest national market is Germany, which has a consumer market of $5.8 billion and a trade market of $2.6 billion. It is followed by France, with a total of $6.8 billion, Britain ($5.2 billion) and Italy ($4.2 billion).

Britain. The magazine market is worth $5.2 billion, consisting of $4.3 billion consumer titles and $0.9 billion trade magazines but advertising revenue and sales are both declining. Many publishers use their magazines to drive spin-offs like exhibitions, books and special offers which add about $2 billion to industry revenues.

China. Consumer, business and technology magazines started to take off in the 1990s and now number over 15,000. The market is worth about $5 billion. The government is gradually liberalizing its control over magazines on science, technology, sport and lifestyles but critical or investigatory reporting is rare. Foreign publishers can publish Chinese editions if they have a licence with a Chinese publisher.

TV and Radio

TV has evolved from a cumbersome technical device to the world's most popular entertainment medium. Its presence in every home in rich countries has substantial influence on lifestyles and entertainment and has financed a generation of celebrities and professional sports-players as well as being an integral part of politics and war. In spite of internet competition, TV viewing continues to rise to record levels and still attracts twice as much advertising worldwide as do newspapers, its nearest rival.

The principle of transmitting sounds and pictures to household receivers remains the same but the technology has changed from VHF to UHF, from analog to digital, and from terrestrial to cable and satellite and the internet. In America and other rich countries people are increasingly likely to pay a premium to watch the programme of their choice at a time of their choice.

TV's future development depends on two technical developments. The first is better-quality and larger TV sets with high-definition (HD) and 3D images. The next is 'connected' sets that can display images direct from the internet and interweave broadcasting's one-to-many services with the internet's capability for one-to-one interactive services.

As a technical invention, broadcasting started as a patent business. The first broadcasts were live because it was technically impossible to record the huge amount of data contained in a moving image until Ampex invented a powerful-enough 2-inch video recording format in 1956. The invention of videotape launched the TV production industry and added a copyright business. A TV programme is treated as a 'film' and qualifies for copyright; and each broadcast counts as a performance. Recently, the growth of multi-channel packages puts more emphasis on branding and marketing. So TV has developed from being only a patent business to being mostly a copyright business and a trademark business.

Radio continues to be a minor success, illustrating the principle that old media seldom die. Global revenues are $47 billion, consisting of $32 billion on advertising and $15 billion on public licence fees and subscriptions to satellite-delivered channels. American radio has an income of $18 billion. Europe's revenues are $15 billion, of which the main markets are Germany ($4.7 billion), France ($2.3 billion) and Britain ($1.8 billion). In Britain, BBC Radio receives $1.0 billion from the licence fee and commercial radio earns advertising revenue of $0.8 billion. Other European markets are much smaller. Japan's radio market is worth $4.5 billion and China's $1.6 billion.

Global TV revenues are $425 billion. The main sources are advertising ($197 billion) and channel subscriptions ($196 billion). Government-levied household licence fees add $31 billion and mobile channels add $1 billion.

There are about 2 billion TV homes. The biggest markets are China (400 million), India (148 million), America (116 million), Russia (65 million) and Japan (60 million). Britain has 26 million TV homes. In revenue terms, the biggest markets by far are America ($142 billion) and Japan ($43 billion), followed by China at about $21 billion. Britain, Germany, Brazil and Italy each have $18–20 billion.

America. The TV market is worth $145 billion. Advertising revenues (spot advertising and sponsorship) of the four main networks (ABC, CBS, NBC and Fox) and the 1,774 local stations total $72 billion and are fairly steady. Subscriptions bring in about the same, $71 billion, and are increasing. The networks lost audience share for decades but their revenues increased when they found ways to charge cable and satellite networks for re-transmitting their signals.

Europe. The total market is worth $105 billion, about two-thirds coming from pay-TV subscriptions and government licence fees and one-third from advertising. The Big Four markets are France with $18.9 billion fees and $4.9 billion advertising, Britain with $12.6 million fees and $5.7 billion advertising; Germany with $12.1 billion fees and $5.7 billion advertising; and Italy with $6.3 billion fees and $5.9 billion advertising. These four countries alone make up nearly three-quarters of Europe's total TV revenues.

The *British* market is worth $18.3 billion, consisting of a household licence fee (of which $4.3 billion is spent on TV), subscriptions for cable and satellite channels ($8.3 billion) and advertising ($5.7 billion). TV viewing has held up well and conventional so-called linear viewing, as distinct from on-demand viewing, reached an all-time record of four hours a day in 2011.

Since the birth of Channel Four in 1982, and the government's subsequent regulation of the business terms of trade between producers and broadcasters, Britain has had a thriving independent production sector and is a major exporter of programmes, especially studio-based formats and drama.

China. Market expenditures are about $22 billion, of which advertising contributes $14 billion and fees $8 billion. The government makes additional annual grants of about $6 billion for infrastructure and programming.

CCTV has 18 channels but its programming is relatively bland and regional companies compete strongly on news and entertainment. Hunan Satellite Broadcasting, the second largest station, produces *Super Girls*, later re-named *Happy Girls*, and *XFactor*. Programming restrictions, and the country's high use of online media, have led to a rapid rise in the market for online video services ranging from Chinese re-runs to user-generated material and American series. The online market was worth $1.6 billion in 2012. The largest networks are Youku and Tudou which merged in 2012 and have 450 million regular users and a combined market share of 31 per cent.

INNOVATION

Innovation today is becoming broader and more interesting than when it meant R&D into technology and was restricted to research in laboratories. Today, innovation covers hi-tech products ranging from materials to biotech as well as processes such as logistics, education and healthcare. It includes incremental change as well as big step-changes. Its purposes can be social welfare as much as commercial profit. China Bridge's design of a mobile phone for partially sighted people caught people's attention as much for its social benefits as its commercial value. There is growing interest in 'frugal' innovation, such as Tata's ingenious 'one lakh' car (about $3,000), and in sustainable innovation, such as the 'cradle-to-cradle' movement and the Maker Movement.

Every country wants to be more innovative and it is tempting to see innovation everywhere. The European Union likes to describe itself as an Innovation Union. The result is a kind of inflation in which every change is called an innovation (in the same way as designers, claiming every example of clever thinking as design, create a kind of design inflation). A Global Innovation Index compiled by WIPO and the INSEAD Business School defines innovation as 'the implementation of a new or significantly improved product, a new process, a new marketing method or new organizational method in business practices, workplace organization or external relations'. It is hard to see what is not included.

This section covers three kinds of innovation. It starts with research, which is still the most widespread way of producing innovation, and then looks at software and dotcoms.

Research

The research and development (R&D) carried out by governments, companies, universities and non-profit organizations can be divided into basic 'blue sky' research, applied research and development research. Basic research is favoured by academics who want to be free from commercial criteria while companies are more interested in commercial applications and business development. It is mainly a patent business. Not all R&D leads to a patent, as the research may be 'blue sky' or theoretical or lead to a dead-end, but almost all patents grow out of research.

R&D can be measured in several ways. The most common criteria are market expenditure and the number of patents (in this section, as throughout, the word patent refers to invention or utility patents and not petty, design or plant patents). R&D expenditure shows the work done (or at least its cost), which is useful but does not measure the result. The number of patents measures one kind of result but only crudely because it does not indicate a patent's quality or its impact.

The relationship between innovation and patents is further muddled by the growing tendency in America and China to apply for patents on a speculative basis in order to build 'patent thickets' to block out other inventors or promote the patent-holder in the eyes of investors or government funders. It is clear that patents are only one indicator. Nonetheless they provide a historical record in easy-to-compare numbers and investors like them, as do governments, for that reason.

Global: R&D market expenditure. Global spending increased at a slightly faster rate than national GDP for several decades until the 2008 crisis. America, Japan and Europe increased their gross expenditure on R&D (known as GERD) by about 5 per cent a year between 2000 and 2008. China, Brazil and Russia did even better, doubling their expenditure over the same period, and raising their combined contribution from 15 per cent of global expenditure in 2000 to 28 per cent in 2010. The world's total GERD rose from $1,250 billion in 2010 to $1,469 billion in 2012.

Table 5: The top global R&D markets (NSF, 2011)

Countries	R&D	
	$ bn	*Percentage of GDP*
America	419	2.7
China	197	1.6
Japan	160	3.5
Germany	91	2.9
Korea	56	3.5
France	50	2.2
Britain	42	1.8
India	41	0.8
Russia	37	1.5
Brazil	26	1.3
Canada	29	2.0
Rest of the world	321	n/a
Total	1469	n/a

The financial crisis saw a temporary fall in America's expenditure, the first for 20 years, and a bigger fall in Japan. In both countries, the immediate cause was a drop in corporate budgets followed by government cuts. China continues to spend more each year and overtook Japan in 2012 to become the second biggest R&D market after America.

The American research institute Battelle uses this NSF data to forecast GERD will grow to $1,496 billion in 2013. This is an impressive increase from the $800 billion spent ten years earlier. It forecasts China will overtake Europe in 2019 and America in 2023.

Of the $1,469 billion, industry contributes about 75 per cent. The biggest spenders are Toyota, Roche, Microsoft, Volkswagen, Pfizer, Novartis, Nokia, Johnson & Johnson, Sanofi and Samsung. The list is dominated by old companies with the exception of Microsoft, although its 40-year history is a long time in software. Their annual budgets range from Samsung's $6.8 billion to Toyota's $9.9 billion.

A list of newer software and dotcom companies is notable for being even more dominated by American companies. Europe is slipping (Vivendi's position is partly due to its purchase of American companies). China appears for the first time. All companies appear to be spending less:

Table 6: Software/Dotcom expenditure on R&D

Company	Country	$ bn
Intel	America	5.3
Cisco	America	5.2
Google	America	3.0
Qualcomm	America	2.3
LG	Korea	2.2
Huawei	China	2.1
Amazon	America	1.6

(*Continued*)

Table 6: (*Continued*)

Company	Country	$ bn
Apple	America	1.6
Yahoo!	America	1.3
Vivendi	France	1.3
Electronic Arts	America	1.3

If we look at these companies closely we see that they are more likely to be spending differently than spending less. All the American companies on the list started as a small group of young graduates in which everyone was expected to pitch in and be smart, and they still operate this way. For them, R&D is a routine part of the job. It helps that they can afford to go it alone without government subsidy and do not need to make artificial budgetary divisions between routine business and research in order to qualify for grants. They are also not required to do expensive clinical trials or product testing.

What is not shown by these figures is how these companies benefit from R&D done by their suppliers. Apple benefits when developers carry out R&D on apps which Apple then makes available to iPhones and iPads. Facebook benefits when companies like Playfish supply a game, because Playfish does all the work but Facebook gets more users. Facebook spends only 10 per cent of its revenues on R&D, generating higher than average margins, and achieving profits of 57 per cent, and often finds it quicker and cheaper to buy in research (when it wanted more expertise in mobile services it bought Instagram for $1 billion).

Another reason why software companies and dotcom companies appear to spend less is that they know research is only half the battle and they will have to spend just as much defending their patents in court. In 2011, Apple and Google spent more on patent lawsuits and patent purchases than on R&D.

Global: Patents. Companies made a total of 2.14 million patent applications in 2011. The largest number of applications was made in China (526,000), followed by America's 503,582 and Japan's 342,610. The Chinese figure was a staggering increase from the 63,000 applications made in 2002 (WIPO). The next largest numbers of applications were made in Germany, France, Britain, Switzerland, Netherlands and Russia.

A total of 7.3 million patents were in force in 2010 (WIPO). Of these, 2.1 million had been granted by the American PTO, 1.4 million by the Japan Patent Office and 697,000 by the China Patent Office.

America: R&D and Patents. In 2012, R&D expenditures rose to $419 billion. After a steady increase from $302 billion in 2004 to $404 billion in 2008, expenditures had stuttered in 2009 as companies cut back. Although licensing data is unreliable, it is reckoned that licence revenues are worth $300–350 billion a year. What is most remarkable about these figures, as well as their absolute size, is that they have increased 250 per cent since 1995. Corporate industry provides 64 per cent of all expenditure.

Table 7: Patents granted by American Patent and Trademark Office, by nationality of applicant (2012)

Country		Number of patents	Percentage of total
America		121,026	48
of which			
California	32,107		
Texas	8,367		
New York	7,640		
Mass.	5,734		
Washington	5,390		
Japan		50,677	20
Germany		13,835	6
South Korea		13,233	5
Taiwan		10,646	4
Canada		5,775	2
France		5,386	2
Britain		5,213	2
China		4,637	2
Italy		2,120	1
Rest of the world		20,607	8
Total		253,155	100

The company that made the most applications in 2012 as in most previous years was IBM, which filed 6,457. It was followed by Samsung (5,043), Canon (3,173), Panasonic (2,748), Toshiba (2,415) and Microsoft (2,610). Google made 1,151 and Apple made 1,136 applications.

Europe: R&D and Patents. Europe's expenditure on R&D was $346 billion, 1.9 per cent of GDP, most of which was spent in three countries, Germany, France and Britain, with smaller amounts in Italy, Spain, Sweden, Netherlands and Switzerland. By most measures, the innovation leaders are the Nordic trio of Sweden, Finland and Denmark, Germany's massive powerhouse and Britain and France but remarkably the EU's own survey admits that Switzerland, which like Norway is not part of the EU, continues to outperform all 27 member states. It casts an odd light on the EU's policies if a non-member beats them all.

Britain: R&D and Patents. Expenditure on R&D was $42 billion. The main spenders are business (64%), followed by universities (26%), government departments (9%) and non-profit organizations (1%). The total was 1.7 per cent of GDP, which is a remarkable decline from the 2.4 per cent spent in 1980. However, Britain still ranks high in terms of the quality of its research. With only 1 per cent of the world's population, it has 4 per cent of the world's researchers and produces 6 per cent of research papers and 10 per cent of the most-cited papers.

But the number of patents granted continues to fall from 10,000 at the beginning of the decade to 2,992 in 2011. Not only do British companies spend less but their research is less commercial and produces fewer patents. In 2011, British companies scored fewer than half the patents at home than did New York. R without the D.

China: R&D and Patents. China continues to consolidate its position as the second-largest sponsor of R&D, measured by the number of researchers (926,000), the expenditure on R&D ($197 billion, 1.6% of GDP) and the number of patents. It overtook Japan in 2010 to become the world's second-largest patent office and overtook

America in 2011 to become the largest. The national priorities are energy, information, health and the environment. The Chinese Academy of Sciences alone spends $36 billion but it knows money is not the best measure and complains its researchers are not innovative enough. Whereas Britain is good at blue sky research but not good at implementation, China has the opposite problem.

China has set a target of two million patents of all kinds by 2015, which David J. Kappos, director of the US Patent and Trademark Office, described as 'mind-blowing'. The target is likely to be achieved, although the State Intellectual Property Organization (SIPO) is frequently criticized for handing out patents too liberally. Having listened to Americans say for years that patent numbers are a mark of success, China is determined to be number one.

Japan has a smaller R&D budget than America but it spends more per capita and, year after year, files more patent applications. The Japanese Patent Office (JPO) received 344,000 in 2010, the overwhelming majority from Japanese applicants, which is partly the result of Japan's liking for formality but also due to the sheer volume of high-class research. The JPO estimates Japan's patent-based products to be worth over $2 trillion.

Software

The process begins with human-readable source code, which is a set of rules to instruct a computer to perform mathematical operations. After further steps of human-managed compilation and machine-managed execution the code delivers a program or application. Programmers play around with these processes and outcomes and sometimes also with the original source code. The difference between open source software (FOSS) and proprietary software is whether users are allowed open access to the source code.

The development of code and programming languages has been one of the outstanding achievements of the past 50 years. The people who developed COBOL, Fortran, C and Java as well as program languages like HTML must be counted as among the most creative

THE CREATIVE ECONOMY

people of the 20th century as, later, were Tim Berners-Lee, who wrote the first protocols for the World Wide Web, and the Americans who took his idea further. The innovations in commercial algorithms for dotcoms and operating systems show the same breakthrough ingenuity and novelty.

I have included digital markets that are part of an existing sector (for example, digital music is included in 'Music' (see p. 168)) but coders and programmers have their own habitats and niches, characteristic attitudes and business models, and merit a separate category. They also have their own distinctive approach to intellectual property. All countries recognize computer programs as a literary work for copyright protection and America also awards patents to a program-and-its-effect, while Europe has a separate copyright-like law to protect databases. But the collaborative nature of coding has led coders to take the lead in developing innovative licences like the General Public Licence and Creative Commons that allow others to use code and digital media in a user-friendly, non-commercial way.

The *global* hardware, software and related industries are worth $1.6–1.8 trillion, depending on how communication costs are allocated, and software makes up about $310 billion. The main markets are America, which accounts for 45 per cent of the total, Europe (25%) and Asia (20%). The American market is increasing but Asian markets are increasing more rapidly. The largest software companies are Microsoft, which has software revenues of $33 billion, followed by IBM ($14 billion), Oracle ($14 billion), SAP ($8 billion) and EMC ($4 billion). All these and other software companies listed below have significant revenues from other sources.

America. The American software market is worth $137 billion. Between 2000 and 2008 it grew at 12 per cent a year, two and a half times faster than the economy as a whole, but growth has slowed recently. The main companies are Microsoft, IBM, Oracle, EMC and Symantec. The industry employs 1.1 million people, who remarkably have average earnings of $85,000 a year, more than twice the national average of $37,000. It is the only American industry which has bucked the country's trend to a trading deficit in the face of Chinese competition.

Europe. The European software market is worth about $78 billion. The largest market is Germany, followed by the big three of Britain, France and Italy. The main companies are SAP, Sage, Dassault, Software AG and Misys.

Britain. The software market is worth $31 billion, of which leisure software is worth about $5 billion. The largest computer company is ARM (since Autonomy was sold to Hewlett-Packard in 2011 for $10 billion). The largest software companies are Sage, Misys, Logica and Acision.

China. It is difficult to estimate market size because many transactions take place between government organizations and are confidential. It has been estimated that the software market reached $35 billion in 2012, with probably an equal amount spent on unlicensed software. Compared to America and Europe, China spends proportionally less on software, about 10 per cent of the total. The national industry is booming and 1.5 million new software-related jobs were reportedly added between 2005 and 2010. The Ministry of Information Industries says the software and information industry earned $167 billion in 2010, of which software contributed $26 billion. The major companies are Neusoft, Ufida, Shanghai Baosight, CDC and Kingdee.

India. The Indian software market has grown quickly, especially in services. The leading companies are Tata, Infosys, 3i Infotech, Teledata and Persistant. The India Software Association estimates software sales provided 5.4 per cent of GDP and employment has risen from 160,000 in 1996 to 600,000 in 2011.

Dotcoms

Dotcoms are companies that are wholly online. We estimate a global market of $242 billion. Assessing national markets is difficult because many American companies use complicated financial structures to transfer revenues to low-cost territories in order to minimize tax.

The world's largest dotcoms by revenue are listed below:

Table 8: The world's largest dotcoms

Name	Country	Founded	Revenues ($ bn)	Business
Amazon	America	1994	61	e-commerce
Google	America	1998	50	search
eBay	America	1995	14	auctions
Tencent	China	1998	7	network
Yahoo	America	1995	5	network
Facebook	America	2004	5	network
Alibaba	China	1999	4	e-commerce
Netflix	America	1997	4	media
Baidu	China	2000	4	search
NetEase	China	1997	1	portal

Most of these companies have diversified. As well as buying Blogspot (now ranked 11th worldwide) in 2003 and YouTube (ranked 3rd) in 2007, Google has become the world's most astonishing source of new ideas from machine translation to mapping and driverless cars. Amazon is similarly adventurous with the Kindle and other devices and building up one of the world's biggest cloud servers. In China, Tencent's QQ.com (ranked 9th), which had 810 million active accounts in June 2013, is host to a range of networking, games, music and shopping services.

Their revenues come primarily from e-commerce or advertising. E-commerce sites attract the highest revenue overall and per-user due to their high transaction costs. Search engines earn the second largest amounts because advertisers want to pay to be top of the search rankings and because people who are searching for information are in the mood to look at advertisements. Social networks earn much less because their users want to connect with their friends in a semi-private space and do not want to be distracted, and so Facebook and Tencent are relatively constrained. Twitter earned very little until it decided bravely to incorporate ads as a normal tweet. Other sources of revenue are sponsorship, brand promotion and virtual gifts, which bring in about $3 billion globally. Linked-In's freemium services such as InMail and JobSearch earn $400 million.

America dominates the global dotcom market even more securely than Hollywood dominates the global film market. Their market values continue to soar even as their revenues stay low. Facebook's market capitalization reached $104 billion on its initial flotation in 2012 in spite of suspicions it was unprepared for the mobile web. Other leading network dotcoms are Twitter (10th) and Linked-In (13th), which have high visibility and traffic but relatively low revenues. Wikipedia is ranked 6th but is financed by donations ($34.8 million in 2012) and has no commercial revenues.

Europe. There are no European dotcoms in the global top 100. Most users prefer to use American dotcoms. Britain's then most popular dotcom, Gumtree (31st when ranked with all websites), was sold to eBay in 2005. The next most successful, IMDB, was sold to Amazon. Online media do better. In Britain, the BBC (7th nationally), the *Daily Mail* and the *Guardian* rank high even as they lose money.

China. The most popular Chinese dotcoms are Baidu (6th worldwide), Tencent's QQ (9th), Taobao (11th), Sina (16th) and 163 (31st). The leading micro-blogging site is Sina's Weibo, which has over half the market. Alibaba dominates China's e-commerce although its site ranks only 71st globally. It started as a business-only service but now enables users to sell to the public (Tmall) and the public to sell to each other (TaoBao). Its total transactions exceed Amazon and eBay combined.

THE GLOBAL TOTAL

Markets are growing at 2 per cent a year in America and Europe and twice as fast in Asia and elsewhere although this average hides wide variations. Recorded music and printed books, newspapers and magazines have been badly hit by online media. But the losses are temporary. Our desire for knowledge and entertainment are as strong as ever and new businesses will emerge.

They will emerge online. Dotcoms need little start-up money and can grow even if revenues are low (Facebook earns much less each year than do Europe's struggling newspaper owners). But the result is ferocious competition.

In all regions, economies will grow as more people move up the hierarchy of desires, are free to use their talents and have easier access to markets.

Table 9: The core markets (2012, $ billions)

	America	Europe*	Britain	China	Global
Arts and Culture					
Art	18	21	13	14	56
Books	37	48	6	13	135
Crafts	6	6	1	8	42
Film	33	25	6	3	90
Music	15	19	4	*	49
Performance	18	18	4	4	52
Video games	15	18	4	8	61
Design					
Architecture	26	15	3	24	95
Design	41	39	8	25	165
Fashion	8	15	4	7	45
Toys/Games	21	17	4	9	60
Media					
Ad agencies	24	20	7	3	58
Magazines	30	29	5	5	98
Newspapers	32	52	9	18	164
Radio	18	15	2	2	47
TV	145	105	18	22	425
Innovation					
R&D	419	310	42	197	1,469
Software	137	78	31	35	310
Dotcoms	n/a	n/a	n/a	n/a	242
Total	1,043	850	171	397	3,663

* The figures for Europe include Britain

** Under $0.5 billion

9
Cities: The Spaces In-between

A BOAT ON A ROOF

Cities and new ideas feed off each other. Cities provide hot-house conditions for change and diversity, generating fashions, entertainments and glamour in unstable combinations, marked by extremes of wealth and poverty, physical intimacy, noisy and full of follies. Creativity is sharpened, made more public and finds more buyers. The boundary between ecology and economy, between lifestyle and business, can be hard to detect and is often a matter of individual inclination. The shift from large-scale manufacturing to brain-scale thinking increases the city's attractions and volatilities and changes its mood and purpose.

In the summer of 2012 two of us stayed overnight in a boat called *Roi des Belges*, which had been designed to be placed high on the roof of the Southbank Centre in central London, overlooking the banks of the River Thames. Putting a boat on top of a concert hall is crazy, of course, but it worked, somehow. She had been commissioned by the radical arts group Artangel and designed by artist Fiona Bannerman and architect David Kohn. The boat's theme was the dark, mysterious journey told in Joseph Conrad's story *Heart of Darkness*, about the Belgian Congo in Africa, which became the source of Francis Ford Coppola's film *Apocalypse Now*. Previous occupants (sailors?) during its 12-month stay included Laurie Anderson and Jeanette Winterson.

The boat's prow hung out over the roof's edge and gave us a bird's-eye view of London from Big Ben to St Paul's Cathedral and, below, one of London's most popular open places. That evening, Artangel held its summer party in a nearby garden designed and looked after by homeless people and former drug addicts. Immediately below us and out of sight the Southbank Centre was hosting a Global Poetry Be-In of poets from 140 countries, which had been launched by a plane dropping 100,000 poems. The boat and the surroundings were an extreme example of Londoners' talent for using an existing building and its open spaces (open spaces are important) to host and orchestrate a bewitching series of happenings.

London's Southbank Centre, now over 60 years old, covers 21 acres and claims to be Europe's largest purpose-built cultural district. It was built for the 1951 Festival of Britain as a celebration of national hope after the terrors of war but since being re-opened in the 1960s its brutalist concrete architecture had aged badly and it had acquired a reputation for uncaring and bureaucratic owners. Music-lovers ducked inside to go to performances and did not want to hang around. Over the years there were numerous plans to revive the site, including a grand scheme by Richard Rogers, but the buildings' elephantine bulk seemed to deflect new ideas.

The problem seemed intractable and Londoners had almost given up hope when a new trio of businessman Clive Hollick, chief executive Michael Lynch and artistic director Jude Kelly switched the focus from the buildings to the spaces between them and to what the public could do in those spaces. They responded to changes in the licensing laws and encouraged cafes and restaurants. They welcomed stallholders and pop-up stores. They built stairs to the roofs for gardens (and boats). They built ramps for skateboarding. They invited in the London Eye ferris wheel, whose rent helped cover the costs. Two new walkways were built across the river.

None of these changes were artistic, cultural or creative in the strict sense of those words. They had no obvious connection with the Southbank Centre's official functions of music and arts. They were not part of any government plan. On the contrary, the new managers applied for a five-year immunity from government registration to give them the freedom they wanted. Their plan succeeded and the public came to love the new scene because they could be part of the action.

The original buildings were an excellent example of top-down government planning. The regeneration of its surrounding spaces showed how people want to live in cities today.

Our brains develop faster in families that like to play together and learn together, we work better in companies that treat us as grown-ups and expect us to have our own ideas, without being asked, and we thrive in neighbourhoods and cities that have a Quad culture of change and diversity, and learning and adaptation.

THE RUSH TO THE CITY

By 2011, half the global population was living in cities and the proportion is expected to rise to 60 per cent by 2025. Probably for the first time in history, very few cities anywhere are losing population. The change is obvious in Europe and America but most dramatic in Asia, Africa and South America. There, vast numbers of young people whose parents work in the fields or in a factory see the city as a source of higher wages and more opportunities. Through the 2000s about 50 million people moved from the countryside to the city every year. This is the equivalent of seven cities the size of Rio de Janeiro or Bangkok or 75 cities the size of Manchester. It is estimated that 350 million Chinese migrated, many illegally, to the big cities on the Eastern seaboard between 1980 and 2010. It was as if the entire population of Russia moved to Western Europe.

The underlying cause is the search for work. This draws Poles to London, Western Chinese to the Eastern seaboard, gauchos to Buenos Aires or São Paulo and Indian Ph.D. graduates to California. Mixed up with the search for work is the desire for new experiences and opportunities.

The desire to move often starts online and on holidays and takes root when a teenager goes to a distant college or university. It is a desire to savour other ways of living, which are also ways of learning, and a search for places where one can work out whatever one wants to do and what one is good at. In the city, wages are higher, advancement faster and the choice of friends and lovers more private.

People who work in one city often forge relationships in other cities for play and holidays. A banker in São Paulo has a weekend house in Rio de Janeiro, where his mother runs an art gallery. Two designers in London have an apartment in Paris for weekends. Young executives working in Shenzhen go to Hong Kong for the weekend. A Washington DC official heads to New York. India's most famous film star has an apartment in Mayfair, London. It's not just the rich. University students from Asia want to visit London, Paris and Rome but have little interest in their rural countryside. Londoners love New York City but seldom visit rural America. The ideal of the countryside as the place for holidays or retirement still exists in countries with a rural aristocracy but has dwindled almost everywhere else. In China and India the countryside is seen as a place of exile and poverty or for excursions.

The speed of this enthusiasm for city life nearly caught city planners by surprise. After the rapid industrialization and urbanization of the 19th century, most cities had become crowded, noisy and dirty and people wanted to escape to the suburbs. London's population shrank between 1950 and 1980 by one-quarter. Crime rose, schools emptied and tax revenues fell. In America, more people lived in suburbs in the 1950s than in the cities. They went to the city to work but they socialized in the suburbs where houses were bigger and cheaper and more suitable for young families with children.

City planners turned away from the old cities and started to design new towns and cities on green-field sites such as Le Corbusier's Unité d'Habitation, Britain's Milton Keynes, Doxiadis's grand schemes for Islamabad and William Levitt's Levittown in Long Island, New York. Technology companies began to prototype the so-called 'smart house', which they claimed would liberate people from city offices, save on travel, reduce pollution and enhance the quality of life.

It never happened that way. The reason became clear from two experiments in Canada and Scandinavia at the same time. The Ottawa government wanted to help an Eskimo group, the Inuits, to sustain their remote communities when many young Inuits were leaving. Telesat Canada designed an Anik satellite network to provide them with a telephone service and TV channels ('anik' means little brother in Inuit) but instead of making the Inuits happy to stay, it opened their eyes to what was happening in the rest of the country, and more people decided to leave.

A few years later, Sweden, Norway and Finland made the same discovery. Like Canada, their mountainous lands go far into the Arctic and they decided to build a land-based telephone network which became the world's first mobile telephone network (thus opening the way for Nokia to take a lead in making handsets). Its greatest impact was again to encourage people to move to the city.

The suburbs were a blip. They marked an unsustainable vision of a society centred on large manufacturing factories at the moment those factories were losing their dominant role and societies were in transition. The nature of work was changing. The increase in the ubiquity of telephones, multi-channel TV and then the internet, as well as cheap air travel, opened people's minds to other lifestyles. There was a rise in the number of people who went to university, often in a strange city, and did not want to go back to their parents' lifestyles in the suburbs or the countryside. They were more interested in service industries like media, advertising and marketing, which were based in the city centre. They discovered the inner cities' housing stock had become cheap. The result was a resurgence of urban life.

This sudden growth of cities threatens their quality of life. The swelling population puts pressure on water, housing, schooling, healthcare, transport and waste. Immigration from other countries puts pressures on taxation and public spending and causes ethnic tensions. As a dozen or so cities in Asia and Africa expand to 30 and 40 million people we can expect major problems of city governance and perhaps an increasing exodus to smaller cities or even back to the countryside.

CREATIVE CITIES

The economies of cities grow in line with their access to resources and customers, which in turn attracts groups of traders, who then come to have lower transactional costs compared to their competitors in smaller towns. As each trader specializes they become more innovative and more competitive. This process, first described by Jane Jacobs, hasn't changed but what has changed is the nature of the resources and what customers want.

The increase in our own knowledge and in the possibility of accessing other people's knowledge has the perhaps surprising effect of making ideas more complex rather than more comprehensible. If diversity is low and the number of ideas is low, then each idea will be familiar and more easily manageable. If diversity is high and the number of ideas is greater, each idea is more likely to be complex and perhaps beyond the grasp of any one person. The spread of network technology makes it easier for people in one place to talk to others anywhere in the world, which increases diversity and complexity, which in turn increases uncertainty and ambiguity. It also tends to increase the speed with which decisions must be made. The result can be overwhelming. To compensate, people need to surround themselves with a chosen core of intimates who are local and supportive.

We can judge a city by its ability to sustain these relationships, measured partly by the size of the population but mainly by the opportunities to find like-minded people. It is likely to have a younger and better educated population than the national average as well as a higher proportion of immigrants both from the rest of the country and from foreign countries. Its colleges and universities will have a higher proportion of foreign students and its companies will recruit more often from other countries. It will be more diverse ethnically in terms of both residents and temporary visitors and have a mix of cultures and experiences. A 2012 London census showed a complex variety of ethnic groups, with people regarding themselves as 'White British' making up only 45 per cent of the population, probably the first time the figure has been under 50 per cent. Some London boroughs have to cope with pupils speaking over 100 different languages.

It helps if the population is diverse, and if it actively welcomes oddities and is curious about differences. What is wanted is not a bland acknowledgement of difference for its own sake but a restless search for other people's attempts to think of new interpretations, new meanings and new kinds of understanding. The first step is multiculturalism, respecting people's different histories, and helping people to treat each other fairly. The second is about their attempts to shape the future.

Creativity is an edgy business. Richard Florida, who invented the idea of a creative class, says: 'Without diversity, without weirdness, without difference, without tolerance, a city will die. Cities don't need shopping malls and convention centres to be economically successful, they need eccentric and creative people.'

In a creative city, a phrase coined by Charles Landry, people are not only open to new ideas, they actively seek them out. The population continually switch between making their own work and experiencing the work of others, between selling and buying. They are creative both in their business as ideas people and as buyers, audiences, consumers and users of other people's ideas, whose interests can be just as eccentric and weird as any creator. It is not an either/or situation. Creative people think creatively whether giving or receiving.

When Artangel opened the box office for its roof-top boat it sold a year's worth of tickets in one day. Another quirky London company, Secret Cinema, charges about £30 for a ticket, three times the normal cinema price, without telling the customers the name of the film or where it will be held. On my first visit, I was asked to wear dungarees and meet other audience members on the forecourt of Euston Station. Their tickets sell quickly, too.

This willingness to join in a creative process can be seen in the sort-of play *You Me Bum Bum Train*, which was designed by two illustrators, Kate Bond and Morgan Lloyd, to be performed by a cast of over 200 for an audience of one. This reversal of the normal ratio between actors and audience prompted the actors' union Equity to complain the actors were not being paid union rates, which was true but irrelevant. The actors and the much larger number of volunteers love its quirkiness, and there is no shortage of people wanting to join in. This trend towards larger, role-playing casts and smaller audiences can be seen not only in London but in Berlin, New York and elsewhere. Odyssey Works in Oakland, California constructs intricate weekend-long 'realities' consisting of life-like installations and performances for only one person. Their success depends on large numbers of open-minded volunteers such as are only found in a large city.

Cities provided social networks long before the internet was invented and their networks are richer, more diffuse and more multi-sensual than the most active Facebooker can create. These incidental serendipitous meetings may lead nowhere or may lead somewhere interesting. Some people like this thrill of the unknown and the chance to decide who to be with, and where, and what to do, but others are nervous and find it exhausting.

A city needs to be big enough to support an immeasurably large number of such networks. We will each bring our own perspective, curiosities and hopes and provide each other with entry points, sign-posts and stepping stones. A city ecology becomes exceptionally fruitful when the number is indefinitely large and more than any single person can know or count. The more the merrier. My own standard is that whatever I am interested in, whatever I want to do, I want there to be a hundred people thinking along the same lines and already doing it.

It is better to wander in and out of a variety of networks, to meet strangers as well as friends, and be challenged by people with new and different ideas, than remain stuck in one or two. This is apparent when people remain too long in one cluster, as often happens if their attitudes or their hours of work are out of sync with others. Brian Uzzi and Jarrett Spiro have mapped the relationship between the closeness of people working in Broadway theatre and their success rate: too close and the flop rate soars. They say it is better to keep moving in and out of many different networks. One of the most powerful stimulants of creativity and innovation is the outsider.

Creativity begins at home, so to speak, and the right place, in terms of this match, is one's own backyard where one feels at home. But on occasion everyone needs to leave their comfort zone to explore other places and make new relationships. Creativity thrives on difference.

Digital media, in all their forms, are a test-bed of these differences. People working in media and entertainment need to know how people are behaving online now and what tech people expect to happen in the next few years. Music, film, TV and games companies are acutely aware of the huge gap between their numbers and tech numbers, summed up in the difference between the 8 million people that bought 2012's best-selling digital track, or the million that streamed traditional TV, and the 500 million daily users of Facebook and Google. They wonder how they can get close to the tech numbers. This is why Troy Carter, Lady Gaga's manager, spends as much time with tech people and innovation specialists as he does with music people because, he says, he has to look outside the music business to make Lady Gaga as successful as she should be.

Carter's Atom Factory business is based in Culver City, Los Angeles, rather than in New York, which is the traditional home of America's music companies and radio networks. He knows that if you want to understand what's happening in digital media and entertainment you have to talk to tech people and innovators. He is typical of someone trying to be in the right place at the right time. Swedish entrepreneur Niklas Zennström and Danish Friis decided to leave their country and move to London to launch their start-up Skype, as did the Swedish Daniel Ek, who founded Spotify, for the same reason.

Princeton sociologist Martin Ruef has shown that entrepreneurs are more likely to succeed if they surround themselves with a high level of novel and conflicting information. He uses principles of social evolution to test how entrepreneurs choose a place (a habitat) and then make themselves fit for the niche they want to create. His work on start-ups shows they avoid pressures to conform or to follow conventional wisdom. Usually, they have one or two people nearby, intimates, who support them in working out their own ideas. This is how creativity operates inside the brain: a tension between what we know already and what we perceive or hear that is different.

THREE KINDS OF CULTURE

One way to measure this network variety is by looking at what is meant by a city's culture. The most common meaning of culture is arts-and-aesthetics but other meanings help us to understand how cities work. Anthropologists use the word to mean a set of beliefs, behaviours and attitudes, a way of life, and biologists and ecologists have a third meaning of a biological medium that contains nutrients for growth, such as a culture to grow cells. We can combine these views to treat a creative city as a medium, an ecosystem, for mixing arts-and-aesthetics and ways of living.

The Mayor of London and BOP Consulting held a forum on the culture of global cities during the London 2012 Olympics. After looking at 12 cities including London, Berlin, New York, Paris, São Paulo, Shanghai, Sydney and Tokyo, its research confirmed that what turns a city into a world city is more its culture than its location or size or political power or wealth, symbolized by exceptional museums, art galleries and theatres, and renowned universities and specialist colleges in art, music and design such as London's Central St Martins College of Art and Design and New York's Juilliard School. London and Paris have four world heritage sites each and over 20 million annual visitors to each city's top five museums. This is culture on a grand scale.

But big stately buildings are not enough. There is another layer, or ingredient, of other, smaller places and organizations, usually privately owned. BOP's 60 indicators range from fringe theatres to bookstores, both new and second-hand, night-clubs, restaurants, bars and video-game arcades. Brazilians love to dance and São Paulo has over 2,000 night clubs while Tokyo has only 73, but Tokyo does have more restaurants and more bars than any other city. There are some surprises. It is Tokyo (1,675) and Shanghai (1,322) rather than London or New York which have the largest number of bookstores, both new and second-hand and, of all 12 cities, Johannesburg surprisingly has the largest number of second-hand bookstores (943).

Some of the most famous big buildings, including London's South Bank Centre, Sydney's even more outstanding Opera House and Bilbao's Guggenheim Art Museum, work best as stimulants to their neighbourhood. All three were prodigious achievements but they stood a little apart and lonely in their early years. In retrospect we can see that they were the prologue, the starting gun, for a new kind of neighbourhood. Sydney's harbour from the Rocks to Woolloomooloo started to become alive only when other buildings opened their doors and cleared the decks for people to enjoy themselves. The Bilbao museum became the trigger for a mile-long urban regeneration along the Nervion river bank, which then curled back into the city.

The third layer is even more affective: people's appetite for informal grass-roots, street-level, pop-up micro-activities, each of which may be short-lived but which adds up to a continuous stream of events and experiences in a market-place of endless information which sharpens the producers' and makers' skills and buyers' appetites. Taking part is an attitude of mind which can be found in people of all ages but it is most noticeable in young people, who are the most active learners and adaptors. Their mimicry and collaboration, expressed in online networks, curation and tweeting, is a hallmark of urban creativity. Shanghai has over 50,000 students on specialist arts and design courses, and many times this number of young people working in creative sectors who are learning, experimenting and making. China has a total of 650,000 arts and design students in all, many of whom want to go to live and work in Beijing, Shanghai and four or five other cities. Worldwide, these growing numbers of inquisitive and restless young people are the champions of the scale and scope of the new economy.

Most of the major cities' grand institutions were founded over 100 years ago (Tate Modern is an offshoot of the 110-year-old Tate Britain), as were most of their major art, music and design colleges. Then, they were isolated pioneers. What has happened recently, as we saw with the South Bank Centre, is a change of attitude which reflects the first proposition of universality and the increase in scale and scope. No longer do these places appeal only to specialists but they sell themselves to anyone who wants to experience the new mood. Tate Modern in the evening is as much a place for meeting people and for entertainment as for appreciating art (not all visitors welcome the change).

The fourth ingredient is the commercial market-place. It is implicit throughout because the exchanges that take place need to be economically sustainable, whether 'free' street theatre, 'free' entry to museums, or commercial transactions between seller and buyer or user and user. A creative city needs private risk-taking and commercial success. It is not a coincidence that the cities regarded as most creative have many companies that are extremely competitive and world-class. These companies provide a dual role: they compete vigorously to sell in the market-place and their employees and others are discriminating critics and buyers of what else is on offer.

The Rise and Fall of the City

The newly graduated students who began to re-colonize the inner city from the 1960s onwards found places in transition. Some cities had lost their original purpose and seemed unable to change. The worst hit, because they were locked into coal, iron and steel, were cities based on ship-building and manufacturing in the north of Britain, Germany's Ruhr region, northern France, China's northern mining towns and what became known as America's rust-belt.

It is no longer true, as company chairman Alfred P. Sloan claimed, that when General Motors sneezes, America gets a cold, but it is true that if GM get into trouble everyone in Detroit suffers. The city grew as a result of innovations in flour milling, shipping, engineering and copper. It became one of America's best-known ecologies of engineering talent, inventive businesses, good universities and energetic people. Then two trends intervened which were initially welcomed but which crippled the city. First, GM, Ford and Chrysler became so successful that Detroit became a one-industry town and diversity shrank. It was ill-prepared for the Japanese who started to sell small, cheap and energy-efficient competitors in the 1980s.

At the same time, the car people moved to new family houses in the suburbs and put their business life and their social life in separate compartments. Managers, engineers, union officials and workers moved in smaller and smaller circles. Between 1950 and 2000 the city's population halved as people moved to the suburbs. By 2005, houses in Detroit were selling for a median price of $25,000. The heart of the city slowed to a murmur. There were hotspots in the still-good universities, a residue of engineering expertise and the city's fabled Motown and Techno music scene, but the lack of diversity and the lack of novelty, of difference, of weirdness, crippled people's imagination.

Slowly, Detroit is getting back on its feet (in 2011 the *Economist* was inspired to the headline, 'The parable of Detroit: So cheap, there's hope'). The urban imagination is working again. Urban farms are sprouting on the empty streets and Detroit is one of the few cities that can genuinely count food as a creative sector. Its Maker Movement looks back to Americans' frontier mentality and the 1960s' *Whole*

Earth Catalog and forward to today's CAD and 3D design tools. Many of the motor industry's small suppliers are re-directing their skills to the consumer market and one company that made protective materials for assembly lines is now making its own fashion clothing. The big three manufacturers are learning. Ford's newly appointed corporate futurist, Sheryl Connelly, admits cheerfully she is not a 'car person' and says, 'I never look at the car industry. Ford already has people to do that. I look outside.' In Detroit, looking outside had become a radical act.

Whole cities seldom fail completely nowadays and places like Detroit, Glasgow and Essen are becoming adept at regenerating themselves. What happens more often is that the city as a whole keeps going but districts fall in and out of favour as people make decisions about where to live and where to work. There is a well-known five-phase regeneration model that can be found in most cities. One, over time, a district's buildings become undesirable and rents fall. If they remain empty, they become derelict. Two, young creative people who have little money and want big, simple spaces move in. Three, these newcomers attract clubs, bars and restaurants that are arty, fashionable and fun. Four, therefore, the area is rejuvenated and rents rise. Five, the next generation of young people cannot afford the high rents and move on to establish themselves somewhere new.

This happened in New York when New York's abstract painters moved into the old Cast Iron warehouse district in SoHo. It happened in London in the run-down houses of Notting Hill in the 1960s and in St Catherine's docklands and warehouses in the 1970s, which became the natural habitat of the city's largest-ever concentration of artists' studios and led to Damien Hirst's Freeze show. It happened in the conversion of Moscow's ZIL factory, a constructivist masterpiece by the Vesnin Brothers, and Red October factory into cultural centres and in Shanghai's old meat-packing district, which became the city's largest art cluster, M50.

It happened again in London in the 1990s when a swathe of run-down office buildings to the north of the City of London's financial district became unsuitable for modern needs and fell into disrepair. They offered welcome habitats for artists looking for large spaces with high ceilings necessary for the newly fashionable large canvases, video work and installations. Hoxton's regeneration followed the regular model. The artists moved to where they could live and work; designers and architects followed; cafes and galleries started up; the neighbourhood became funky; other people moved in; and rents rose.

But then something new happened. Hard on the heels of the artists came a second wave of digital companies. My digital streaming company Tornado moved to Old Street in 2001 because rents were cheap and we knew other like-minded companies nearby in Hoxton, Shoreditch, Spitalfields, Clerkenwell, Farringdon and St Luke's. A medley of young start-up companies later lodged in workplaces, co-working spaces, members' clubs and incubators with names like the Trampery, TechHub, the Hoxton Mix and London HackSpace. Google opened Google Campus as a launch-pad for local start-ups. The New York-based General Assembly, which describes itself as a 'global net-work of campuses', has a branch in Clerkenwell with funding from the Russian DST Global fund, which also backed Facebook and Spotify.

What happened next was again unusual. The area began to attract large international companies. The bastion known as the City of London a few hundred yards to the south, which has been London's financial centre since the 1600s, began to diversify. Many of its major corporations had moved their large trading floors and back offices eastwards to Canary Wharf and the smaller companies moved westwards to town houses in Mayfair. The City district is losing its single-minded mono-culture and financial companies are now part of a medley alongside Google, Bloomberg, News Corp, Oracle, Expedia and other tech-based firms.

These shifts are partly explained by the underlying trend in the northern hemisphere for a city's centre of gravity to move to the east. For centuries, richer people moved upwind to avoid the city's noxious smells and, in the northern hemisphere, that meant westward. When sewer systems were built (London's were completed in the 1870s), the immediate cause was removed but by then the western districts had their own attractions and the eastern districts were run-down. Since then, as pressure for living space grew, people began to look again at re-occupying the cheaper districts in the east.

These trends are driven by private initiatives. In Britain both the national and city governments were slow to discover what was happening and, when they did, there was little they could do to help. The government began to promote Tech City around Hoxton in 2010 and offered financial support but little money arrived. It built its 2012 Olympic Park in the Lee Valley on the edge of London as a way of financing local infrastructure but, like most Olympics Parks, it is located too far away for post-Games business and its long-term value is dubious. The truth is, governments have little influence on these urban shifts. There is a fairly standard tool-kit of policies and regulations but, even so, many governments fail to do what they can. The causes of change are private companies, both British and American, that have moved in and the street-level micro-activism generated by youth culture in the arts, culture, media and software sectors.

Physio, not Surgery

The most effective interventions use the planning equivalent of physiotherapy rather than surgery and work with what is already happening. The trailblazer of this approach is architect Jaime Lerner who became the Mayor of Curitiba in Brazil. Lerner does not shun large, expensive infrastructure projects and started his term of office by installing a rapid transit system and closing roads to traffic but he prefers more subtle interventions, known as 'acupuntura urbana', which involves small but dramatic interventions at precise points on the city's meridians to affect its energies and flows. He appeals to people's emotions. He knew the South Bank Centre would only solve its problems when it stopped worrying about the buildings and started thinking about what people want to do in the spaces in-between.

Mayors like to use these urban acupuncture needles because they are cheap and can be easily reversed if they fail. Memorable interventions include Valparaiso's project to paint old houses in vivid colours, Montreal's commission to a local artist to turn street markings into enigmatic symbols, Kirovograd's planting of one million marigolds as a curtain-raiser to its revamp and Wuxi's laying of cobblestones and colour washes on house exteriors and building old-style archways between spaces.

These street-level changes mark a new self-consciousness in the relationship between a city's government and its inhabitants' creative energies. The recent reawakening of Berlin illustrates the shift. Berlin's arts and culture flourished prodigiously during the brief Weimar republic, between 1919 and 1933, in spite of Germany's political and economic terrors. It was home and an extraordinary outburst of art, design, dance, cabaret, satire, theatre, film and photography led by Fritz Lang, Otto Dix, George Grosz, Arnold Schoenberg, Walter Gropius and Bertolt Brecht as well as Professor Albert Einstein at the university. The thinking was fiercely independent and provocative and the tone was cheeky and transgressive. There are interesting comparisons between Berlin and Shanghai at the time (especially after the Russian and German Jewish refugees arrived in China) but then Berlin became isolated by war and division and culture was marginalized.

With reunification, the city government announced 'Creative Berlin' and attracted thousands of young people who came for its new openness and freedom and cheap rents. It has more start-ups than any other city in Germany, although it also has 20 per cent unemployment, twice the German average. The *Berliner Zeitung* newspaper once said: 'Berlin's drama is that its creative richness is inseparable from its economic poverty', and Mayor Klaus Wowereit notoriously described the city as 'poor but sexy', a slogan that Berliners put proudly on their T-shirts. What is happening now lacks the political challenge of the 1920s and has not (yet) produced the same quality of work. It is government-embraced, better behaved, more aligned with business and more attractive to visitors. The old Berlin was a city of the 1920s, as tough, energetic and depraved as anything then happening in Moscow, Chicago or Shanghai. Today, Berlin symbolizes the more collaborative, calmer 2010s and is a beacon of both grand culture and street-level experiments, drawing in Germans as well as people from the rest of Europe.

Kate Levin, New York's energetic Commissioner of Cultural Affairs, says that about half of the services supported by her department are indistinguishable from social services and likes to quote one project which provides gardening facilities inside prisons. São Paulo takes the same approach towards craft workshops in the favelas, which can be called art or social inclusion (which is how the city government justi-fies its grant). The results are the same: thinking, doing and making as a microcosm of change and diversity, learning and adaptation. In these cities, the Quad happens on a larger scale than elsewhere and with effects that are multiplied more quickly and more randomly. The number of networks and the permeable boundaries between them is one of their most seductive qualities. The larger the population, the faster and more disruptive the mix. Ideas come from anywhere and go anywhere and that is truer in the city than anywhere else.

10

My Brain, My Asset

INDIVIDUAL VOICE VS GROUP POWER

The most common bargain in the creative economy is between a person who has an idea and another person or a company who has the means to take it further. It is an unavoidable step in the move from the inner mindscape to a market. The bargain may turn on advice or money or something else. The first person wants to ensure the idea survives without being diluted or mucked around but others will only become involved if they have some control over what happens next.

The 'individual voice' refers to the first person's unique tone and point-of-view and the phrase 'group power' to describe the person on the other side of the table who has the assets to take the idea to the next stage. The bargain between an individual voice and group power depends upon both sides agreeing what the assets consist of, both their own and the other person's. They try to estimate an asset's value today and its ability to produce something in the future and, having compared the relative values, decide whether to use it now or store it for tomorrow. If it is stored then its value, like that of any asset, may go up or down.

The creative economy is the first economic system whose most valuable assets are people and their personal qualities of imagination and curiosity, their relationships, their intellectual property and their ability to make a fair deal. Historically, most assets took the form of money (known as financial capital) and land, buildings and equipment (physical capital). Understanding the nature of assets helps us to understand how economies operate and to intervene effectively when they wobble or do harm.

THE START OF CAPITAL

The historian Fernand Braudel showed that capital is inevitable in a society that has to 'grapple with the necessities and disputes of exchange, production and consumption'. He agreed with Karl Marx, who said in his book *Capital* that 'the modern history of capital dates from the creation in the 16th century of a world-embracing commerce and a world-embracing market.' Braudel recounts how the word 'capitalist' began to be used in the 17th century and 'capitalism' in the late 19th century. Economists began to talk about the trinity of land, labour and capital.

The relative value of capital assets changes continually to reflect society's priorities. The evolution from hunting to farming, the growth of trade, manufacturing and services and the emergence of the information society: each new system required a new kind of capital. Hunters need only short-term access to land but farmers who grow seeds want fields for at least a year (the ownership of land became the most secure asset of all). The Italian traders in Venice, Genoa and Livorno who first used the word needed ships, warehouses and store-chests. Manufacturers need factories and machines.

The need for large-scale finance for these factories led to the emergence of full-time capitalists who believed growth depended on capital-intensive economies of scale, which reduced the costs of producing each unit as volume grew, and on greater specialization. These economies of scale demanded more money, larger factories, more workers and bigger machines in line with Ricardo's theories of economies of scale.

Capital Families

When Gordon Moore of Intel made his calculation of computer power, which says chip speeds double every 18 months, he was not thinking about such economies of scale (although they were present to a small degree) but about people learning how to perform their tasks more skilfully and more quickly. He realized Intel's group power and its main source of competitive advantage was its people's ability to work together and learn from each other. The factory-owner's traditional requirements for punctuality, obedience and repetition had become commodities, to be supplied by automation. Moore was especially interested in the relation between the two opposites of collaboration and competition; when to share and when to overtake. He saw how increases in people's know-how produced an increase in earning capacity which was cumulatively more advantageous than the old economies of scale.

The growth of sectors providing experiences, such as art, culture, design and media, depends more on using people's imagination to increase their intangible values than on reducing the costs of physical inputs. People have a trunk-load of this human capital that they pick up throughout their lives, ranging from slippery bits of half-remembered knowledge to formal qualifications and facts, judgement and wisdom, if they are lucky. The growth of higher education directly increased the numbers of people who knew more and, equally important, were minded to learn more. In turn, companies began to see people as their chief asset. Advertising and design agencies were the first, leading one agency executive to say his company's assets walk out of the door every evening and go home.

The monumental research of Fritz Machlup, published as *The Production and Distribution of Knowledge in the US*, presented convincing evidence that this added value of intangibles matched physical inputs in terms of its contribution to economic output. As a result, companies put a higher priority on investments in personal development and in-house training and governments followed by increasing education budgets for secondary education and expanding the proportion of teenagers going to higher education.

By 2008 the American economist Alan Greenspan, former chairman of America's Federal Reserve Bank, said: 'Virtually unimaginable a half-century ago was the extent to which concepts and ideas would substitute for physical resources and human brawn in the production of goods and services.' Accenture, a management consultancy, calculates that the proportion of intangible assets in the value of companies in America's S&P 500 shot up from 20 per cent in 1980 to around 70 per cent in 2010. In London, the proportion for companies listed on the London Stock Exchange in 2010 was 80 per cent.

Human capital is a strikingly unusual variety of capital. The old financial and physical capital are impersonal and 'out there'. Human capital was the first variety to be recognized as something personal and 'inside'. But it still needs the right context to flourish.

When Jerry Hirshberg was a senior design executive at Detroit-based General Motors the designers were not permitted to touch their own model prototypes. Touching was against union rules (the unions similarly forbade American film directors to move studio props). When Hirshberg was recruited by Nissan to head up its first American outpost, Nissan Design International, he was determined to create an environment where designers could touch and move whatever they wanted. He insisted the new company be set up in San Diego, California, which is as far away from Detroit as possible, and said everyone was free to touch whatever they wished to. He wanted people to work together. What Hirshberg introduced was structural capital.

If human capital is the asset that walks out the door every evening, then structural capital is the ecosystem everyone leaves behind. It starts with a company's organization, whether hierarchical like the old General Motors or flat like Valve; the daily routines that determine what people do during the day; policies on recruitment, remuneration and training; the attitude to working hard and to working late. It includes the management of intellectual property, brands and domain names. It includes the office location, interior design and canteen. Its objective is to provide an environment where people can turn ideas into other ideas and then into products; in other words, a creative ecology. Creativity and innovation spring from local, informal exchanges and are incremental and cumulative, and an organization learns not through sudden or dramatic discontinuities but through a gradual process in the way a sponge absorbs water.

Intellectual Capital

These ideas about human and structural capital were brought together into the single concept of 'intellectual capital' by Leif Edvinsson of Skandia, a Swedish finance company. His phrase hit a chord around the world and among his many honours I like the one awarded in 1998 by the BBC Brains Trust, which chose him as Brain of the Year ahead of runners-up Bill Gates and Paul McCartney, each of whom has his own vault-full of intellectual capital.

Fritz Machlup had already talked of 'intellectual investment' to describe the intelligent use of knowledge. Edvinsson took this one step further and showed that these kinds of investments, though crucial to a company's value, were seldom included in its annual accounts, which recognize the equipment in the research laboratory but not the know-how of the researchers, which is why creative people who regard their knowledge as their most important asset are quick to distrust accountants who give it no value.

It is like valuing a company car in the car park but not the owner's knowledge of where to go. Edvinsson began to refer to the latter as 'hidden assets', saying: 'Most of this is common sense and the challenge is to turn it into common practice.' Writing in London's *Business Strategy Review*, Microsoft's Bill Gates said: 'Our primary assets, which are our software and our software development skills, do not show up on the balance sheet at all. This is probably not very enlightening from a pure accounting point of view.' The Chairman of Coca-Cola has said its intellectual assets are worth more than all its land, offices, factories, vehicles and bottling plants.

After inventing the Walkman and digital video technologies, Sony decided to move into the entertainment business and acquired CBS Records and Columbia Pictures. Yet later Chairman Norio Ohga complained: 'We continue to be rated in Japan as an electronics company rather than a content company. All our entertainment businesses, our music and our picture operations, are undervalued. The share price should be higher. I want to make our hidden assets more visible.'

In a creative economy, a person's imagination is their most valuable asset. In total, it is likely the value of the world's intellectual capital exceeds the value of its financial and physical capital. It is clearly the greater part of arts, culture, design, media and innovation. The world's universities and R&D laboratories have high ratios of intellectual capital. The BBC's hefty intellectual capital includes the world's largest groups of programme-makers and a management structure designed to turn their ideas into programmes but neither the people nor the structures appear on the BBC's balance sheet.

It is the chief resource of companies that depend upon copyrights and patents and of those that depend upon trademarks and brands. If drugs were unpatented and unbranded, consumers, after a moment of delight at cheap prices, would become confused and also, if the drug companies are to be believed, frustrated at the slowness of new drugs coming to the market. If tomorrow's newspapers were undesigned, readers would be overwhelmed by a morass of words.

These assets are often tagged in words like talent or skill but such words ignore the context. The Italian public broadcaster RAI once asked me to contribute to a year-long exercise involving 300 senior managers. We learned three things. One, RAI's massive financial and physical capital, which conveyed an appearance of solidity, was alarmingly insufficient to fuel its purpose of providing programmes that appealed to the audience. Two, many managers had talent and skill which were obvious to them but hidden to others and so wasted. Three, these managers needed an ecosystem, structural capital, so they could not only have ideas but do something about them.

The United Nations' annual wealth report is an ambitious attempt to put some numbers to these varieties of capital. It defines human capital as education, skills, tacit knowledge and health. Of the 20 countries analysed, America scores highest at $118 trillion, about eight times as much as its GDP, followed by Japan ($55 trillion), China ($20 trillion), Germany ($20 trillion) and Britain ($13 trillion). Each country's human capital exceeds its natural and manufactured capital by a significant margin.

WHEN WHAT'S DESIRABLE MEETS
WHAT'S POSSIBLE

I began by showing how Massive Software took an idea from the movies and adapted it to help people get around more safely in real life. About the same time as Massive's Diane Holland was meeting Nate Wittasek, the staff of Birmingham University Hospital Trust, like many of their National Health Service colleagues, were searching for ways to improve clinical efficiency at their flagship Queen Elizabeth Hospital. Slightly on a whim, the medical director and chief executive visited the local BMW car factory. Over the years, the Japanese and German car companies have led global R&D on systems of error capture that cut mistakes down to 0.1 per cent of tasks and enable those mistakes to be rapidly investigated and dealt with. Hospitals face much more complex tasks, of course, but they also have much higher failure rates even in the simplest routine matters. Birmingham CEO Julie Moore realized that her hospital, although dealing with human health, was far too tolerant of mistakes.

The NHS approach to mistakes is to monitor outcomes, and if something really bad happens to trace it back to the original error. Error detection and correction can take hours, if not days, and often results in little improvement. Moore says: 'As long as no one dies or there's no big fuss, nothing gets done.' Walking around BMW, she and medical director David Rosser saw how the NHS could be doing better. BMW has a policy of zero tolerance for errors. It monitors every incident and, where necessary, takes action. After their visit, the hospital worked with CSE Healthcare to develop a Prescribing, Information and Communication System (PICS) to monitor performance and activate remedies. The PICS dashboards, one in every ward, produced startling results (for example, the hospital now treats an incidence of the hospital bug MRSA on average within 10 seconds instead of the previous 30 hours). It is a good example of learning and of adaptation.

But the next step did not go smoothly. Although the NHS encouraged other hospitals to install PICS dashboards, little was done. According to the King's Fund, a leading healthcare think-tank, the NHS's overriding principle is standardization rather than excellence and its bureaucratic liking for benchmarks, best practices and case studies offers little incentive to anyone to do better than average. The spark of personal insight that led Julie Moore and David Rosser to leave the wards and visit a car factory remains unusual. The NHS ecosystem is based on repetition and does not reward change or diversity.

In these circumstances, change is more likely to come from outside. In America, when family physician Jeremy Brenner became involved in a local street shooting he was perplexed and shocked by the system's inability to provide a service that met people's needs. He tried to push the local police to compile computerized crime maps to show vulnerable areas. When they refused, he made his own. The result was a dynamic, real-time map of vulnerable areas that led to three dramatic outcomes: better health services, better policing and much lower costs. Across the country, individuals and non-profit organizations are now analysing data to enable them to identify what people really want (as dotcoms have been doing for years) and then providing it. The gain is healthier people and lower medical costs. Brenner sums up the creative spirit, just as strongly as does artist Elaine Shemilt in her pictures of genetic data (see p. ix), both using their personal instincts and ingenuity to make something more meaningful to others. Creativity depends not only on thinking new thoughts but on doing something about it and turning what is desirable into what is possible; in other words, treating ideas as assets.

It seems reasonable to treat our ideas as assets because they result from investments (attention, time, money) which we can increase or vary and they determine future outputs. Treating ideas as assets helps us to understand the nature of the creative market-place. In financial terms, asset markets are spheres of speculation, a world of one-off deals rather than mass production. Putting an effort into thinking increases its value and effectiveness as surely as do investments in other capital assets.

Demand and supply are fluid. It is a world of personalities and promises, incidents and accidents. Creativity happens when we have an idea, our own or someone else's, add our personal value to it, and make something new and original. There is no official rate of exchange. One person's idea may be uninteresting or useless to another. Money is money, but an idea can be good, bad or indifferent. It can be good one day and bad the next.

Investment strategies vary. We can put cash under the mattress and see its value wither away or we can spend it or by investing we can hope to increase it. Likewise, we can let creative assets lie dormant; spend them; or invest them.

These forms of creativity shade easily into innovation and the boundary lines are blurred. More and more creativity feeds into a larger conversation about new ways of working, new technologies, new algorithms and new processes that unknown others might take on. In 2012 the Shanghai School of Creativity held an international seminar on digital technologies and performance. In the early sessions, the speakers were eager to prove their intellectual credentials and made distinctions about whether this or that decision was art- or technology-based. By the end, they realized such niceties were lost in a greater whole and art and technology were simply different mindsets for what they were trying to do.

An idea gains most when it is managed and made *purposive*. Ideas flourish best in small, flexible ecosystems with full-time thinkers, network offices and clusters who know about rights management and know if and when an idea can or should be turned into property, and the most cost-effective means of doing so.

Something bought over the counter or downloaded becomes mine and that may seem the end of it, and anyway the terms of sale often forbid further use. But the creative instinct, the ecology, does not give up so easily. Thinking about what I have done, what I now have, what I can do next, who else might enjoy it, will inspire me to think how I can use it and so the cycle of creativity begins again.

Throughout this book, I have focused on business and markets but the overall impact of a creative ecology is wider. The way we treat ideas and inventions affects social, cultural and political issues. How we decide the ownership of ideas and inventions, and *who decides*, affects the kind of society we create for ourselves.

A society that stifles or misuses its creative assets cannot prosper but if we understand and manage our creative economy successfully, individuals benefit and society is rewarded. Seeing creativity as a universal human quality, and the beginnings of a process of learning and adaptation, is the first step.

Notes

PREFACE: WHO IS CREATIVE, AND WHY?

p.vii For the **IBM survey**, see *Capitalising on Complexity*, Global CEO Study, IBM, 2010.

p.viii Britain's Propshop Modelmakers had the idea of **printing Bond's Aston Martin** and commissioned Voxeljet, which used its VX4000 printer.

p.ix For **Shemilt's art project**, see Elaine Shemilt, 'A Blueprint for Bacterial Life', Birkbeck College, 2006.

p.x This invitation to the '**creative talent here in Scotland**' was made by Wendy Wilkinson, Deputy Director, Culture Division, Scottish Government, March 2010.

p.x The CIA employee **who started his career developing video games** is Gilman Louie, who ran Tetris, then the world's best-selling computer game, before joining In-Q-Tel as its first CEO.

1. WHEN ORCS WALKED ACROSS OXFORD CIRCUS

p.1 **Tolkien's description of the Orcs** is from Humphrey Carpenter, *The Letters of J. R. R. Tolkien*, HarperCollins, 1981.

p.2 **Peter Jackson** described his jump moment during an interview at the Academy of Achievement, Washington, DC, 3 June 2006.

p.3 **Nate Wittasek** was talking to the author on 13 January 2012.

p.4 See **C. A. Ronan**, *The Cambridge Illustrated History of the World's Science*, Cambridge University Press, 1983.

p.4 See **Edward O. Wilson**, *Consilience: The Unity of Knowledge*, Little Brown, 1998.

p.7 For *creative intensity*, see Hasan Bakshi, Alan Freeman and Peter Higgs, 'A Dynamic Mapping of the UK's creative industries', NESTA, 2013.

p.8 See **Abraham H. Maslow**, *Motivation and Personality*, Harper and Brothers, 1954.

p.8 See **Linus Torvalds** and David Diamond, *Just for Fun*, Harper Business, 2001.

p.8 See **Fred Hoyle**, 'The Universe: Past and Present Reflections', *Engineering and Science*, November 1981.

p.9 For **rich countries' spending on culture and recreation**, see *Family Spending, 2011 Edition*, Office of National Statistics, London; Consumer Expenditure Survey, Bureau of Labor Statistics, Washington DC, 2011.

2. THE TRIPOD

p.11 For **700 new connections a second**, see 'The Foundations of Lifelong Health are Built in Early Childhood', Center on the Developing Child, Harvard University, 2010.

p.12 See **Noam Chomsky**, 'Approaching Universal Grammar from Below', in Uli Sauerland and Hans Martin Gartner, eds, *Interfaces + Recursion = Language?*, Walter de Gruyter, 2007; and **Steven Pinker**, *The Language Instinct*, William Morrow and Company, 2007; and Steven Pinker, *The Language Instinct*, Allen Lane, London 1994.

p.17 See **Bill Gross**, 'The $300 House', *Harvard Business Review Blog Network*, 25 October 2010; http://blogs.hbr.org/cs/2010/10/the_300_house_the_design_chall.html.

p.17 For **the global electricity market**, see Venkataraman Krishnaswamy, 'Closing the Electricity Demand-Supply Gap', World Bank, 2007.

3. THE FIRST TALENT

p.19 **Sam Mendes** was speaking in an interview in the *Sunday Times*, 23 January 2000.

p.19 See **Herman Vaske**, *Why are You Creative?*, How Design, 2002.

p.19 See **Kurt Vonnegut**, *A Man Without a Country*, Seven Stories Press, 2005.

p.20 See **Robert Craft**, *Stravinsky: Chronicle of a Friendship*, Nashville, 1994.

p.21 **Picasso** was speaking in an interview with the *Paris Review*, 32, 1964.

p.21 See **Daniel Kahneman**, *Thinking, Fast and Slow*, Farrar Straus and Giroux, 2012.

p.23 See **C. J. Jung**, *The Development of the Personality*, *The Collected Works*, vol. 17, Routledge, 1954.

p.23 **Antonio Damasio**, author of *The Feeling of What Happens* (1999), made this remark in a lecture at the London School of Economics on 14 January 2000.

p.23 For the **benefits of wandering**, see Richard Fisher, 'Dream a Little Dream', *New Scientist*, 16 June 2012.

p.23 See **Jennifer Wiley** and Andrew Jarosz, *Psychology of Learning and Motivation*, vol. 56, 2012.

p.24 See **Mihaly Csikszentmihalyi**, *Flow: The Psychology of Optimal Experience*, Rider, 1990.

p.24 See **Charles Sherrington**, *Man on his Nature*, Penguin, 1940.

p.25 See **Somerset Maugham**, *The Summing Up*, Heinemann, 1938.

p.25 See **A. N. Whitehead**, *Science and the Modern World*, Macmillan, 1925.

p.25 See **J. R. R. Tolkien**, *The Lord of the Rings*, Allen and Unwin, 1954.

p.26 **Trevor Nunn** made this remark in an interview with the author in 1999.

p.26 See **Johan Huizinga**, *Homo Ludens*, Routledge, 1949.

p.26 See **David Puttnam**, 'Behind and Beyond the Screen', *The Utopian Papers*, Newell and Sorrell, 1996.

p.27 See **Richard Feynman**, *The Pleasure of Finding Things Out*, video, BBC, 1981; book, Perseus, 1999.

p.28 See **Anthony Storr**, The Dynamics of Creation, Secker & Warburg, 1972.

p.28 **F. Scott Fitzgerald**'s short story appears in *The Crack-Up*, New Directions, 1945.

p.28 See **Peter Bazalgette**, 'How to Spot (and Manage) the Creatives', *Broadcast*, 20 November 1998.

p.29 See **K. Anders Ericsson**, *The Road to Excellence*, Psychology Press, 1996; Malcolm Gladwell, *Outliers*, Allen Lane, 2008.

p.29 See **Erving Goffman**, *Where the Action Is*, 1969.

p.29 The comment on **Steve Jobs's methods** was made in 'Breaking the Rules: Apple Succeeds by Defying Core Valley Principles', *WIRED*, 18 March 2008.

p.29 See **Peter Ackroyd**, *T. S. Eliot*, Hamish Hamilton, 1984.

p.30 See **Bob Dylan**, 'It's Alright, Ma (I'm Only Bleeding)', Columbia, 1965.

p.30 See **Kamil Idris**, Introduction to WIPO, *Annual Report* (1999).

p.30 The story about **Laurence Olivier** is told in Richard Findlater, *The Player Kings*, Weidenfeld and Nicolson, 1971.

4. WHERE IDEAS TAKE ROOT

p.33 **John Steinbeck** made this remark in an interview with Robert van Gelder, 1947, quoted in Jay Parini, *John Steinbeck: A Biography*, Trafalgar Square, 1994.

p.34 The Khan Academy and Udacity are examples of Massive Open Online Courses (MOOCs).

p.35 See **Soedjatmoko**, 'The Future and the Learning Capacity of Nations', Louis G. Cowan Lecture, 11 September 1978.

p.37 **Alex Graham** made this remark in conversation with the author, London, 2011.

p.38 See **Kenneth Goldsmith**, *Uncreative Writing*, Columbia University Press, 2011.

p.39 The link between **imitation and mutual enjoyment** has been explored by Fiona Kerr, University of Adelaide, in her work on the neuro-science of management.

p.39 See **Richard Dawkins**, *The Selfish Gene*, OUP, 1976.

p.41 See **Francis Galton**, 'Vox Populi', *Nature*, 28 March 1907; and **Eric S. Raymond**, *The Cathedral and the Bazaar*, O'Reilly, 1999.

p.41 See **Keith Johnstone**, *Impro: Improvisation and the Theatre*, Methuen, 1981.

p.41 For **We-Think,** see Charles Leadbeater, *We-Think*, Profile, 2008.

p.41 See 'The **Valve Handbook** for New Employees', http://newcdn.flamehaus.com/.

p.42 **Nicky Binning** was quoted in Ross Tieman, 'From Teamwork to Collaboration', *Financial Times*, 15 March 2012.

p.43 See **Edward de Bono**, *Six Thinking Hats*, Time Warner, 1985.

p.43 For the **link between memory and engagement**, see Kenneth T. Kishida and others, 'Implicit Signals in Small Group Settings', *Philosophical Transactions of the Royal Society*, 23 January 2012.

p.43 Sociologist Robert Merton has traced the remark **standing on the shoulders of giants** back to 12th-century French philosopher Bernard of Chartres.

p.43 See **Rabindranath Tagore**, *Gitanjali*, Macmillan, 1970.

5 . MANAGING IDEAS

p.48 See **Joseph Schumpeter**, *Capitalism, Socialism and Democracy*, Allen & Unwin, 1943.

p.48 The data on **new ways of working in Europe** is from *Fifth European Working Conditions Survey* (2012), Eurofound; the data for other countries is from OECD Factbook, 2012.

p.49 For **lower tax rates for multinationals**, see media release, Committee on Fiscal Affairs, OECD, Los Cabos, June 2012.

p.50 See **Daniel Bell**, *The Matching Scales*, Louis G. Cowan Lecture, 12 September 1979.

p.50 See **Peter Drucker**, *The Landmarks of Tomorrow*, Harper and Brothers, 1959.

p.52 **Ralph Waldo Emerson** was quoted in Bliss Perry (ed.), *The Heart of Emerson's Journals*, Dover, 1995.

p.52 **BT/Management Today survey** was discussed in 'Information Strategy', *Economist*, March 1997.

p.55 See **Ernest Hall**, *In Defence of Genius*, Arts Council of England, 1996.

p.55 **Hermann Hauser** made this comment at a CREATEC board meeting in 1998.

p.55 **Jeff Bezos** made this remark in an interview with *Upside*, October 1996.

p.56 **Kasparov** made this comment before his match with Deep Blue 3 in 1997.

p.56 See **Ayelet Fishbach** and Jinhee Choi, 'When Thinking about Goals Undermines Goal Pursuit', *Organizational Behavior and Human Decision Processes*, 118 (2012), 99–107.

p.56 **Trevor Bayliss** was quoted in *The Times*, 14 March 2000.

p.57 **Paul Orfalea** was quoted in Schumpeter, 'In Praise of Misfits', *Economist*, 2 June 2012.

p.57 For the **high incidence of dyslexia in entrepreneurs**, see Julie Logan, *Dyslexic Entrepreneurs*, Cass, 2010.

p.57 **Art Barron**'s comment about not having a strategy was made during a meeting in London on Channel Five, in 1994; see also John Howkins, 'Why Michael Porter is Wrong', BOSS, *Australian Financial Review*, September 2006.

p.57 See **Scott Cook**, 'Emergent Strategies', *Harvard Business Review*, June 2011.

p.58 **Terry Kelly** was quoted in Stefan Stern and Peter Marsh, 'The Chaos Theory of Leadership', *Financial Times*, 2 December 2008.

p.58 See **John Kao**, *Jamming: The Art and Discipline of Business Creativity*, HarperBusiness, London, 1996.

p.60 The **Ashridge Business School survey** was mentioned by Pam Jones in 'Leading Complex Teams: A Model for the Future', a lecture given at the World Future Annual Conference, 29–31 July 2007.

p.61 Alfred Marshall, *The Principles of Economics*, Macmillan, 1890.

p.61 See **Charles Leadbeater**, *Living on Thin Air*, Viking, 1999.

p.62 For **outsiders in Hollywood**, see *Wall Street Journal*, 10 April 1994.

p.62 **Barry Diller** was quoted in *Financial Times*, 10 March, 1990.

p.62 For **YouTube video-makers**, see Rob Walker, 'On YouTube, Amateur is the New Pro', *The New York Times*, 28 June 2012.

p.66 **Duncan Niederauer** was quoted in *Economist*, 16 June 2012.

p.66 For **crowd-funding regulations**, see Steven Bradford, 'Crowd funding and the Federal Securities Laws', *Columbia Business Law Review*, 2012 (1) 2012.

p.66 For **UKIE's new regulatory framework** for crowd-funding, see *Crowd Funding Report: A Proposal to Facilitate Crowd-funding in the UK*, UKIE, 2012.

p.68 **David Puttnam**'s remarks were made in a speech at the National Film and Television School on 25 July 2012.

p.69 For **Europe's inability to create a rival to Silicon Valley**, see 'Lessons from Apple', *Economist*, 9 June 2007.

p.70 This section on **negotiating deals and contracts** is based on Richard E. Caves, *Creative Industries: Contracts Between Art and Commerce*, Harvard University Press, 2001, and John Howkins, *Creative Ecologies: Where Thinking is a Proper Job*, UQP, 2009.

p.71 For *Star Wars* **revenues from merchandising**, see Alex Ben Block, 'The Real Force Behind Star Wars', *Hollywood Reporter*, 17 February 2012.

p.74 **Jonathan Ive** was speaking at the Global Business Summit on ICT, London, 3 August, 2012.

p.77 **Albert Einstein** was quoted in *Observer*, 15 January 1950.

6. OWNING IDEAS

p.79 For comments about the **subtleties of intellectual property law**, *see Intellectual Property and the National Information Infrastructure*, Information Infrastructure Task Force, 1994; *Folsom v. Marsh*, 9 F. cas. 342, 344 (CCD Mass. 1841); and Mark Twain's *Notebook, 1902–1903.*

p.79 **President Obama**'s remarks were made on the White House blog, 14 January 2012.

p.79 See **Ian Hargreaves**, *Digital Opportunity*, IPO, 2011.

p.83 For **Disney's application for a trademark,** see US Patent Application no. 77618057. Disney has extended its application five times but at the time of writing the mark had not been granted.

p.85 For **product designers' attitude to design rights,** see BOP Consulting, '*Design Economics: International Comparisons,* IPO, 2012.

p.86 **Thomas Jefferson**'s letter to Isaac McPherson, dated 13 August 1813, can be found in Merrill D. Peterson (ed.), *Thomas Jefferson: Writings,* Library of America, 1984.

p.87 **Martin Luther** was quoting Matthew 10:8.

p.87 The **writers' complaint,** quoted here, became the Act's opening words.

p.88 **Daniel Defoe**'s comment about a book being the author's own property is quoted in Raymond Williams, *The Long Revolution*, Chatto and Windus, 1961; his remark that writing was a very considerable branch of commerce was made in *Applebee's Journal*, 1725.

p.90 For the full report, see *The Internet and Copyright,* Green Paper, Department of Commerce, 1999.

p.90 See **John Perry Barlow**, 'The Economy of Ideas', *WIRED*, 2.03, March 1994.

p.92 The FBI's estimate of Megaupload's **advertising and premium services revenues** was given in a press release by the US Department of Justice, 19 January 2012.

p.92 For the **consequences of extensive infringement of copyright,** see Stephen Siwek, *The True Cost of Copyright Industry Piracy to the US Economy*, Institute for Policy Innovation, 1997; while Rob Reid's video *Copyright Math* (2012) gives a satirical but fact-based alternative view.

p.93 For **media piracy in poorer countries,** see Joseph Karaganis, 'Media Piracy in Developing Countries', SSRC, 2011; www.piracy.ssrc.org.

p.93 **David Petrarca,** speaking at Perth Writers' Festival, was quoted in *Sydney Morning Herald*, 26 February 2013.

p.95 Microsoft, 'Halloween Report', internal document, 1997.

p.95 See **Eric S. Raymond**, *The Cathedral and the Bazaar*, O'Reilly, 1999.

p.96 A full report of the **CODE** conference is at www.cl.cam.ac.uk/conference/code.

p.96 For more information about **ENCODE**, see www.encodeproject.org/.

p.97 Hans Rosling's comment was quoted in 'Making Data Dance', *Economist*, 9 December 2010.

p.97 See **Directive Supporting Access to Publicly Funded Research**, White House, 22 February 2013; and 'Open Data Policy: Managing Information as an Asset' (M-13-13), White House, 9 May 2013.

p.97 See **Tim Berners-Lee**, *TED Talk*, 2009.

p.99 For the **role of patents in smartphones,** see Geoff McCormick, 'Patents Wars: Stripping the iPhone Bare', *BBC News*, 16 February 2012.

p.99 For the judgement that **Samsung is not as cool as Apple**, see www.bailii.org/ew/cases/EWHC/Patents/2012/1882.html.

p.100 **Judge Posner**'s comment was reported by Reuters on 5 July 2012.

p.102 See **Andrew Gowers**, *Review of Intellectual Property*, TSO, 2006.

p.104 See **James Gleick**, 'Patently Absurd', *The New York Times*, 12 March 2000.

p.105 See **Lawrence Lessig**, *Code and Other Laws of Cyberspace*, Basic Books, 1999.

p.105 **Eric Schmidt** was interviewed in *Wall Street Journal*, 4 December 2012.

p.106 See **European Patent Office**, *Patents for Software?*, 2012.

p.108 **Dr Pennapa Subcharoen** is quoted in D. R. Mankekar, *Media and the Third World*, Indian Institute of Mass Communication, 1979.

p.109 The declaration '**Anything under the sun . . .**' is recorded in S Rep. No. 1979, 82nd Congress, 2nd Session, 5 (1952).

p.110 For the American court decision on the **exclusive ownership of one's body parts**, see *Moore vs University of California*, 51 Cal. 3d 120; 271 Cal. Rptr. 146; 793 P.2d 479. See also James Boyle, *Shamans, Software and Spleens*, Harvard University Press, 1996.

p.110 The quote '**An element isolated from the human body** . . .' is from EU Directive 98/44, Article 5.2.

p.112 For Myriad, see Association for Molecular Pathology vs Myriad Genetics Inc., Supreme Court, 12–398, 13/6/13.

p.116 See **Immanuel Kant**, *The Critique of Judgement*, translated J. C. Meredith, Hackett, 1997.

p.119 See **Presidential Task Force on National Information Policy**, report, White House, 1976.

p.120 See **Jeffrey Sachs**, 'Helping the World's Poorest', *Economist*, 14 August 1999.

p.121 The **feasibility study for Britain's copyright hub** was chaired by Richard Hooper; see Richard Hooper, *Copyright Works*, IPO, 2012.

p.122 The story of WIPO and **Open Source software** is told in Lawrence Lessig, 'Open Source, Closed Minds', *E-Week*, 1 October 2003; www.lessig.org/content/columns/cio3.pdf.

p.124 **Nokia**'s head of Litigation Unit, Richard Vary, gave these figures in his presentation to the UK Intellectual Property Office, 'Bifurcation: Bad for Business', on 12 April 2012.

7. SEARCH, LEARN, MIX AND SHARE

p.128 The **comparison between apps and online** was supplied by Flurry, a mobile analytics company, 2013.

p.128 The **data about online shopping** is from 'Are You Giving Your Customers What They Really, Really Want?', WorldPay, 2012.

p.128 For the **impact of online social media** on the Arab Spring, see Chris Zambelis, 'Information Wars: Assessing the Social Media Battlefield in Syria', Combating Terrorism Center (CTC), 2012.

p.130 See **Gary Wolf**, 'The Data Driven Life', *The New York Times Magazine*, 28 April 2010; see also www.quantifiedself.com.

p.132 For **Stealth and Shark** and other trading algorithms, see Scott Patterson, *Dark Pools*, Random House, 2012.

p.132 Companies' intimations of **marital break-ups** were described in Oliver Burkeman, 'Reality Check', *Guardian*, 15 March 2011.

p.134 See **David Isenberg**, 'The Rise of the Stupid Network', Computer Telephony, August 1997. Available at isen.com/stupid.

p.135 See **Peter Martin**, *Financial Times*, 20 October 1998.

p.138 See **John Naughton**, 'Everything You Ever Need to Know About the Internet', *Observer*, 20 June 2010.

p.142 **Johnny Black** made this comment in an email to the author, 4 May 2012.

p.142 **Erin McKeown** was speaking at the Copyright 2012 Conference, New York, March 2012.

p.143 The **data on album sales** is from New Music Seminar, June 2012; http://newmusicseminar.com/.

8. HEARTLANDS: ART, DESIGN, MEDIA AND INNOVATION

p.145 The main sources used in this chapter, **Heartlands: Art, Design, Media and Innovation,** include: Department of Commerce (US); Department for Culture, Media and Sport (UK); European Union; HIS Screen Digest; National Bureau of Statistics, China (www.stats.gov.cn/english); OECD; PwC; State Administration for Radio, Film and Television (SARFT); United Nations (UNESCO, WIPO); World Bank; Xinhua; and company annual reports. Sector-specific sources are given below at the start of each section.

p.145 Global economic **output** (2012) from World Bank data.

p.148 **America's supposed decline** was discussed in Edward Luce, *Time to Start Thinking: America in the Age of Descent*, Atlantic Monthly Press, 2012.

p.151 For the **gap between digital media and cultural heritage,** see John Howkins, 'Digital Divide', WIPO, 2010.

p.153 For the **Department of Commerce's treatment of creative outputs**, see 'Preview of the 2013 Comprehensive Revision of the National Income and Product Accounts', Bureau of Economic Affairs, Department of Commerce, March 2013.

p.153 For **Britain's R&D spending**, see Peter Goodridge and Jonathan Haskell, 'Film, Television & Radio, Books, Music and Art: UK Investment in Artistic Originals', IPO, 2011; 'Copyright Adds £3 billion to National Accounts', IPO, 8 June 2012.

p.153 For **Britain's new approach**, see Hasan Bakshi, Alan Freeman, and Peter Higgs, 'A Dynamic Mapping of the UK's Creative Industries', NESTA, 2013, and Hasan Bakshi, Ian Hargreaves, and Juan Mateos-Garcia, 'A Manifesto for the Creative Economy', NESTA, 2013.

p.153 The **luxury market** is described by Dr Thitiporn Sanguanpiyapan in her report *A Love Affair with Luxe*, 2008.

p.154 **Art**. Sources include: *Art Newspaper*; Artprice and auction results.

p.155 For the **global market**, see Clare McAndrew, *The International Art Market*, TEFAF, Maastricht, 2013.

p.155 For **the value of the British art market**, see Arts Economics, 'The British Art Market: A Winning Global Entrepôt', BAMF, 2011.

p.158 **Books**. Sources include: *Bookseller*; Bowker; Nielsen; Publishers Association of China and *Publishers Weekly*.

p.161 For **China's share in the global book market**, see David Graddol, 'The Future of English', British Council, 1997.

p.162 **Craft**. Sources include: Bundesverband Kunsthandwerk; Crafts Council; and Craft and Hobby Association.

p.164 **Film**. Sources include: British Film Institute (BFI); British Screen Advisory Council (BSAC); CMM Intelligence, Beijing; European Audiovisual Observatory; Film Business Asia; KPMG; Motion Picture Association of America (MPAA); Nielsen; Nigerian Films and Video Census Board; *Screen International*; and *Variety*.

p.165 For **Netflix's spending on licences**, see Brooks Barnes, 'Web Deals Cheer Ailing Hollywood', *The New York Times*, 11 March 2012.

p.166 The **data on the six major Hollywood studios** is given by Benjamin Swinburne, from Morgan Stanley, in *Economist*, 25 February 2013.

p.168 **Music**. Sources include: *Billboard*; British Phonographic Industry (BPI); China Performing Industry Association; International Federation of the Phonographic Industry (IFPI); PRS for Music; and Recording Industry Association of America (RIAA).

p.169 For **the 2012 list of the Music Power 100**, see *Billboard*, 27 January 2012.

p.171 For **the British music market share**, see 'Adding Up the Music', PRS for Music, 2011.

p.171 For **people working in the music industry** or identifying themselves as musicians in Britain, see Creative & Cultural Skills Council, 'The Music Blueprint', 2011.

p.171 For **the music market in China,** see *People's Daily*, 21 March 2013.

p.171 For **Modern Sky's** offer of free downloads, see *BBC News*, 21 February 2008.

p.172 **Performance**. Sources include: Broadway League; China Performing Industry Association; IBDB; Society of London Theatre (SOLT); *Variety*; *Stage*; and individual producers.

p.172 The data on *Les Misérables* is taken from the company's website and press reports.

p.174 For the **number of theatre-goers in China**, see 'Theatre in China', Guangzhou Public Opinion Research Centre, 2012.

p.174 **Video Games**. Sources include: Entertainment Software Association; Interactive Entertainment Association (UK); TIGA; and Information Industry Association.

p.177 **Architecture**. Sources include: American Institute of Architecture (AIA); *Architects' Journal*; *Building Design*; Royal Institute of British Architects (RIBA); and Union Internationale des Architectes (UIA).

p.178 'Global Construction Perspectives and Oxford Economics', *Global Construction 2020*, PwC, 2011.

p.180 **Design**. Sources include: China Industrial Design Association (CIDA); design-china.co; Design Council; Icograda; Industrial Designers Society of America (IDSA); International Council of Societies of Industrial Designers (ICSID); Japan Institute of Design Promotion; and eightsix. org.

p.180 See **Lazlo Moholy-Nagy**, *Vision in Motion*, Paul Theobald, 1947.

p.181 For the **performance of design-intensive companies**, see *Multidisciplinary Design Education in the UK*, Design Council, 2010.

p.181 **Designers' confusion about design rights** was reported in BOP Consulting, *Design Economics*, IPO, 2011.

p.182 For the data on **design schools in China**, see 'Design in China: Mapping Report', MovingCities, Shanghai, 2012.

p.183 **Fashion**. Sources include: British Fashion Council; *Women's Wear Daily*; and company reports.

p.183 For **Inditex** quote, see www.inditex.com/en/who_we_are.

p.184 For the **American fashion industry**, see 'Strengthening New York City's Fashion Wholesale Market', New York City Economic Development Corporation, 2009.

p.185 The data for **the fashion market and online shopping** is taken from 'The Future of Fashion', London Fashion Week, 2012.

p.185 For **China's market share in fashion**, see Vincent Lui and others, 'Dressing Up: Capturing the Dynamic Growth of China's Fashion Market', BCG Perspectives, 2011.

p.186 **Toys**. Sources include: British Toy and Hobby Association (BTHA); International Council of Toy Industries; and Toy Industries of Europe (TIE).

p.187 For **UNICEF's criticism of British parents**, see 'Child Well-Being in UK, Spain and Sweden', UNICEF/HMSO, 2012.

p.187 **Advertising**. Sources include: *Advertising Age*; Advertising Association; American Advertising Association; Institute of Practitioners in Advertising; Nielsen; and World Advertising Research Centre.

p.190 **Newspapers and Magazines**. Sources include: Groupe Publicis; International Federation of Periodical Publishers (FIPP); International Publishers Association; Newspaper Association of America; Periodical Publishers Association; and *Publishers Weekly*.

p.192 The data for the **Chinese newspaper market** is from *Global Times*, 8 May 2012.

p.194 **TV and Radio**. Sources include: European Audiovisual Observatory; Federal Communications Commission; Ofcom; State Administration of Radio, Film and Television; BBC; and CMM Intelligence, Beijing.

p.197 **R&D.** Sources include: Department for Business, Innovation and Skills (BIS); Department of Commerce; European Commission; National Science Foundation; Battelle; and national patent offices.

p.198 **Battelle's forecast** is published in '2012 Global R&D Funding Forecast', Battelle, 2011.

p.198 For the **big R&D spenders**, see 'The R&D 2010 Scorecard', Department of Business, Innovation and Skills.

p.200 For **Apple's and Google's patent activities**, see Charles Duhigg and Steve Lohr, 'The Patent, Used as a Sword', *The New York Times*, 7 October 2012.

p.201 For the **number of patents in force in 2010**, see 'Statistical Communiqué on National Economic and Social Development', National Bureau of Statistics, 22 February 2012.

p.202 For **Europe's expenditure on R&D and patents**, see 'Innovation Union Scorecard 2012', European Commission.

p.202 For **Britain's expenditure on R&D and patents**, see Janet Finch, *Accessibility, Sustainability, Excellence: How to Expand Access to Research Publications*, Research Information Network, 2012.

p.202 For data on **Chinese Academy of Sciences' R&D expenditure**, see *People's Daily*, 17 September 2012.

p.203 For **China's patents target**, see 'National Patent Development Strategy 2011–2020', SIPO, 2012.

p.203 **Software.** Sources include: Business Software Alliance; Gartner; Ministry of Information Industries, China; NASSCOM, India; and company reports.

p.205 For the **growth in the Indian software market**, see 'The Software Industry and Developing Countries', UNCTAD, 2012.

p.205 **Dotcoms.** Sources include: Alexa.com and company reports.

9. CITIES: THE SPACES IN-BETWEEN

p.211 For **population movement to cities**, see go.worldbank.org/QHKRLTGH70.

p.214 See **Jane Jacobs**, *The Economy of Cities*, Random House, 1969.

p.215 See **Richard Florida**, *The Rise of the Creative Class*, Basic Books, 2001.

p.215 See **Charles Landry**, *The Creative City*, Earthscan, 2000.

p.216 See **Brian Uzzi and Jarrett Spiro**, 'Collaboration and Creativity: The Small World Problem', *American Journal of Sociology*, September 2005.

p.217 **Troy Carter** is discussed in Neal Pollack, 'How Lady Gaga's Manager Reinvented the Celebrity Game with Social Media', *WIRED*, 21 May 2012.

p.217 See **Martin Ruef**, *The Entrepreneurial Group*, Princeton University Press, 2010.

p.217 I expand on the **three dimensions of culture** in John Howkins, *Creative Ecologies*, UQP, 2009.

p.218 For the **forum on the culture of global cities** held in 2012, see BOP Consulting, *World Cities Culture Report 2012*, Greater London Authority, 2012.

p.220 '**The parable of Detroit . . .**' was a headline in *Economist*, 22 October 2011.

p.221 **Sheryl Connelly**'s remark was made in 'Dreaming Up the Shape of Cars to Come', *New Scientist*, 21 August 2012.

p.222 For a **city's centre of gravity moving to the east**, see John Howkins, 'Why Cities Move from West to East', Architectural Association, 1970.

p.223 For a summary of government policy toolkits, see 'Driving Growth Through Local Government Investment in the Arts', London Government Association, 2013.

p.224 **Mayor Klaus Wowereit** was speaking in a television interview in 2004.

p.224 **Kate Levin**'s comment was made during the presentation of *World Cities Culture Report 2012* in Shanghai, April 2012.

10. MY BRAIN, MY ASSET

p.227 See **Fernand Braudel**, *Civilisation and Capitalism*, Collins, 1984.

p.227 See **Karl Marx**, *Capital*, William Glaisher, 1918.

p.228 See **Fritz Machlup**, *The Production and Distribution of Knowledge in the US*, Princeton University Press, 1962.

p.228 **Alan Greenspan**'s comment was quoted in Richard Bolton, Barry Libert and Steve Samek, *Cracking the Value Code*, HarperCollins, 2000.

p.229 See **Jerry Hirschberg**, *The Creative Priority*, Viking, 1998.

p.230 See **Leif Edvinsson**, *International Journal of Strategic Management*, 30 (3), June 1997.

p.230 See **Bill Gates**, 'Business @ the Speed of Light', *Business Strategy Review*, February 1999.

p.230 **Norio Ohga**'s comment was made during a speech at Sony's Annual General Meeting, 1998.

p.231 For the **United Nations' data on annual wealth**, see *Inclusive Wealth Report 2012*, Cambridge University Press.

p.232 A good summary of the **problems facing the NHS** is given in David Prosser, 'The Role of Information in Ensuring Quality and Patient Safety', Mid Staffs Public Inquiry, 19 October 2011.

p.232 **Julie Moore**'s comment was made in 'From Petrol to Prescriptions', *Economist*, 16 June 2012.

p.233 **Jeremy Brenner**'s story is told in Atul Gawande, 'The Hot Spotters', *New Yorker*, 24 January 2011.

Bibliography

Academy of Sciences, *The Digital Dilemma: Intellectual Property in the Information Age*, National Academies Press, Washington, DC, 2000.

Amabile, Teresa, *The Social Psychology of Creativity*, Springer-Verlag, New York, 1983.

Anderson, Chris, *Makers: The New Industrial Revolution*, Random House, New York, 2013.

Antons, Christopher, *Traditional Knowledge, Traditional Cultural Expressions and Intellectual Property Law in the Asia-Pacific Region*, Kluwers, 2009.

Arai, Hisamitsu, *The Japanese Experience in Wealth Creation*, WIPO, Geneva, 1999.

Attali, Jacques, *Noise: The Political Economy of Music*, University of Minnesota Press, Minneapolis, 1985.

Bakhshi, Hasan, Freeman, Alan, and Higgs, Peter, *A Dynamic Mapping of the UK's Creative Industries*, NESTA, London, 2013.

Bakhski, Hasan, Hargreaves, Ian, and Mateos-Garcia, Juan, *A Manifesto for the Creative Economy*, NESTA, London, 2013.

Bandura, Albert, *Self-Efficacy: The Exercise of Control*, Worth, 1997.

Benkler, Yochai, *The Wealth of Nations: How Social Production Transforms Markets and Freedoms*, Yale, New Haven, 2006.

Benthall, Jonathan, *Science and Technology in Art Today*, Thames & Hudson, London, 1972.

Berreby, Peter, 'The Hunters-Gatherers of the Knowledge Economy', *Strategy and Business*, 3/1999.

Bettig, Ronald V., *Copyrighting Culture*, Westview, Boulder, 1996.

Boden, Margaret, *The Creative Mind: Myths and Mechanisms*, Routledge, London, 2004.

Bogle, John, *Enough: True Measures of Money, Business and Life*, John Wiley, New York, 2008.

Bohm, David, *On Creativity*, Routledge, London, 1998.

Boorstin, Daniel J., *The Creators*, Random House, 1992.

Boorstin, Daniel J., *The Image*, Vintage, 1997.

BOP Consulting, *Mapping the Creative Industries: A Toolkit*, British Council, 2010.

BOP Consulting, *World Cities Culture Report 2012*, Greater London Authority, 2012.

Boyle, James, *The Public Domain*, Yale, New Haven, 2008.

Burke, Sean, *Authorship*, Edinburgh University Press, Edinburgh, 1995.

Branscomb, Anne Wells, *Who Owns Information?*, Basic Books, New York, 1995.

Brewer, John, and Porter, Roy (eds), *Consumption and the World of Goods*, Routledge, London, 1993.

Burman, Edward, *Logan Pearsall Smith: An Anthology*, Constable, London, 1989.

Bruce, Tina, *Cultivating Creativity*, Hodder & Stoughton, London, 2004.

Bruce, Tina, *Early Childhood Education*, fourth edition, Hodder, London, 2011.

Buzan, Tony, *The Power of Creative Intelligence*, Thorsons, London, 2001.

Byttebier, Igor, and Vullings, Ramon, *Creativity Today*, BIS, Amsterdam, 2007.

Castells, Manuel, *The Information Age*, 3 vols, Blackwell, Oxford, 1996–8.

Caves, Richard, *Creative Industries: Contracts between Art and Commerce*, Harvard, Cambridge, 2000.

Choo, Chun Wei, *The Knowing Organisation*, Oxford University Press, Oxford, 1997.

Christensen, Clayton M., *The Innovator's Dilemma: When New Technologies Cause Great Firms to Fail*, Harvard, Cambridge, 1997.

Claxton, Guy, *Hare Brain, Tortoise Mind: How Intelligence Increases When You Think Less*, Ecco Press, New York, 1999.

Cleveland, Harlan, *The Knowledge Executive*, Dutton, New York, 1985.

Coombe, Rosemary, *The Cultural Life of Intellectual Properties: Authorship, Appropriation and the Law*, Duke University Press, Durham, 1998.

Cornish, W. R., Llewelyn, David, and Aplin, Tanya, *Intellectual Property*, 7th edition, Sweet and Maxwell, London, 2010.

Creative Nation: Commonwealth Cultural Policy, Australian Government Printing Service, Canberra, 1994.

Csikszentmihalyi, Mihaly, *Creativity: Flow and the Psychology of Discovery and Invention*, HarperCollins, New York, 1996.

de Blij, Harm, *Why Geography Matters More Than Ever*, Oxford University Press, Oxford, 2012 de Bono, Edward, *Serious Creativity*, Harper Collins Business, London, 1995.

de Bono, Edward, *Lateral Thinking*, Penguin, London, 2009.

Dewulf, Simon, and Baillie, Caroline, *How to Foster Creativity*, Department for Education and Employment, London, 1999.

Doidge, Norman, *The Brain that Changes Itself*, Penguin, London, 2008.

Drahos, Peter, 'Intellectual Property and Human Rights', *Intellectual Property Quarterly* (1999), 3.

Ducharme, Louis-Marc, *Measuring Intangible Investment*, OECD, Paris, 1998.

Dutton, Denis, *The Art Instinct*, Oxford University Press, Oxford, 2009.

Dyson, George, *Turing's Cathedral*, Penguin, London, 2012.

Yearbook, European Audiovisual Observatory, Strasbourg, 2012.

Fairtlough, Gerard, *Creative Compartments: A Design for Future Organization*, Adamantine Press, London, 1994.

Febvre, Lucien, *The Coming of the Book*, Verso, London, 1984.

Fishbach, Ayelet, 'Goal Dilution', *Journal of Personality and Social Psychology* (2007), 92 (3).

Flint, Michael, and others, *A User's Guide to Copyright*, 6th edition, Tottel, London, 2006.

Florida, Richard, *The Rise of the Creative Class*, Basic Books, New York, 2002, revised 2012.

Florida, Richard, *Who's Your City?*, Basic Books, New York, 2009.

Fonseca Reis, Ana Carla, and Kageyama, Peter (eds), *Creative City Perspectives*, Garimpo de Solucoes and Creative City Productions, São Paulo, 2009.

Fung, Alex, Lo, Alice, and Rao, Mamata, *Creative Tools*, Hong Kong Polytechnic, 2005.

Glaeser, Edward, *Triumph of the City*, Macmillan, London, 2011.

Goldsmith, Kenneth, *Uncreative Writing*, Columbia University Press, New York, 2011.

Goldstein, Paul, *Copyright's Highway*, Hill & Wang, New York, 1996.

Guo, Meijun (Marina), *Creative Transformation*, China Economic Publishing House, Shanghai, 2011.

Hardwick, Philip, Khan, Bahadur, and Langmead, John, *An Introduction to Modern Economics*, 5th edition, Longman, London, 1999.

Hargreaves, Ian, *Digital Opportunity*, Intellectual Property Office, London, 2011.

Hartley, John, and Potts, Jason, *Creative City Index*, Queensland University of Technology, Brisbane, 2012.

Hartley, John, and others, *Key Concepts in Creative Industries*, Sage, London, 2012.

Hawken, Paul, *Blessed Unrest: How the Largest Movement in the World Came into Being, and Why No One Saw It Coming*, Viking, New York, 2008.

Hirshberg, Jerry, *The Creative Priority*, Penguin, London, 1998.

Howe, Michael J. A., *Genius Explained*, Cambridge University Press, Cambridge, 1999.

Howkins, John, *Creative Ecologies: Where Thinking is a Proper Job*, UQP, Brisbane, 2009.

Huizinga, Johan, *Homo Ludens*, Routledge, London, 1949.

Hyde, Lewis, *The Gift: How the Creative Spirit Transforms the World*, Random House, New York, 1979.

International Financial Statistics Yearbook, 2012, International Monetary Fund, Washington.

Jacobs, Jane, *The Economy of Cities*, Penguin, London, 1972.

Garnett, Kevin, Davies, Gillian and Harbottle, Gwilym, *Copinger and Skone James on Copyright*, Sweet & Maxwell, London, 2010.

Jardine, Lisa, *Ingenious Pursuits*, Little Brown, London, 1999.

Johnson, Steven, *Where Good Ideas Come From*, Penguin, New York, 2010.

Johnstone, Keith, *IMPRO: Improvisation and the Theatre*, Methuen, London, 1981.

Jussawalla, Meheroo, and others, *The Cost of Thinking*, Ablex, Norwood, 1988.

Kanter, Rosabeth Moss, *SuperCorp: How Vanguard Companies Create Innovation, Profit, Growth and Social Good*, Crown, New York, 2008.

Kao, John, *Jamming: The Art and Discipline of Business Creativity*, HarperBusiness, London, 1996.

Kay, John, *The Truth about Markets: Their Genius, Their Limits and Their Follies*, Penguin, London, 2003.

Keane, Michael, *Creative Industries in China*, Polity Press, Cambridge, 2013.

Kelley, Tom, and Littman, Jonathan, *The Art of Innovation: Success Through Innovation the IDEO Way*, Profile, London, 2002.

Kelly, Kevin, *New Rules for the New Economy*, Fourth Estate, London, 1998.

Kline, Stephen, *Out of the Garden: TV and Children's Toys*, Verso, London, 1993.

Koestler, Arthur, *The Act of Creation*, Hutchinson, London, 1964.

Kruger, Paul, and Piscke, Jörn-Steffen, *Observations and Conjectures on the US Employment Miracle*, Working Paper no. 6146, US National Bureau of Economic Research, Washington DC, 1997.

Krugman, Paul, *The Self-Organizing Economy*, Blackwell, Oxford, 1996.

Landry, Charles, *The Creative City*, Earthscan, London, 2000.

Lanier, Jaron, *You Are Not a Gadget: A Manifesto*, Penguin, London, 2011.

Leadbeater, Charles, *We-Think*, Profile, London, 2008.

Lessig, Lawrence, *Free Culture: How Big Media Uses Technology and the Law To Lock Down Culture and Control Creativity*, Penguin, New York, 2004.

Lévi-Strauss, Claude, *The Jealous Potter*, University of Chicago Press, Chicago, 1996.

Li, Wuwei, *How Creativity is Changing China*, Bloomsbury Academic, London, 2011.

Lin, Carol Yeh-Yun, and Edvinsson, Leif, *National Intellectual Capital: A Comparison of 40 Countries*, Springer, Heidelberg, 2011.

Lipson, Hod, and Kurman, Melba, *Fabricated: The New World of 3D Printing*, John Wiley, New York, 2013.

McLuhan, Marshall, *The Gutenberg Galaxy*, University of Toronto Press, Toronto, 1962.

Maddison, Angus, *Contours of the World Economy 1–2030 AD*, Oxford University Press, Oxford, 2007.

Mann, Peter H., *Books, Buyers and Borrowers*, Andre Deutsch, London, 1971.

Maslow, Abraham, 'A Theory of Human Motivation', *Psychological Review*, 50(4), 1943.

Mason, Hugh, and Chong, Mark, *Brainfruit*, McGraw-Hill, Singapore, 2012.

May, Christopher, *A Global Political Economy of Intellectual Property Rights: The New Enclosures?*, Routledge, London, 2000.

Mayer-Schönberger, Viktor, and Cukier, Kenneth, *Big Data: A Revolution That Will Transform How We Live, Work and Think*, John Murray, London, 2013.

Montgomery, Lucy, *China's Creative Industries*, Edward Elgar, London, 2010.

Naughton, John, *A Brief History of the Future: The Origins of the Internet*, Weidenfeld & Nicolson, London, 1999.

Naughton, John, *From Gutenberg to Zuckerberg: What You Really Need to Know about the Internet*, Quercus, London, 2012.

Nordström, Kjell, and Ridderstråle, Jonas, *Funky Business: Talent Makes Capital Dance*, Financial Times/Prentice Hall, London, 2000.

OfCom, *Communications Market Report*, London, 2012.

Parrish, David, *T-Shirts and Suits*, Merseyside, Liverpool, 2007.

Petty, Geoffrey, *How to Be Better at Creativity*, Kogan Page, London, 1997.

Pine, B. Joseph II, and Gilmore, James, *The Experience Economy*, Harvard Business School Press, Cambridge, 1999.

Ploman, Edward W., and L. Clark Hamilton, *Copyright*, Routledge & Kegan Paul, London, 1980.

Pope, Rob, *Creativity: Theory, History and Practice*, Routledge, London, 2005.

Prahalad, C. K., *The Fortune at the Bottom of the Pyramid*, Prentice Hall, New York, 2004.

Prahalad, Deepa, and Sawhiney, Ravi, *Predictable Magic*, Wharton, Philadelphia, 2011.

Pritzker, Steve, and Runco, Mark, *Encyclopedia of Creativity*, Academic Press, Amsterdam, 1999.

Raleigh, Thomas, *An Outline of the Law of Property*, Clarendon, Oxford, 1890.

Rifkin, Jeremy, *The Age of Access*, Penguin, London, 2000.

Rivette, Kevin G., and Kline, David, *Rembrandts in the Attic*, Harvard Business School Press, Cambridge, 1999.

Rogers, Everett, and Kincaid, Lawrence, *Communication Networks*, Free Press, New York, 1981.

Rogers, Everett, and Larsen, Judith, *Silicon Valley Fever*, Basic Books, New York, 1984.

Roszak, Theodore, *Where the Wasteland Ends*, Faber & Faber, London, 1972.

Ruskin, John, 'Unto This Last', *Cornhill Magazine*, London, 1860.

Schumpeter, Joseph, *Capitalism, Socialism and Democracy*, Allen & Unwin, London, 1943.

Smith, Chris, *Creative Britain*, Faber & Faber, London, 1998.

Steiner, George, *Grammars of Creation*, Faber & Faber, London, 2001.

Stiglitz, Joseph E., *Public Policy for a Knowledge Economy*, speech at the Centre for Economic Policy Research, London, 27 January 1999.

Storr, Anthony, *The Dynamics of Creation*, Secker & Warburg, London, 1972.

Tapscott, Don, *The Digital Economy*, McGraw Hill, New York, 1995.

Tharp, Twyla, *The Creative Habit: Learn it and Use it for Life*, Simon & Schuster, New York, 2007.

Titmuss, Richard, *The Gift Relationship: From Human Blood to Social Policy*, Pantheon, New York, 1971.

Törnqvist, Gunnar, *The Geography of Creativity*, Edward Elgar, London, 2011.

UNCTAD, *Creative Economy Report 2010*, Geneva, 2010.

Van Kranenburg, Rob, and others, *The Internet of Things*, Berlin Symposium on Internet and Society, 2011.

Vaske, Hermann, *Why Are You Creative?*, How Design, 2002.

Von Krogh, Georg, Ichijo, Kazuo, and Nonaka, Ikujiro, *Enabling Knowledge Creation*, Oxford University Press, Oxford, 2000.

Walker, David, *Understanding Pictures*, University of Massachusetts, Amherst, 1979.

Wiener, Norbert, *The Human Use of Human Beings*, Doubleday, New York, 1954.

Wilde, Oscar, *The Decay of Lying*, in *Complete Works of Oscar Wilde*, Collins, London, 1966.

Williams, Raymond, *Culture and Society 1780–1950*, Penguin, London, 1961.

Wilmut, I., Campbell, K., and Tudge, C., *The Second Creation: The Age of Biological Control by the Scientists who Cloned Dolly*, Headline, London, 2000.

Wilson, Edward O., *Consilience: The Unity of Knowledge*, Abacus, London, 1998.

Wolf, Michael, *The Entertainment Economy*, Penguin, London, 1999.

Zohar, Danah, *Rewiring the Corporate Brain*, Berrett-Koehler, San Francisco, 1997.

Acknowledgements

This book could not have been written without the help of many people all over the world who are thinking about creativity: how it starts, how it grows and how it becomes more valuable to us and to others. I am indebted to them all and hope they find this book a useful addition to the conversation. I am especially grateful to my colleagues at BOP Consulting in London and my colleagues in Shanghai and Beijing. I would like to thank my agent, Michael Sissons, PFD, and my editor Stuart Proffitt, Penguin, who warmly supported the idea from the very beginning. Many thanks, as always, to Ariane Bankes who was my shipmate on *Roi des Belges* and other journeys.

Index

Page numbers in *italic* refer to tables.

ALLEN LANE
an imprint of
PENGUIN BOOKS

Recently Published

Hooman Majd, *The Ministry of Guidance Invites You to Not Stay: An American Family in Iran*

Roger Knight, *Britain Against Napoleon: The Organisation of Victory, 1793-1815*

Alan Greenspan, *The Map and the Territory: Risk, Human Nature and the Future of Forecasting*

Daniel Lieberman, *Story of the Human Body: Evolution, Health and Disease*

Malcolm Gladwell, *David and Goliath: Underdogs, Misfits and the Art of Battling Giants*

Paul Collier, *Exodus: Immigration and Multiculturalism in the 21st Century*

John Eliot Gardiner, *Music in the Castle of Heaven: Immigration and Multiculturalism in the 21st Century*

Catherine Merridale, *Red Fortress: The Secret Heart of Russia's History*

Ramachandra Guha, *Gandhi Before India*

Vic Gatrell, *The First Bohemians: Life and Art in London's Golden Age*

Richard Overy, *The Bombing War: Europe 1939-1945*

Charles Townshend, *The Republic: The Fight for Irish Independence, 1918-1923*

Eric Schlosser, *Command and Control*

Sudhir Venkatesh, *Floating City: Hustlers, Strivers, Dealers, Call Girls and Other Lives in Illicit New York*

Sendhil Mullainathan & Eldar Shafir, *Scarcity: Why Having Too Little Means So Much*

John Drury, *Music at Midnight: The Life and Poetry of George Herbert*

Philip Coggan, *The Last Vote: The Threats to Western Democracy*

Richard Barber, *Edward III and the Triumph of England*

Daniel M Davis, *The Compatibility Gene*

John Bradshaw, *Cat Sense: The Feline Enigma Revealed*

Roger Knight, *Britain Against Napoleon: The Organisation of Victory, 1793-1815*

Thurston Clarke, *JFK's Last Hundred Days: An Intimate Portrait of a Great President*

Jean Drèze and Amartya Sen, *An Uncertain Glory: India and its Contradictions*

Rana Mitter, *China's War with Japan, 1937-1945: The Struggle for Survival*

Tom Burns, *Our Necessary Shadow: The Nature and Meaning of Psychiatry*

Sylvain Tesson, *Consolations of the Forest: Alone in a Cabin in the Middle Taiga*

George Monbiot, *Feral: Searching for Enchantment on the Frontiers of Rewilding*

Ken Robinson and Lou Aronica, *Finding Your Element: How to Discover Your Talents and Passions and Transform Your Life*

David Stuckler and Sanjay Basu, *The Body Economic: Why Austerity Kills*

Suzanne Corkin, *Permanent Present Tense: The Man with No Memory, and What He Taught the World*

Daniel C. Dennett, *Intuition Pumps and Other Tools for Thinking*

Adrian Raine, *The Anatomy of Violence: The Biological Roots of Crime*

Eduardo Galeano, *Children of the Days: A Calendar of Human History*

Lee Smolin, *Time Reborn: From the Crisis of Physics to the Future of the Universe*

Michael Pollan, *Cooked: A Natural History of Transformation*

David Graeber, *The Democracy Project: A History, a Crisis, a Movement*

Brendan Simms, *Europe: The Struggle for Supremacy, 1453 to the Present*

Oliver Bullough, *The Last Man in Russia and the Struggle to Save a Dying Nation*

Diarmaid MacCulloch, *Silence: A Christian History*

Evgeny Morozov, *To Save Everything, Click Here: Technology, Solutionism, and the Urge to Fix Problems that Don't Exist*

David Cannadine, *The Undivided Past: History Beyond Our Differences*

Michael Axworthy, *Revolutionary Iran: A History of the Islamic Republic*

Jaron Lanier, *Who Owns the Future?*

John Gray, *The Silence of Animals: On Progress and Other Modern Myths*

Paul Kildea, *Benjamin Britten: A Life in the Twentieth Century*

Jared Diamond, *The World Until Yesterday: What Can We Learn from Traditional Societies?*

Nassim Nicholas Taleb, *Antifragile: How to Live in a World We Don't Understand*

Alan Ryan, *On Politics: A History of Political Thought from Herodotus to the Present*

Roberto Calasso, *La Folie Baudelaire*

Carolyn Abbate and Roger Parker, *A History of Opera: The Last Four Hundred Years*

Yang Jisheng, *Tombstone: The Untold Story of Mao's Great Famine*

Caleb Scharf, *Gravity's Engines: The Other Side of Black Holes*

Jancis Robinson, Julia Harding and José Vouillamoz, *Wine Grapes: A Complete Guide to 1,368 Vine Varieties, including their Origins and Flavours*

David Bownes, Oliver Green and Sam Mullins, *Underground: How the Tube Shaped London*

Niall Ferguson, *The Great Degeneration: How Institutions Decay and Economies Die*

Chrystia Freeland, *Plutocrats: The Rise of the New Global Super-Rich*

David Thomson, *The Big Screen: The Story of the Movies and What They Did to Us*

Halik Kochanski, *The Eagle Unbowed: Poland and the Poles in the Second World War*

Kofi Annan with Nader Mousavizadeh, *Interventions: A Life in War and Peace*

Mark Mazower, *Governing the World: The History of an Idea*

Anne Applebaum, *Iron Curtain: The Crushing of Eastern Europe 1944-56*

Steven Johnson, *Future Perfect: The Case for Progress in a Networked Age*

Christopher Clark, *The Sleepwalkers: How Europe Went to War in 1914*

Neil MacGregor, *Shakespeare's Restless World*

Nate Silver, *The Signal and the Noise: The Art and Science of Prediction*

Chinua Achebe, *There Was a Country: A Personal History of Biafra*

John Darwin, *Unfinished Empire: The Global Expansion of Britain*

Jerry Brotton, *A History of the World in Twelve Maps*

Patrick Hennessey, *KANDAK: Fighting with Afghans*

Katherine Angel, *Unmastered: A Book on Desire, Most Difficult to Tell*

David Priestland, *Merchant, Soldier, Sage: A New History of Power*

Stephen Alford, *The Watchers: A Secret History of the Reign of Elizabeth I*

Tom Feiling, *Short Walks from Bogotá: Journeys in the New Colombia*

Pankaj Mishra, *From the Ruins of Empire: The Revolt Against the West and the Remaking of Asia*

Geza Vermes, *Christian Beginnings: From Nazareth to Nicaea, AD 30-325*

Steve Coll, *Private Empire: ExxonMobil and American Power*

Joseph Stiglitz, *The Price of Inequality*

Dambisa Moyo, *Winner Take All: China's Race for Resources and What it Means for Us*

Robert Skidelsky and Edward Skidelsky, *How Much is Enough? The Love of Money, and the Case for the Good Life*

Frances Ashcroft, *The Spark of Life: Electricity in the Human Body*

Sebastian Seung, *Connectome: How the Brain's Wiring Makes Us Who We Are*

Callum Roberts, *Ocean of Life*

Orlando Figes, *Just Send Me Word: A True Story of Love and Survival in the Gulag*

Leonard Mlodinow, *Subliminal: The Revolution of the New Unconscious and What it Teaches Us about Ourselves*

John Romer, *A History of Ancient Egypt: From the First Farmers to the Great Pyramid*

Ruchir Sharma, *Breakout Nations: In Pursuit of the Next Economic Miracle*

Michael J. Sandel, *What Money Can't Buy: The Moral Limits of Markets*

Dominic Sandbrook, *Seasons in the Sun: The Battle for Britain, 1974-1979*

Tariq Ramadan, *The Arab Awakening: Islam and the New Middle East*

Jonathan Haidt, *The Righteous Mind: Why Good People are Divided by Politics and Religion*

Ahmed Rashid, *Pakistan on the Brink: The Future of Pakistan, Afghanistan and the West*

Tim Weiner, *Enemies: A History of the FBI*

Mark Pagel, *Wired for Culture: The Natural History of Human Cooperation*

George Dyson, *Turing's Cathedral: The Origins of the Digital Universe*

Cullen Murphy, *God's Jury: The Inquisition and the Making of the Modern World*

Richard Sennett, *Together: The Rituals, Pleasures and Politics of Co-operation*

Faramerz Dabhoiwala, *The Origins of Sex: A History of the First Sexual Revolution*

Roy F. Baumeister and John Tierney, *Willpower: Rediscovering Our Greatest Strength*

Jesse J. Prinz, *Beyond Human Nature: How Culture and Experience Shape Our Lives*

Robert Holland, *Blue-Water Empire: The British in the Mediterranean since 1800*

Jodi Kantor, *The Obamas: A Mission, A Marriage*

Philip Coggan, *Paper Promises: Money, Debt and the New World Order*

Charles Nicholl, *Traces Remain: Essays and Explorations*

Daniel Kahneman, *Thinking, Fast and Slow*

Hunter S. Thompson, *Fear and Loathing at Rolling Stone: The Essential Writing of Hunter S. Thompson*

Duncan Campbell-Smith, *Masters of the Post: The Authorized History of the Royal Mail*

Colin McEvedy, *Cities of the Classical World: An Atlas and Gazetteer of 120 Centres of Ancient Civilization*

Heike B. Görtemaker, *Eva Braun: Life with Hitler*

Brian Cox and Jeff Forshaw, *The Quantum Universe: Everything that Can Happen Does Happen*

Nathan D. Wolfe, *The Viral Storm: The Dawn of a New Pandemic Age*

Norman Davies, *Vanished Kingdoms: The History of Half-Forgotten Europe*

Michael Lewis, *Boomerang: The Meltdown Tour*

Steven Pinker, *The Better Angels of Our Nature: The Decline of Violence in History and Its Causes*

Robert Trivers, *Deceit and Self-Deception: Fooling Yourself the Better to Fool Others*

Thomas Penn, *Winter King: The Dawn of Tudor England*

Daniel Yergin, *The Quest: Energy, Security and the Remaking of the Modern World*

Michael Moore, *Here Comes Trouble: Stories from My Life*

Ali Soufan, *The Black Banners: Inside the Hunt for Al Qaeda*

Jason Burke, *The 9/11 Wars*

Timothy D. Wilson, *Redirect: The Surprising New Science of Psychological Change*

Ian Kershaw, *The End: Hitler's Germany, 1944-45*

T M Devine, *To the Ends of the Earth: Scotland's Global Diaspora, 1750-2010*

Catherine Hakim, *Honey Money: The Power of Erotic Capital*

Douglas Edwards, *I'm Feeling Lucky: The Confessions of Google Employee Number 59*

John Bradshaw, *In Defence of Dogs*

Chris Stringer, *The Origin of Our Species*

Lila Azam Zanganeh, *The Enchanter: Nabokov and Happiness*

David Stevenson, *With Our Backs to the Wall: Victory and Defeat in 1918*

Evelyn Juers, *House of Exile: War, Love and Literature, from Berlin to Los Angeles*

Henry Kissinger, *On China*

Michio Kaku, *Physics of the Future: How Science Will Shape Human Destiny and Our Daily Lives by the Year 2100*

David Abulafia, *The Great Sea: A Human History of the Mediterranean*

John Gribbin, *The Reason Why: The Miracle of Life on Earth*

Anatol Lieven, *Pakistan: A Hard Country*

William Cohen, *Money and Power: How Goldman Sachs Came to Rule the World*

Joshua Foer, *Moonwalking with Einstein: The Art and Science of Remembering Everything*

Simon Baron-Cohen, *Zero Degrees of Empathy: A New Theory of Human Cruelty*

Manning Marable, *Malcolm X: A Life of Reinvention*

David Deutsch, *The Beginning of Infinity: Explanations that Transform the World*

David Edgerton, *Britain's War Machine: Weapons, Resources and Experts in the Second World War*

John Kasarda and Greg Lindsay, *Aerotropolis: The Way We'll Live Next*

David Gilmour, *The Pursuit of Italy: A History of a Land, Its Regions and Their Peoples*

Niall Ferguson, *Civilization: The West and the Rest*

Tim Flannery, *Here on Earth: A New Beginning*

Robert Bickers, *The Scramble for China: Foreign Devils in the Qing Empire, 1832-1914*

Mark Malloch-Brown, *The Unfinished Global Revolution: The Limits of Nations and the Pursuit of a New Politics*

King Abdullah of Jordan, *Our Last Best Chance: The Pursuit of Peace in a Time of Peril*

Eliza Griswold, *The Tenth Parallel: Dispatches from the Faultline between Christianity and Islam*

Brian Greene, *The Hidden Reality: Parallel Universes and the Deep Laws of the Cosmos*

John Gray, *The Immortalization Commission: The Strange Quest to Cheat Death*

Patrick French, *India: A Portrait*

Lizzie Collingham, *The Taste of War: World War Two and the Battle for Food*

Hooman Majd, *The Ayatollahs' Democracy: An Iranian Challenge*

Dambisa Moyo, *How The West Was Lost: Fifty Years of Economic Folly - and the Stark Choices Ahead*